BYE FELIPE

Disses, Dick Pics, and Other Delights of Modern Dating

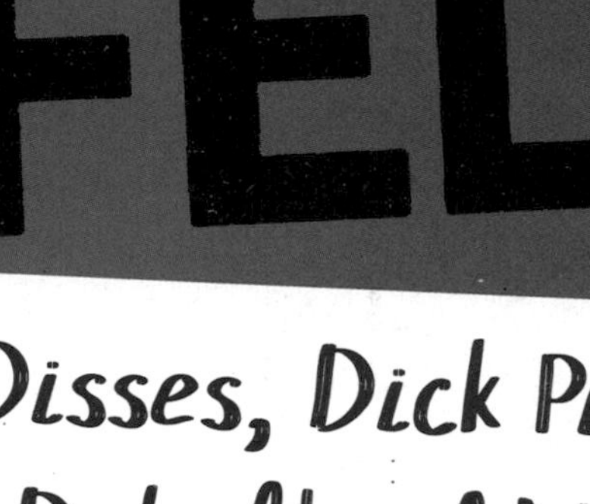

ALEXANDRA TWETEN

RUNNING PRESS

PHILADELPHIA

Running Press
Hachette Book Group
1290 Avenue of the Americas, New York, NY 10104
www.runningpress.com
@Running_Press

Printed in the United States of America

First Edition: August 2018

Published by Running Press, an imprint of Perseus Books, LLC, a subsidiary of Hachette Book Group, Inc. The Running Press name and logo is a trademark of the Hachette Book Group.

The Hachette Speakers Bureau provides a wide range of authors for speaking events. To find out more, go to www.hachettespeakersbureau.com or call (866) 376-6591.

The publisher is not responsible for websites (or their content) that are not owned by the publisher.

Print book cover design by Daniel Cantada.
Interior book design by Daniel Cantada and Corinda Cook.

Library of Congress Control Number: 2018932618
ISBNs: 978-0-7624-6374-9 (paperback), 978-0-7624-6373-2 (ebook)

LSC-C

10 9 8 7 6 5 4 3 2 1

CONTENTS

INTRODUCTION 4

Chapter 1
ONLINE DATING: Y THO? 18

Chapter 2
SWIPE LEFT TO AVOID A TERRIBLE FATE 70

Chapter 3
WHY ARE MEN? 101

Chapter 4
WTF CAN WE DO TO DEAL WITH MEN? 139

Chapter 5
BEING A BOSS: HOW TO TAKE CONTROL
OF YOUR DATING LIFE 211

Chapter 6
WTF DO WE DO NOW? 240

RESOURCES 252

ENDNOTES 254

ACKNOWLEDGMENTS 256

INTRODUCTION

Let's be real. You probably picked up this book because you're a fan of the viral Instagram account @ByeFelipe and already know about the fresh hell that is modern online dating, or you have no idea what "Bye Felipe" means, but the phrase "dick pics" caught your eye and you were intrigued. Either way, hello and welcome! I'm Alexandra, and I started Bye Felipe, a website that calls out men who turn hostile when they're rejected or ignored. It's basically just screenshots of terrible things dudes say to women online, which the women send to me, and I share publicly. Kinda like this:

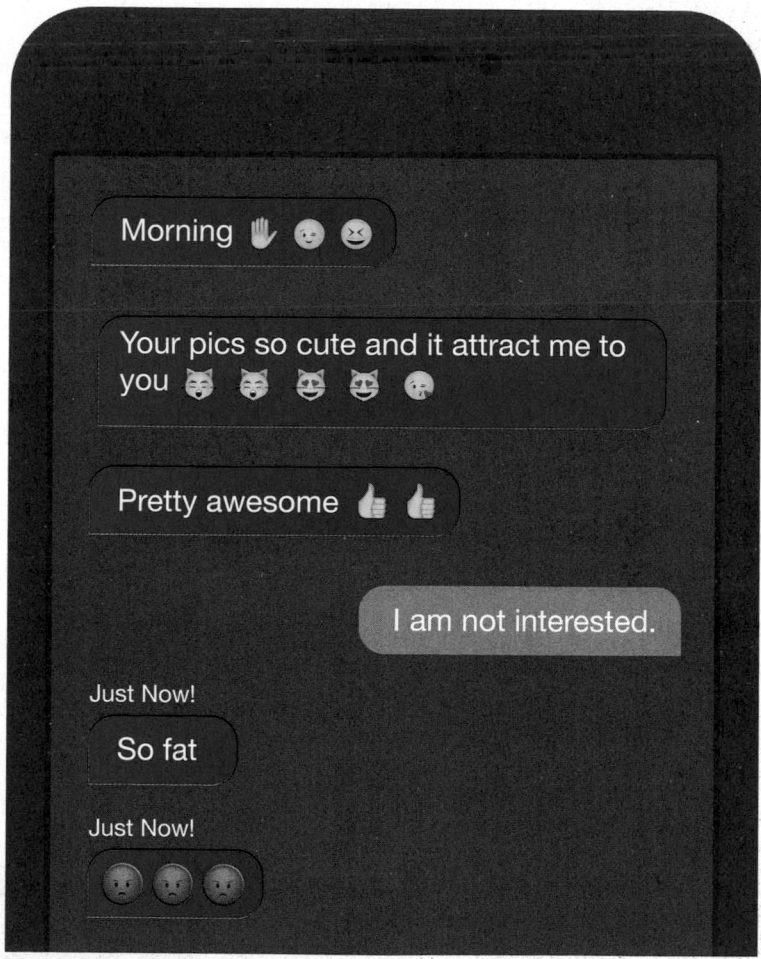

And this:

Now you're probably like, "Oh, I get it, but WTF is this book about?" Well, after years of being inundated with thousands of dreadful examples of men being complete assholes to women for politely declining or ignoring their desperate pleas for attention, I decided there was much more I wanted to say about modern dating (and misogyny) that wouldn't quite fit into a tiny Instagram square. Hence, the idea for this book was born. I wanted to start a conversation about the problems women are experiencing in online dating (and just navigating through life online) because the abuse and harassment don't seem to be letting up anytime soon. I receive about twenty submissions a day with the worst insults from women's inboxes, and with questions about how they should respond or what they can do to combat the abuse.

I also spent the majority of my twenties doing online dating in Los Angeles, and after more than two hundred dates, I've pretty much witnessed it all in terms of straight dudes' bad behavior. It's downright brutal out there if you're a single woman right now. I wanted to write a guide to avoiding all the mistakes I made when I first started meeting strangers from the internet, and wanted to make fun of all the awful men.

Is this book going to tell you how to catch a man? NOPE. There's already enough of that BS out there as it is. Straight and bi women, femmes, queer, nonbinary, and trans people, anyone-who-is-not-a-straight-cis-male, YOU'RE FINE. It's mostly straight cisgender dudes who need to get their acts together. As such, this book is for anyone, regardless of identity, who is an unfortunate target for straight guys.

I wanted you to be able to use this book to learn how to best spot, avoid, and effectively take down asshole dudes you encounter. And I hope you'll have some laughs along the way, because, well, there's pretty much no way to read some of these absurd interactions and not cackle.

You down? OK, cool. Now that you know what to expect, let me answer your next question: How the heck did this all start?

In August 2014, I woke up one day and discovered that my friend Miranda had added me to a secret Los Angeles–based Facebook group called "Girls Night In" (later to be known as GRLCVLT—because we were basically a feminist cult). It was like a giant online sleepover with fifteen hundred ambitious, successful women and non-binary identifying people who talked about anything and everything, from career problems to relationship issues. The group was diverse and included lesbian,

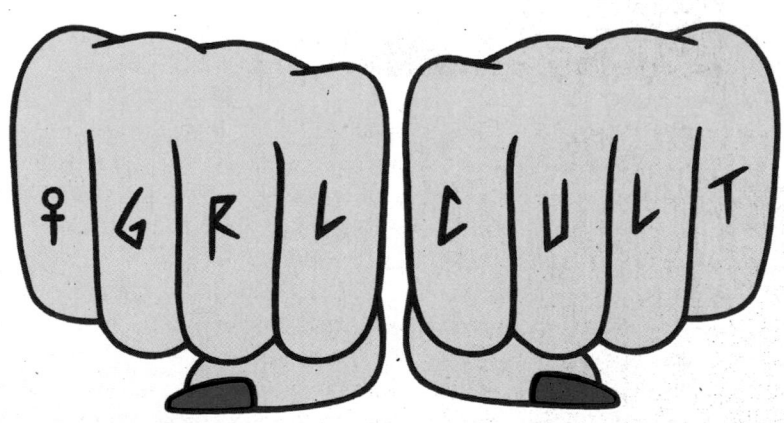

bisexual, and trans women; immigrants; women of color; sex workers; CEOs; models—everyone. However, it was kind of similar to Fight Club: what happens in GNI, stays in GNI. Anyone caught leaking info is kicked out. Hence, there was a sense of freedom, openness, and frankness that you don't find on your regular Facebook feed with everyone's grandparents. It was like a whole new world, a paradise where no man could butt in and derail or explain anything. I'm not exaggerating when I say that being added to GNI changed my life.

One day, a member of GNI posted a screenshot of a message she had received on the dating site OkCupid. It was a dude's dopey, long-winded, boring message, like any of the hundreds you typically receive if you're a woman on a dating site. She didn't respond, and then twelve hours later, he just said "asshole." I thought it was hilarious.

It just so happened that I had received a message a couple of days before that on OkCupid, where the guy had been sending me the same message over and over. When I finally responded and said I wasn't interested, he lashed out. He had sent me multiple messages, starting like this:

Hi there,

We're 89% compatible -- pretty incredible! :)

You're really pretty and seem like a lot of fun. I'm looking for a cute, easy-going woman who I can date and with whom I can explore the town during my free time at night. You seem to be very much my type.

Would you like to chat? :)

Sent on 9/2/2014   Block them   Report

Seems nice, but when you get as many messages as women do on OkCupid (hundreds), you start to develop a spidey sense for generic copy-and-pasted messages that guys send to hundreds of women without reading their profiles. Still, I looked at his profile, and none of his pictures actually showed his face. (Red flag!) Sorry, I'm not trying to date a torso. I ignored the message. However, he kept trying.

Hi there,

Whoa, we're 80% compatible! That's really high... :)

You're really pretty and seem like a lot of fun. I'm looking for a cute, easy-going woman who I can date and with whom I can explore the town during my free time at night. You seem to be very much my type.

Given my profession as an attorney, I don't post too many pics online; however, if you'd like, I can send you a few more.

Would you like to chat? :)

Sent on 9/24/2014   Block them   Report

I continued ignoring them, hoping he would get the hint and go away.

A few weeks later, he tried yet again, and I finally said, "No." And then this happened.

Hi there,

You're really pretty and seem like a lot of fun. I'm looking for a cute, easy-going woman who I can date and with whom I can explore the town during my free time at night. You seem to be very much my type.

People have described me as tall, dark and handsome, but I don't expect you to take my word for it. So if you'd like to see more pictures of me, I can send you a few immediately. I just don't feel comfortable posting too many online because of my profession as a lawyer.

Would you like to chat? :)

Sent on 10/11/2014   Unblock them   Report

No.

Sent from the OkCupid app • 10/11/2014

WHY THE FUCK NOT?!?

If you weren't interested, then you shouldn't have fucking replied at all! WTF!

Sent on 10/11/2014   Unblock them   Report

At the time, I was kind of freaked out. This guy seemed unstable. Was he going to keep messaging me? Would he try to find me? I didn't want to deal with it. So I blocked him. This wasn't the first time a guy had insulted me when I wasn't interested, but it *was* the first time I actually felt queasy from the unprovoked anger and rage of a man on a dating site. As I would later learn, this sort of thing is not rare. I posted the disturbing screenshot from the lawyer in the GNI conversation.

As the thread got going, more women added examples of increasingly offensive messages they'd received on dating sites. They all seemed to have something in common: we'd ignore a guy's messages or politely decline his advances and then get a shitstorm of abuse. We agreed that online dating was often as frightening as it was entertaining.

We talked about the double bind of being a single (straight) woman: You get a message from a guy, and if you answer no, the guy gets angry. But if you ignore it, the guy gets angry anyway. There's no winning! The only way to avoid making an entitled man hostile is to agree with him. Do these men expect us to go on dates with everyone who's interested in us? We also talked about how we hated declining men, because we expect this aggressive reaction. And we normally don't even acknowledge it; it's just an everyday thing that we accept.

We had already come up with our own lingo for dismissing dudes: "Bye, Felipe," a riff on "Bye Felicia," the classic quote from the movie *Friday*. (If you've survived this long without hearing that slang phrase, it's basically a dude's way of dismissing a woman who's an irrelevant whiner.)

It had been our inside joke for a few weeks. Someone's boyfriend is being shady? *Bye, Felipe!* Someone went on a date and he ghosted her? *Bye, Felipe!* A dude got caught cheating? *Girl, you need to Bye Felipe him.* Some asshole sent you a rude message on Tinder because you didn't respond fast enough? *BYE FELIPE.*

This is one of the first screenshots someone added to the original Facebook thread:

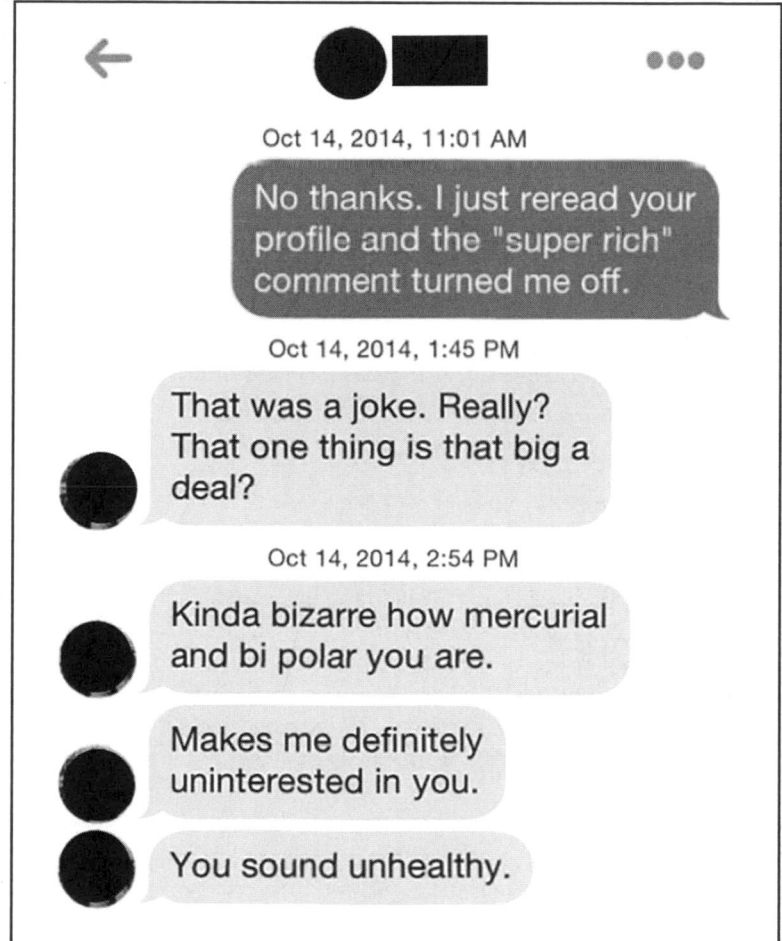

"Someone should make an Instagram with these!" one member said after what seemed like the eight millionth horrible screenshot went up. Making a split-second decision, I did. I created the @ByeFelipe Instagram account as a protest against assholes who insult and even threaten women online and to publicize that abuse like this was common and widespread. I wanted to take the therapeutic experience of GNI and give more women an open forum in which they could post nightmare text exchanges and bond over the horrors of online dating. With the blessing of my fellow GNI members, I uploaded the first few posts.

I'll give you 5 minutes to write something back, if you don't, I'll never talk to you again.....you might be able to play other dudes but not this one!!!

5 minutes is up....don't ever text me again, don't, have fun being a cunt to other people.....besides you're too fat for me anyways!! Delete my number and leave me alone bitch!!!!!

To Bye Felipe:
I accidentally fell asleep in the middle of texting a "nice guy" from Tinder. Woke up to this. #BYEFELIPE #accidentally #ignoredmen 💩

> Here's what I'm thinking. We get to know each other and inevitably hit it off. Then, we go on this epic amazing date and then you'll have the story you want.

Oct 15, 2014, 5:48 PM

> Guess not lol

Oct 15, 2014, 10:00 PM

> Ur not even anything special

> Y ignore me

> U look like a fuckin tranny

Exactly two weeks after I created the Instagram account I awoke to a nonstop stream of push notifications blowing up my phone. I watched, astounded, as likes and comments scrolled across the screen, sometimes too fast to even read. That morning, *The Atlantic* had published an article about online harassment, featuring @ByeFelipe and calling me a "Feminist Tinder-Creep-Busting Web Vigilante." I went into my Instagram settings and turned off notifications. I had no idea the concept would touch a nerve with so many people. I didn't think anyone outside of GNI would even get the joke. But as it turned out, *a lot* of people got it. The followers of

@ByeFelipe grew from about six hundred, just among GNI members, to thirty thousand the following week, and they continued to grow with every news story.

As the account received more and more media coverage (*Buzzfeed, The Huffington Post, Good Morning America, The New York Times*), I received thousands of submissions. They were all examples of truly horrific messages women were dealing with. There were submissions with deluges of insults, from "fat whale" to "cunt" to "whore." There were text messages running multiple pages, describing why they thought these women were awful and unworthy of respect. Occasionally, women would send me the rape threats or physical threats they'd received. This is when I realized the truly incredible magnitude of the hatred women face online on a regular basis.

It became clear that there were certain types of harassers, and there was a distinct pattern of a very large problem. People were constantly asking me, "What causes these responses? Why are men like this?" Maybe if I could find a pattern to the harassment, I could learn the warning signs and make women more aware. Or maybe I could somehow come up with specific defenses to each type. I started putting the submissions into categorized folders when I received them: "Dick Pics," "Nice Guys," "Racists," "Weirdos," etc.

The examples people sent me from dating apps like Tinder were wild. Some of the men's profiles practically screamed "I'm a bigot and I hate women!" Their Tinder taglines were littered with "No fat chicks" and "Too many skanks looking for attention on here." But some men seemed fine at first glance, yet, as soon as you took a shower or accidentally fell asleep while messaging them, their impatient, entitled side would come out. These awful reactions to rejection came from everywhere. Most were from dating sites like OkCupid, Tinder, and Plenty of Fish, but there were also submissions from Facebook, gaming apps, and real-life interactions that the submitters described. The issue is larger than just dating sites, but it is especially pronounced there and it's easier to document.

Four years later, Bye Felipe has more than 400,000 followers on Instagram. I host a popular podcast and have watched Bye Felipe become young women's destination of choice as they ask the age-old questions: What the fuck is wrong with these men? What is it that makes some of them think it's okay and perfectly acceptable to catcall and harass women? To send them dick pics? To turn hostile when we shut them down? To treat us like inanimate objects?

We know that online dating harassment is primarily a woman's problem because a whopping *57 percent*[1] of women report feeling harassed on dating apps, compared to 21 percent of men. Our patriarchal society, rife with misogyny, and the male-dominated culture we all grow up and live in, call on men to be sexually aggressive, unemotional, and violent. This is toxic masculinity, and it is at the root of the interactions I see on Bye Felipe.

Toxic masculinity is responsible for the same general attitude that ended up electing a known and admitted "pussy-grabber" as president of the United States. Evidenced by how the 2016 election turned out, apparently a lot of Americans are VERY okay with misogyny. And make no mistake: Donald Trump is a textbook Felipe. The quotes from the notorious bus video read exactly like a submission I'd get: "I moved on her like a bitch. But I couldn't get there. And she was married. Then all of a sudden, I see her, she's now got the big phony tits and everything." Translation: "I hit on her, but she wasn't interested. Well, she's ugly anyway."

Under President Felipe-in-Chief, the dating landscape feels shittier than ever—and the work of Bye Felipe has never felt more important. The day after the 2016 election, a friend of mine was walking into a Los Angeles 7-Eleven, having just stepped out of her Bernie Sanders–stickered car, when a man in a Make America Great Again hat grabbed her between her legs and said, "Are you scared now, you liberal cunt?" I have heard many stories like this since.

I'm not saying that Bye Felipe alone can solve our culture's perennial problem with misogyny or harassment—or even the more recent problems of online hate and abuse. Women, especially women of color, knew that the world was like this long before the 2016 election. We had the evidence not only in our personal experiences from walking down the street in public, but also in our online inboxes. The ideologies that enabled Donald Trump to take power are the same beliefs that reinforce the notion that women are lesser. From the institutional sexism in pretty much every industry, to the micro-aggressions we deal with on a daily basis, it's a wonder every woman hasn't gone postal at some point.

What I am saying is that drawing together to share our collective experiences feels like survival work now. And laughing about it feels like one of the best ways to cope, because what the hell else are we going to do in the short term? Real long-term solutions involve a comprehensive plan of attack, from demanding safety and security from app makers to changing social norms and public policy. I'll talk about some of this kind of big-picture advocacy work a little later on, but, in the meantime, this book is going to help you laugh and find your people so that your life as a woman online becomes a little more fucking bearable.

For now, there's little you can do to avoid these maniac men if you want to live a normal functioning life in public as a woman in the digital arena. They're everywhere: Tinder, Bumble, Facebook, Twitter, the bar down the street, the White House. So you might as well learn to anticipate them, be prepared with strategies to deflect their insults and threats, and commiserate in knowing that you're not alone.

If you are just dipping your toes into online dating—for the first time, or the first time in a while—this book is for you. This is the book I wish I had had when I was first starting out as a bright-eyed, bushy-tailed Tinder noob. I'll take you through many of the tribulations you'll undoubtedly face in this strange internet dating world, and we'll learn how to get through them together.

CHAPTER 1

Online Dating: Y Tho?

OK, I get it. Why would anyone put themselves through internet dating? You've seen the horror stories, whether they're from Bye Felipe or one of the dozens of viral news stories that come out every few months about a man doing something so ridiculous, you'd think it's a headline from *The Onion*. (Except it's real.) I see your point; however, online dating is not weird anymore, and pretty much everyone is doing it or knows someone who's doing it. And here's why: no one meets in real life. We're all addicted to our phones. Have you ever gone to a coffee shop, talked to a stranger, and then gone on a date with that stranger? If you're under thirty-five (a millennial or younger), probably not.

We do everything with our beloved phones, so why wouldn't we use them to get out of our isolation caves and establish some real human contact? A lot of people just want to find someone to love, and it's hard to meet people otherwise. If you're not in college, and if you don't really have many friends who can set you up with other nice single people, how exactly are you supposed to meet someone in public when their face is buried in their phone at all times? At bars? Only if you want to meet aggressive creepo-s who put the moves on countless women in hopes that one of them will bite. If you turn one of them down, you know he's going to hit on ten more.

The types of guys I'm into would never go up to a woman and aggressively hit on her in public because—and I've heard this from my great guy friends—they "don't want to ruin her day." The normal, self-aware, nonasshole guys usually are not going to hit on you in public. And isn't that kind of a relief? Anytime I'm walking down the street and I pass a man, I'm usually thinking, "Please don't talk to me. Please don't talk to me." Because I know it's almost always going to be something to make me feel uncomfortable—a "Hey, you should smile more" or an unsettling whispered comment about my boobs.

Maybe my millennial generation is a little bit socially inept from all the internet usage we grew up with. But at the end of the day, let's face it, online dating is just more efficient. I like it because it's fast, easy, and I can eliminate deal-breakers before I agree to meet for a date. I also just like meeting lots of new people—and I've met some really interesting and wonderful guys I would have never met otherwise: ER doctors, entrepreneurs, scientists, minor celebrities. There's no way I would have run into these people through friends or in my neighborhood. For whatever reason, we may not have been compatible, but I've made a ton of guy friends from online dating. I've even met some of my best girlfriends through guys I met on an internet date.

The great thing about the current state of internet dating is that there really is a niche app or site for everyone, so if one of them doesn't work for you, try another one. In my quest for love, and in the name of research for this book, I've tested them all so you don't have to.

Guide: Which Dating App Should You Use?

TINDER: Swiping app centered around pictures only. (Swipe left if you're not interested, swipe right if you are. If two people both swipe right, they match and can chat.) Use this one if you're looking for a hookup. Or a date. Or if you want to network. Basically, if you want to meet a stranger for any reason at all based only on their appearance. Pretty much everyone is on it—straights, gays, bi, cis, trans, nonbinary folks. As well as polyamorous couples, monogamous people, cheaters. This requires you to wade through lots of people as there aren't many filters besides age, gender, and location, and a lot of profiles don't show many details. Useful if you're traveling on a backpacker's budget for free food or travel guides. (Just kidding—but not really.)

OKCUPID: Generally more for relationships. Profiles are more detailed, and you can answer questions to get matched with compatible people. The filtering features are nice. I met my ex-boyfriend of two-and-a-half years on OkCupid, and I've met some other quality guys on there, too. Try it if you want to know some weirdly specific facts about a stranger before you meet them, like how they'd answer this question: "While in the middle of the best lovemaking of your life, if your lover asked you to squeal like a dolphin, would you?"

BUMBLE: Like Tinder, but women have to message first, and matches disappear in twenty-four hours if you don't talk. It was started by Whitney Wolfe Herd, the woman who co-founded Tinder. She later had a falling out with the other douchebro founders of Tinder, sued for sexual harassment, and won a settlement. In my opinion, Bumble is OK. But I know lots of women who swear by it. The gender roles of messaging are reversed, which is kind of cool, but you have to message a bunch of guys before one of them responds. About 10–15 percent of guys I match with usually respond, which seems like more effort than with other apps.

HAPPN: Kinda like Tinder, but it shows you everyone you've "crossed paths" with. It's supposed to work if you pass someone on the street or see them at the same restaurant, and you think they're hot, but you're too afraid to talk to them. You can check Happn and, if they're also on it, match with them to chat. I have never once actually used it in the scenario it was created for. In reality, it brings up a list of people who have probably driven past your apartment at one point. That said, I've still met a few solid dudes on Happn.

HINGE: When I first started using Hinge a few years ago, it was all rich bros from Santa Monica, which is not really my scene, and it was premised on having Facebook friends in common, which was nothing special. However, they have since completely overhauled the app and are now more focused on creating relationships. You have to have six photos or videos on your profile and complete three writing prompts like "I'd donate my kidney for___." (I said, "putting Trump in jail.") It's a middle ground between Tinder, where you don't know anything about the person, and OkCupid, where the profiles are long and tedious. There's also a place to indicate important deal-breakers, like whether you want kids and if you smoke weed or not.

MATCH.COM: Everyone says that you should join Match if you want to get married, because you have to pay for it, and dudes who pay for their dating apps are SERIOUS (apparently). In my experience, Match is the worst matching algorithm, created on a website that looks like it was designed in 2003 with the blandest guys who hardly fill out their profiles and don't have a clue about how to start a conversation besides copying and pasting something generic and calling you beautiful. It's also full of outdated profiles of people who haven't been on the site in months. I joined for six months (FOR SCIENCE!) and didn't see one guy I would ever want to go on a date with. Try it if you're looking for someone with a personality like plain oatmeal.

THE LEAGUE: It's supposed to be for people who went to prestigious colleges, but they let me on it (I went to a non-Ivy League university), so IDK. I got approved a year after I signed up because they say they go through each application by hand. You can pay to get approved sooner, but I'm glad I didn't because they gave me three matches a day, and they all seemed like rich douchebros. Maybe that's someone's type, but not mine. Try it if you're super into dudes who went to the Ivy League.

COFFEE MEETS BAGEL: This app/site works by sending guys a selection of twenty-one women. The guys indicate who they're interested in, then they provide the chosen women with the guys who liked them, so you get the final say. It's nice to only be presented with guys who you already know are interested. It's more relationship-oriented.

HUGGLE: This one was co-founded by Stina Sanders, a model who publicly shared a dick pic someone sent her, in order to call out his sexism. The app is based on places you go, and you can only message someone if you have a public place in common. The reasoning behind it is, Sanders says, that guys are less likely to send dick pics to people they see in real life. Huggle is also focused on helping people make platonic friends at the places they frequent. Try it if you're new to a city and want to make friends with the regulars at your favorite coffee shop.

RAYA: "The secret Tinder for celebrities." You allegedly have to have some sort of clout to join this app. Anyone can apply, but they're going to judge you based on how many Instagram followers you have, if you're a famous person, and if you have phone number references from three people who are already Raya users. I tried to apply once with the @ByeFelipe Instagram account and was waitlisted. However, I know some regular people who got on it in the beginning and have played around with their accounts. It's mostly a sprinkling of DJs, models, actors, and a few sort-of famous people like Moby. They try to keep it a secret, and you get kicked off if you take a screenshot of any profile.

PLENTY OF FISH: The bottom of the barrel. I don't really know why anyone uses this. I get a lot of Bye Felipe submissions from POF, if that tells you anything about the types of guys who use it.

FEELD: This is the threesome app. It used to be called 3nder (yes, thrinder), but then Tinder sued them so they had to change the name. If you've ever wanted to go on a date with a couple, this is your app. However, I've tried it out and matched with some pretty hot single dudes who were nice. People are very up front about their sexual kinks and talk about hooking up right away, so if you're looking for something casual, this might be good to try. I've also never experienced a Bye Felipe situation on this app.

JSWIPE: Like Tinder for Jewish people. I haven't tried this one, but it exists.

JDATE: Like OkCupid for Jewish people. Also have not tried it (because I'm not Jewish).

ZOOSK & BADOO: They say they have millions of users, but too many features are behind paywalls, no one fills out their profiles, and the interface is bad. No thanks.

EHARMONY: For the olds. Like, people over fifty.

HER: Tinder for women-identifying people only.

GRINDR: Gay hookup app. I have heard from friends that a lot of guys lead with dick pics there.

WHAT'S YOUR PRICE: If you wanna get paid $200 to have dinner with a (probably creepy) rich guy. No judgment though; sometimes you need some quick cash. I have friends who have done this. Just be *extra* careful.

FARMERS ONLY: Their tagline is "City folks just don't get it!" Not gonna lie—I signed up just to see what was on there. (I am from a town of 50 people in the middle of nowhere Minnesota, so I *do* get it.) The guys looked very sweet and emotionally available, and are into things like horses, blacksmithing, and making wagon wheels, if that's your scene.

I know that reading the horror stories from Bye Felipe can make it seem as if online dating isn't worth it. But my original reason for showing these messages was not that people shouldn't use Tinder or other dating apps. It was that we need to take a look at our society and culture, and figure out why the hostile men do this, so we can try to change it. It was about starting a conversation about gender roles and why the patriarchy is bad for men *and* women.

Though online dating is inherently easy, it also has challenges. There are more chances to meet a gem of a man who could be your best friend, but there are also more chances for you to meet someone sleazy. Let me show you what I mean.

Backtrack: It was the summer of 2013 in Los Angeles. I sat on my bed in my new studio apartment near Hollywood Boulevard, swiping through photos of "eligible" men on my phone. A man's shirtless gym selfie appeared. NOPE. The next guy was wearing sunglasses in every single one of his photos. NOPE. One blurry profile picture only featured half of a guy's face. NOPE. Group of dudes on the beach—who was I supposed to be looking at? I didn't have time to figure it out. NOPE.

I was rebounding hard. My live-in boyfriend of two-and-a-half years had broken up with me a few months before. Lucky for me, the dating app Tinder had just reached critical mass in Los Angeles. All I needed was for someone to buy me a beer, tell me I'm pretty, and try to make out with me. Too young. NOPE. There is no way that old man is twenty-nine. NOPE.

Then, there he was. My thumb lingered over a scruffy, dark-haired babe who actually seemed to know how to dress himself. He was HOT. Like, almost too hot. His main profile picture was him holding a pool cue at a bar and giving a half-smile to the camera. I knew that dimple in his cheek was trouble from the get-go. For the purposes of this story, I'll call him "Ryan."

Would I? Should I? What the hell. Yep, I swiped right.

The screen lit up. "It's a match!" My heart fluttered a little. Ryan would be the second person I ever communicated with on Tinder. (I'll tell you about the first one later. It is a story that involves feces.)

> Hi.
> You're quite attractive.
> I'm kinda silly.
> What's your favorite drink in the whole wide world?
> Hot chocolate is acceptable. :)
> "Currently, water," I replied. "I'm pretty hungover from last night."

We started chatting, and I eventually gave him my number. He made it clear early on that he was freshly out of a relationship and wasn't looking for anything serious. "I just want to let you know, since there are a lot of douchebags out there," he said. Wow! So courteous.

He lived in the valley, but he claimed that he came down to LA every weekend, so we could meet up then. Being fresh out of a relationship myself, I didn't really mind that he gave me the all-too-common disclaimer. After all, he was RULL good-looking.

A few days later, I agreed to Skype with him—mostly to see if he was as attractive as his photos and to determine if he was not a douchebag, as he claimed. He seemed nice enough, and we chatted a bit before the compliments started flowing (my kryptonite). I was pretty flattered.

"You're really beautiful. I love your eyes and your hair," he said.

Then he admitted that he was really turned on. I myself wasn't so much, but I wasn't offended.

He asked if I wanted to see his penis.

"Uhhhhhhh . . . Oh, umm, I don't know," I squeaked out. I don't even remember the details of the entire exchange, but I ended up conceding "for science!" to see how this would end up. (A lot of my experiences with online dating have happened because this is my general attitude.) I'm always curious about human nature and want to know why people do weird things, so I try new things and observe. I'm the Margaret Mead of Tinder, you could say.

It was most definitely weird. I ended up watching him masturbate. I was not turned on, but I was kind of fascinated: Why did he think this was a good idea?

This wasn't the last time a guy I matched with on Tinder masturbated in front of me via the internet. It happened *two more times* with other guys within the first few months. I was so confused. I thought, "THIS IS INSANE. WHY is this happening to me? What is it about me that makes dudes want to fap it immediately? Do they love making women uncomfortable? What do they get out of it?"

I was repulsed, but I knew Ryan was harmless, in the sense that he probably wasn't going to physically harm me, so I tried to just forget about him. However, he contacted me again a few months later since I forgot to block his Skype handle. I figured it was a good time to ask him my questions. Here's our conversation:

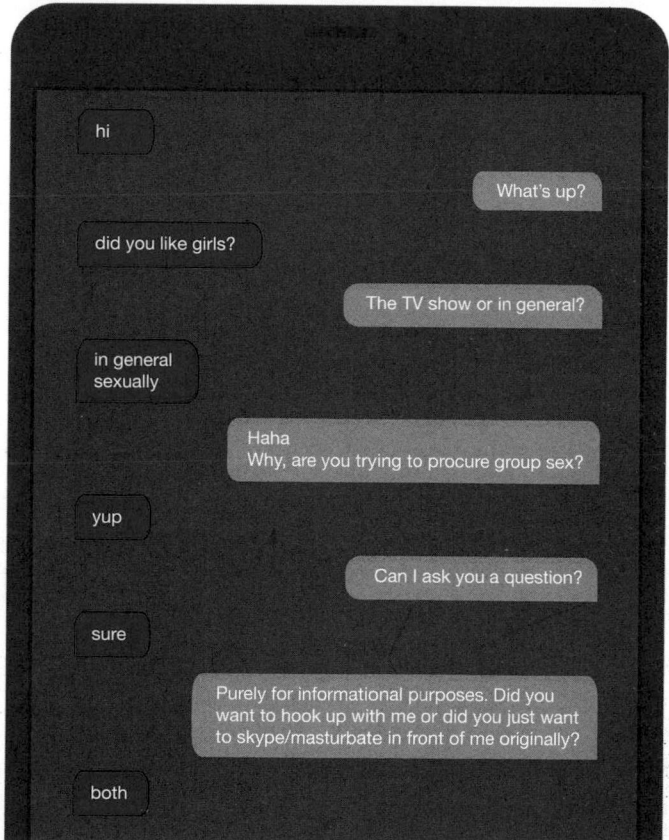

hi

What's up?

did you like girls?

The TV show or in general?

in general sexually

Haha
Why, are you trying to procure group sex?

yup

Can I ask you a question?

sure

Purely for informational purposes. Did you want to hook up with me or did you just want to skype/masturbate in front of me originally?

both

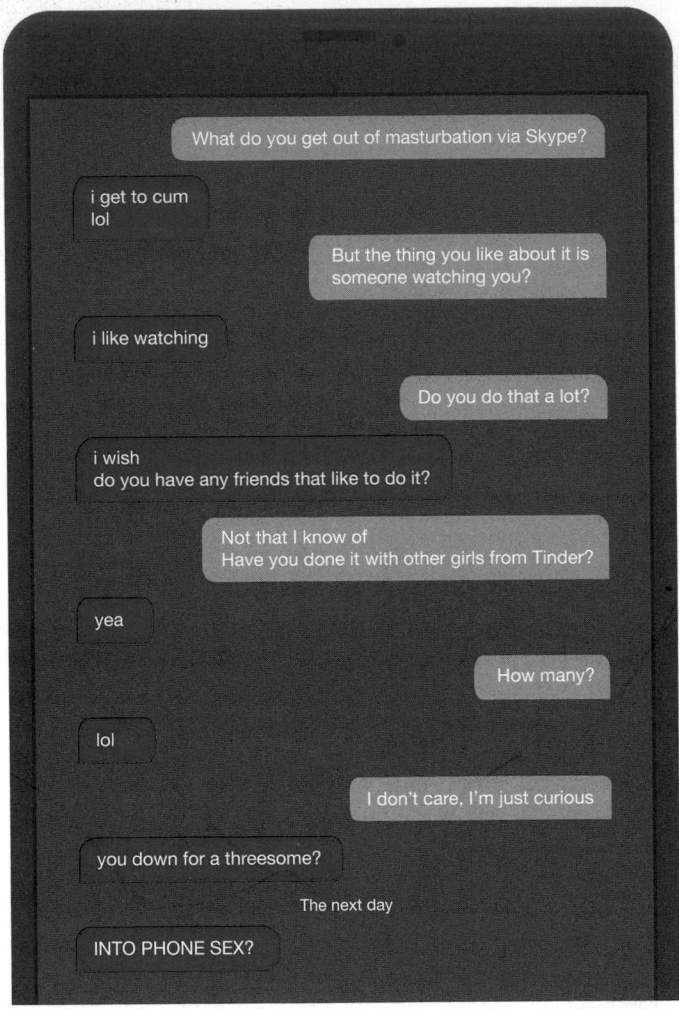

Clearly, Ryan was just a typical sex-obsessed hornball of a guy. The kind of guy who interrupts a normal conversation with an off-the-wall sexual comment, completely ruining the mood and making you regret even talking to him in the first place. At the time, it was shocking, but now after regularly trudging through the trenches of Tinder, I've come to discover that this type of behavior is quite common. There's even a Tumblr blog dedicated to this phenomenon called "Straight White Boys Texting."

Straight White Boy Texting

1. adj/noun: A style of texting popularized primarily by straight white boys (but can be used to pertain to people of all sexual orientations and genders) wherein the sender abruptly transitions the conversation from normal and polite to raunchy and gross. It is characterized by the texter displaying a blind sexual urgency and a complete disregard for social cues and norms, e.g., "He asked what I had for lunch, and then out of nowhere, asked if I was DTF. It turned into a Straight White Boys Texting situation."

Here are a few more examples of "Straight White Boy Texts" I have received. In this one, I matched with him on Tinder because he had posted a cute profile picture of himself with an adorable orange cat lying on his shoulders. It starts off innocently enough, until he asks me to meet up at midnight.

> Hello

> Hi

> What's going on cutie

> Was just about to fall asleep

> Do u live in Santa Monica

> No, Hollywood/Los Feliz.

Apparently, the thought of me going to sleep was all it took to put him over the edge?

I matched with this next guy despite his being an "actor, writer, carpenter, voice and breath coach looking for adventures." I think mostly because his pictures were hot. He had nice hair and a good beard. What transpired in the conversation was . . . odd, to say the least.

And, yes, *of course*, he was white. Hey, dude, maybe don't involve me in your bizarre racial cuckolding kink right off the bat? Thanks. (Obviously, I'm not against interracial relationships, but this was just straight up racial fetishizing.)

As you can see, the jumping to sexual lingo prematurely on Tinder is definitely *a thing*, but if you need more examples, just check out the SWBT blog. One thing to note is that while many straight white boys do text like this, not all of them are guilty. Boys (and nonboys) who are of other orientations and races are not immune to doing it, either, but it was a joke and it stuck. According to the creator of the Straight White Boys Texting Tumblr blog, "While originally coming up with a more inclusive name could have been better in hindsight, it's a bit late."[2]

Straight White Boys Texting was an obvious precursor to Bye Felipe, as it was started a few months earlier, but it didn't quite capture the hostility I came to experience and expect from clueless men in my online dating life. The idea would come after going on many more dates and connecting with women who had also been experiencing nightmare men.

I didn't really give Ryan or the other horny dudes a second thought after these experiences, until a year later, when I joined Girls Night In, the secret girl group on Facebook. One day, a member posted something about a guy she'd matched with on Tinder. I instantly recognized the opening line: "I kinda want to make out with you."

IT WAS RYAN. We all immediately chimed in with groans of recognition. It seems he had matched with pretty much everyone who was on Tinder at the time, and used the same lines, immediately killing the mood with his crude version of sexting.

Ryan has since shown up in over a hundred posts. Every time, he sends women the exact same messages—kind of like a horny robot. "STAY FAR AWAY FROM HIM! He's on EVERY dating site ever. Claims to be 'good Christian man with strong Christian values,'" someone said in the group.

"He's sent me dick pix when I haven't asked for them. He has stalked me, AND has stalked one of my close friends. I asked one of my friends who was a mutual friend of his on FB, and he said he's A CREEP! STAY AWAY LADIES!"

"I've matched with him a few times as well. He's super creepy!! Sends nasty dick pics and begs to hook up. He's a disgusting individual. So glad someone posted this. I was going to report him next time he tried to match with me."

Now, whenever someone in our group matches with Ryan on Tinder, they'll recognize him by reputation immediately. Even when they call him out, he's never flinched.

The following exchanges were all courtesy of Ryan on various women's Tinder accounts.

As you can see, he only has two pickup lines: "I kinda want to make out with you," and "What's your favorite drink in the whole wide world?" Once you respond to those, he goes straight for the dick pic or says he "wants to fuck." A classic straight white boy move.

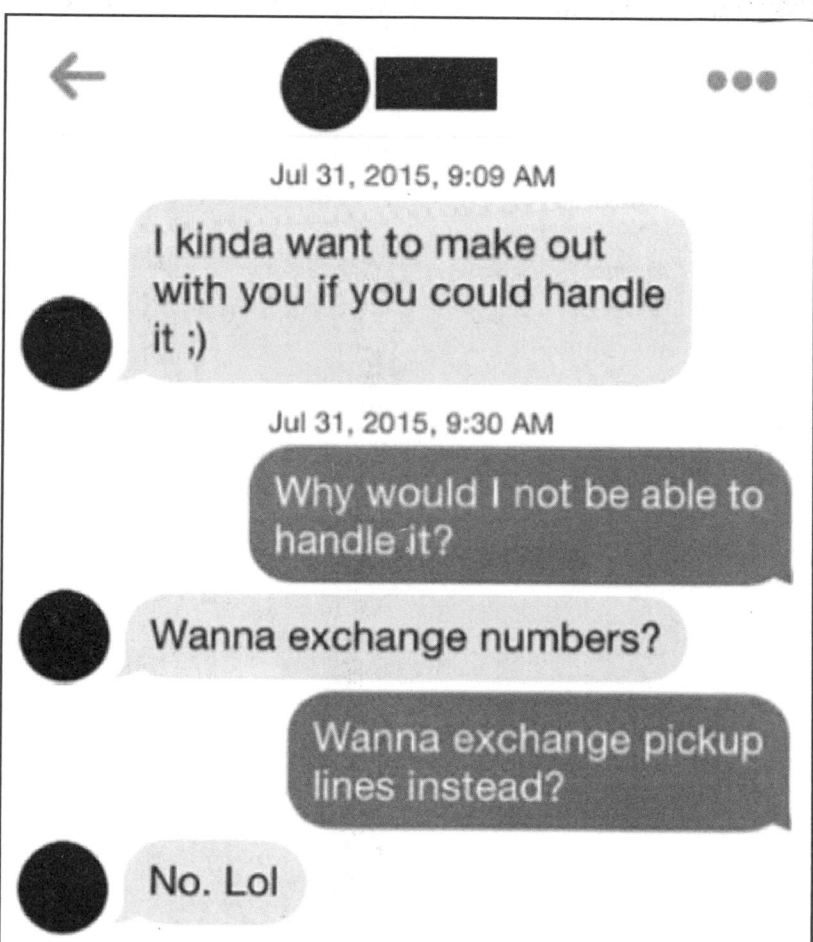

And another one of his classic pickup lines on Tinder:

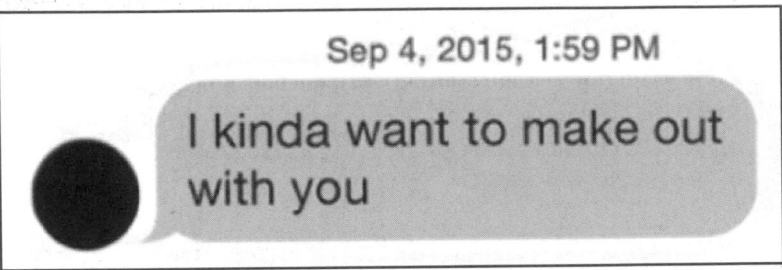

After matching on Tinder, Brianna exchanged numbers with Brian and got this unfortunate straight white boy response.

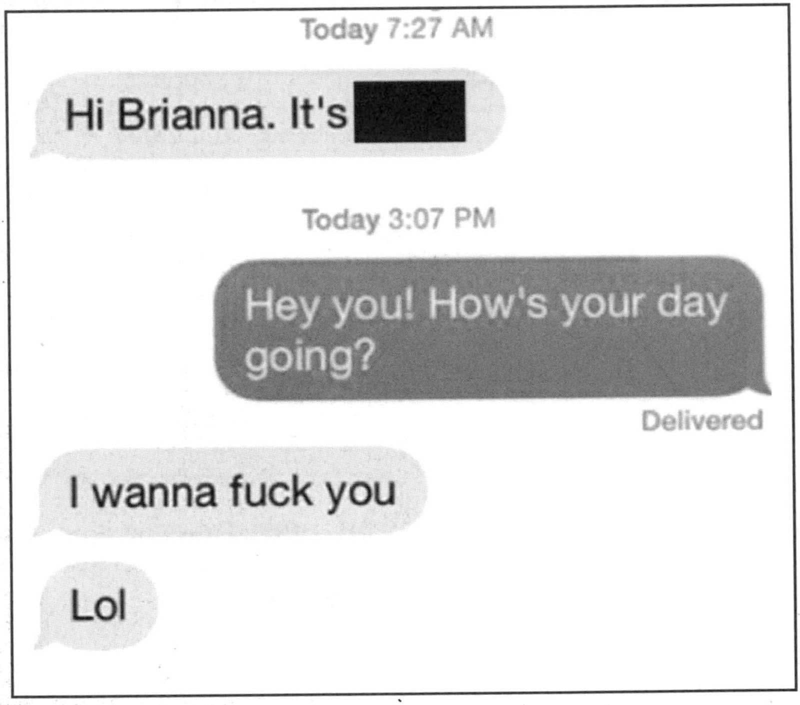

Today 7:27 AM

Hi Brianna. It's ▮

Today 3:07 PM

Hey you! How's your day going?

Delivered

I wanna fuck you

Lol

And here he is with a dick pic no one asked for:

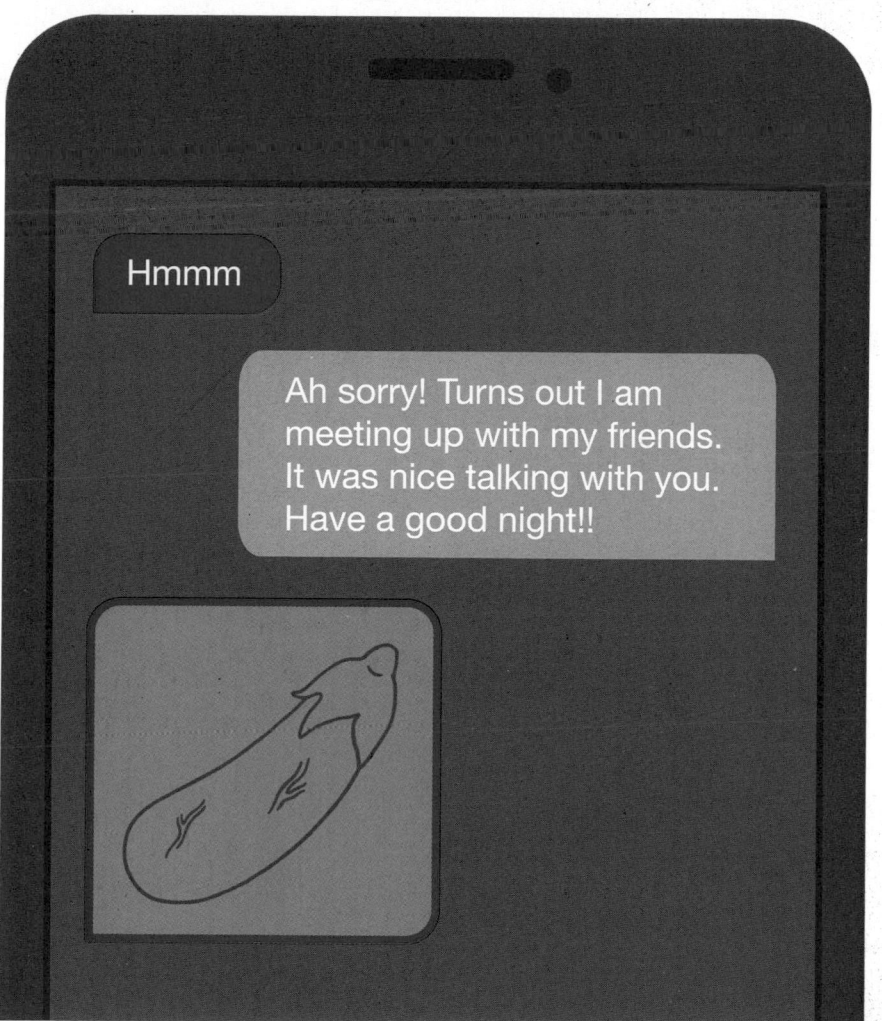

And he was on OkCupid, too. The following exchanges are from four different women:

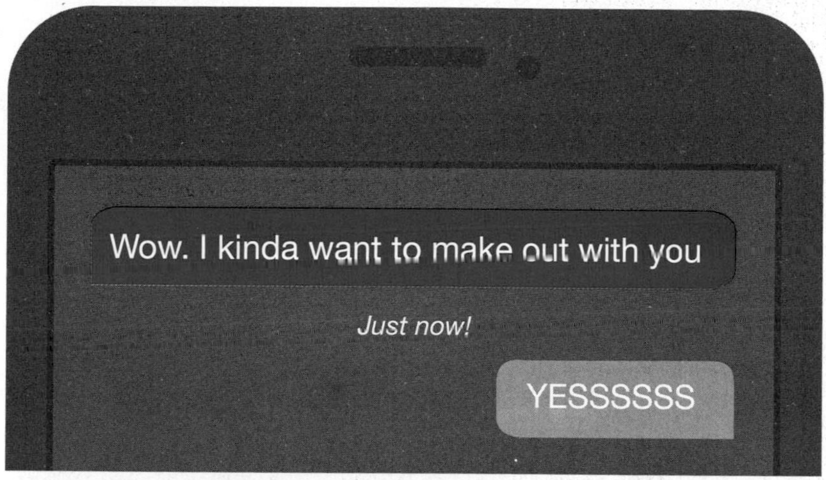

Wow. I kinda want to make out with you

Just now!

YESSSSSS

Sept 10

Hi. You're quite attractive. I'm kinda silly. What's your favorite drink in the whole wide world? Hot chocolate is acceptable ;)

Sept 11

Oh Ryan . . .

Wanna exchange numbers?

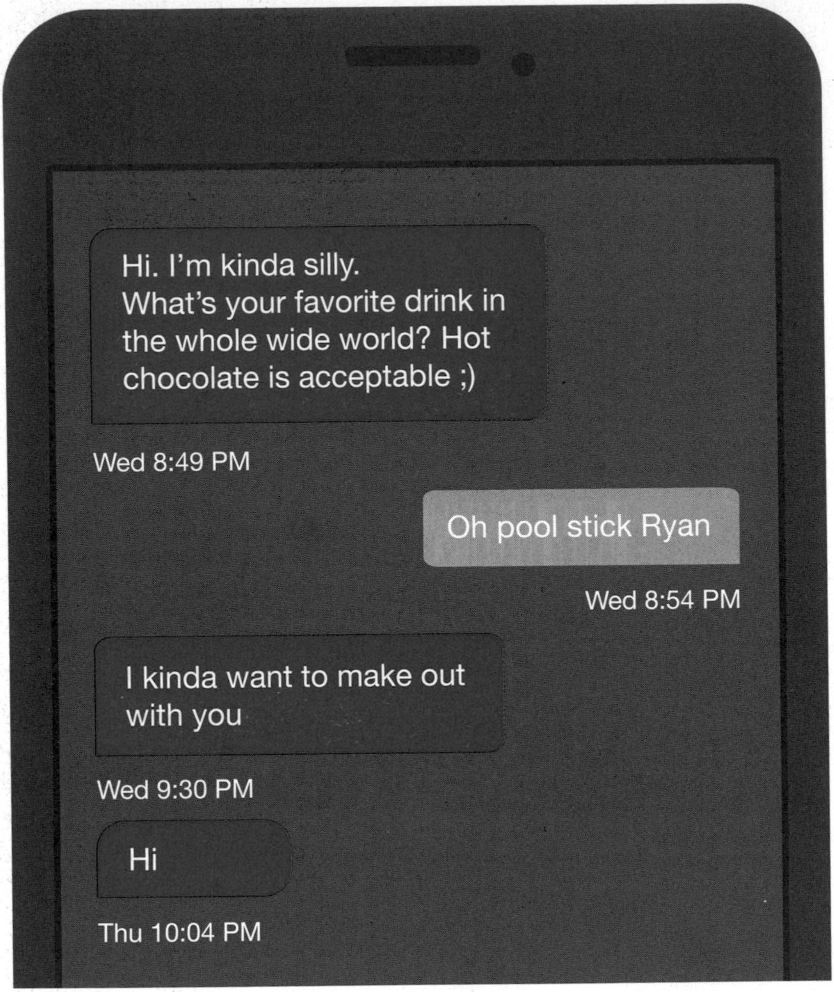

Hi. I'm kinda silly.
What's your favorite drink in
the whole wide world? Hot
chocolate is acceptable ;)

Wed 8:49 PM

Oh pool stick Ryan

Wed 8:54 PM

I kinda want to make out
with you

Wed 9:30 PM

Hi

Thu 10:04 PM

YOU GOT RYAN'D

HOW IS THIS A REAL PERSON? He's a good-looking, conventionally attractive guy. Whenever I tell other women about this story and then show them a picture of Ryan, they say, "THAT'S Ryan?! He's so *hot*. Why does he do that?" My answer is always "I have no idea." He could definitely go on dates with a great number of women in the Los Angeles area. All he'd have to do is behave like a normal human being.

(Maybe he's actually an alien from another planet?) What is he doing on Tinder? It seems like his approach always fails horribly, but he keeps doing the same thing. Is he just there to "exchange numbers"? Will he only be satisfied when he's completely disgusted every person who will listen to him? As far as I know, he's still out there proclaiming to the ladies of Los Angeles that he "kinda" wants to make out with them. Maybe it works on some women, and it's just a numbers game to him. Honestly, I have no idea what's wrong with Ryan. He probably has some personal issues that he needs to work through.

Since that first fateful Tinder interaction with Ryan, I continued to persevere into the online dating muck. Why? For love. People in my generation are looking for the right person. We're picky and don't want to settle for less than the best. The thing about online dating is that it's easy to get burned out. Either you go on a bunch of dates and none of them work out, or you have a bad experience, like getting your heart stomped on, or you end up dealing with bozos who send mean messages. But I always take a break and come back because otherwise I'd never meet anyone. Plus, more than one-third of marriages now start online.[3]

At this point, I've seen it all. In addition to receiving a constant stream of examples of terrible dating behavior delivered to my Bye Felipe inbox daily, I've also been on more than two hundred dates with dudes I've met from OkCupid, Tinder, and a bunch of other sites. Of course, most dates and online interactions go fine—most men are perfectly polite but, for whatever reason, we just didn't click. But all that experience has also given me a superpower: the ability to spot some types of Felipes in the wild from miles away. I now have a pretty good intuition for screening them out, and that's why I want to share with you my method for weeding out the terrible ones.

I've categorized the Bye Felipe submissions into ten types of garbage diarrhea men to be extra wary of. We need to have terms for these problem guys if we want to discuss how to deal with them. Which brings us to the first type:

1. Boring Bob

This is your basic Bye Felipe submission. Boring Bob just isn't very imaginative or intelligent. He thinks that because we live in a society where women are mostly valued for their appearance, he'll be able to make you feel bad for rejecting him by saying you're fat or ugly. But the joke's on him, because you know you're hot—otherwise, why would he be hitting on you in the first place? That's why it's hilarious.

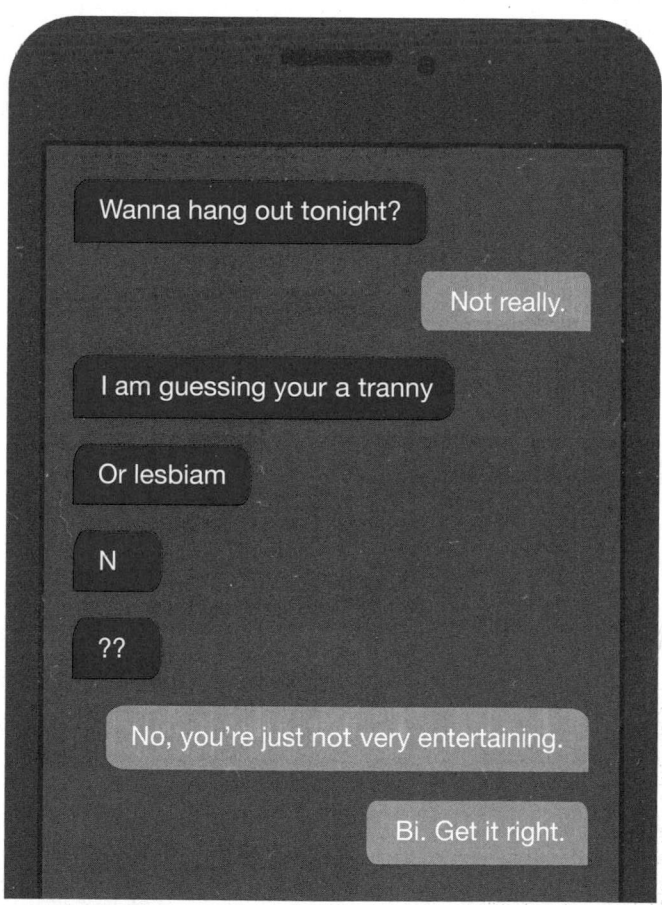

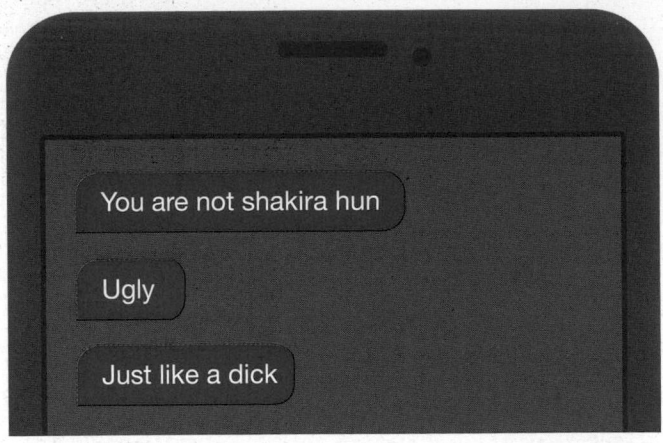

OK, so because she doesn't want to hang out with you, Boring Bob, she's either transgender (which is not a very good insult, because trans folks are beautiful, and there's nothing wrong with being trans) or a lesbian because anyone who doesn't like you must not be interested in any man? And of course, she's "ugly." But there's no reasoning with Felipes. They're just too dense to understand that women don't owe them shit.

This other Boring Bob doesn't understand that women get hundreds of messages on OkCupid, and there's no way we can respond to all of them. I'm not really sure why it's so hard to accept that if a person doesn't reply, they're not interested. And after only twenty minutes?!

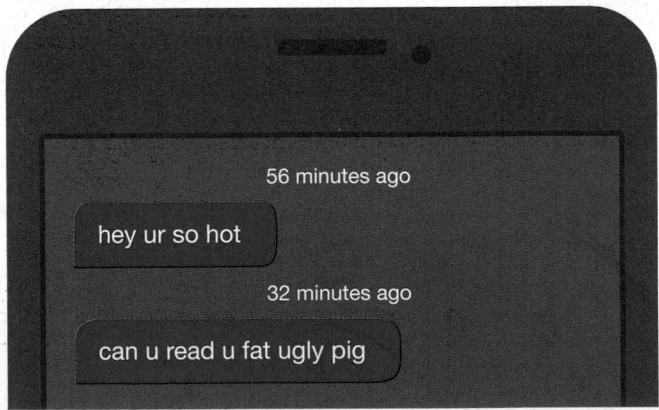

This Tinder Boring Bob asked her to come over prematurely, and suddenly she's too fat.

> Idk what you think is gonna be happening lol

Boning

> Yea no

July 30, 2016, 1:32 AM

Youre fat

Stay away from soda

And fast food

The first time you experience someone calling you fat or ugly when you don't respond, you might feel angry, hurt, or offended. But around the fifth time, you just want to yawn. Why is that always the go-to insult?

See Exhibit A:

> So, you're too good?

> No, I'm not too good, but I'm just not interested.

> Because your fatass isn't. Disgusting blob of lard.

> Interested in diet tips?

> Hope diabetes kills you soon.

> Not particularly. I don't really associate with cyber bullies. Have a blessed day!

And Exhibit B: Notice his screenname contains "thegentleman." He's really proving it to be true.

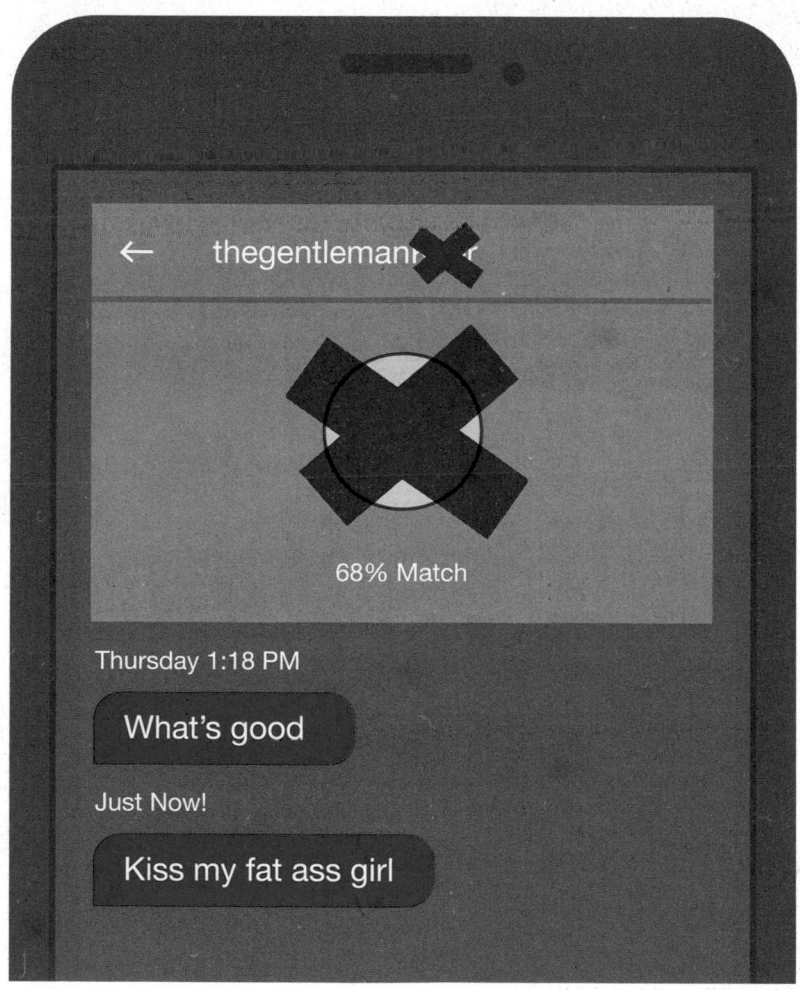

2. Nice Guy™ Nick

We've all experienced a Nice Guy™ Nick. You know, the one who meets the minimum standards of a decent human being and thinks he deserves a trophy because he "respects women," except in the same breath he'll tell you you're a 5/10. Actual nice people never have to tell you that they're nice because they know that being "nice" is a given. Proclaiming that you are a "nice guy" is like saying, "I breathe air and I don't murder!" Cool, same as 99.9999 percent of people on Earth!

Observe this standard OkCupid Nice Guy™ move of trying to bargain for your friendship, telling you he's not a creep, and then proceeding to be a creep.

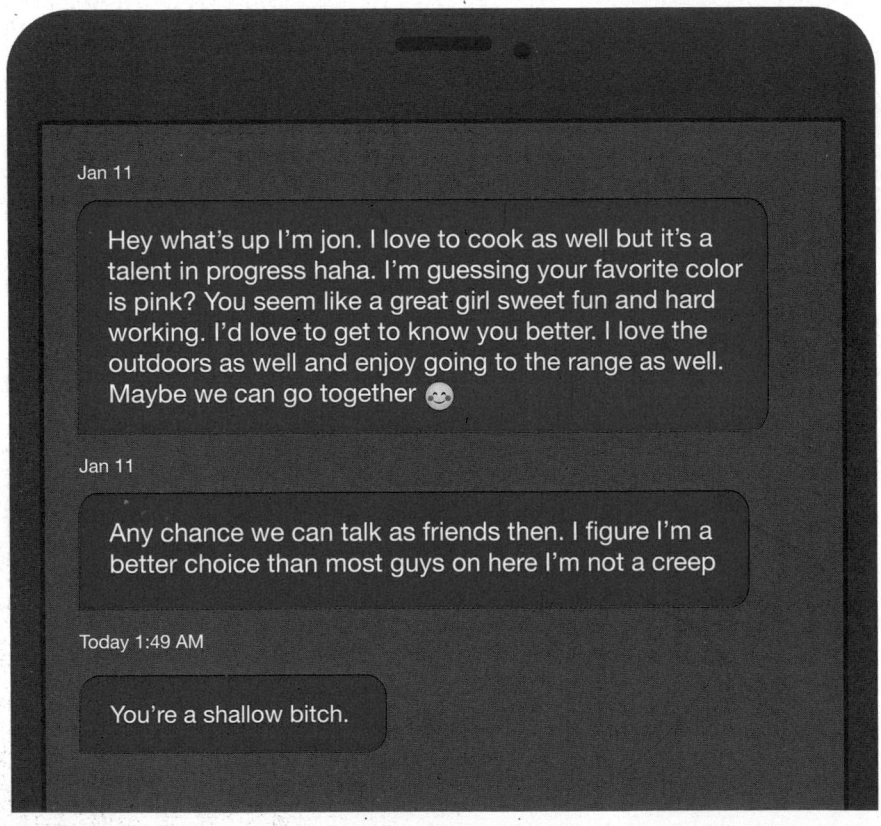

Jan 11

Hey what's up I'm jon. I love to cook as well but it's a talent in progress haha. I'm guessing your favorite color is pink? You seem like a great girl sweet fun and hard working. I'd love to get to know you better. I love the outdoors as well and enjoy going to the range as well. Maybe we can go together 😊

Jan 11

Any chance we can talk as friends then. I figure I'm a better choice than most guys on here I'm not a creep

Today 1:49 AM

You're a shallow bitch.

He DESERVES your attention because he didn't send you a dick pic!

> Hey how are you? I'm so bad at this online thing. I don't get a lot of responses. I don't know if I'm just coming off the wrong way or what. I'd really like to chat and see if we click. I don't know what I have to say to make that happen, but I'd love to hear back from you.

> So. . . WTF? you can't just say not interested? you're gonna visit my page and make me feel like a piece of shit wondering why I wasn't worth 3 fucking words? This site is driving me crazy. I am a super fucking nice guy. I have a great high paying job, my life is in order and I'm just trying to meet some people. I'm so tired of this "visit" and no response rejections. Am I just crazy, is it not insanely rude to just completely ignore someone after they read your profile and spend time trying to spark some form of conversation politely? I'm not sending dick pics to people! I'm not going "hey great boobs bitch wanna fuck? I though you seemed awesome. sorry I wasted my time reading your profile.

They never consider that maybe our inboxes are full of this stuff and we don't have time to respond to every person. Maybe we're just not attracted to them? And if we say they're not our type, we're afraid of getting an expletive-laden response?

If you're lucky, they'll be upfront about their own Nice Guy™ tendencies in their dating profiles:

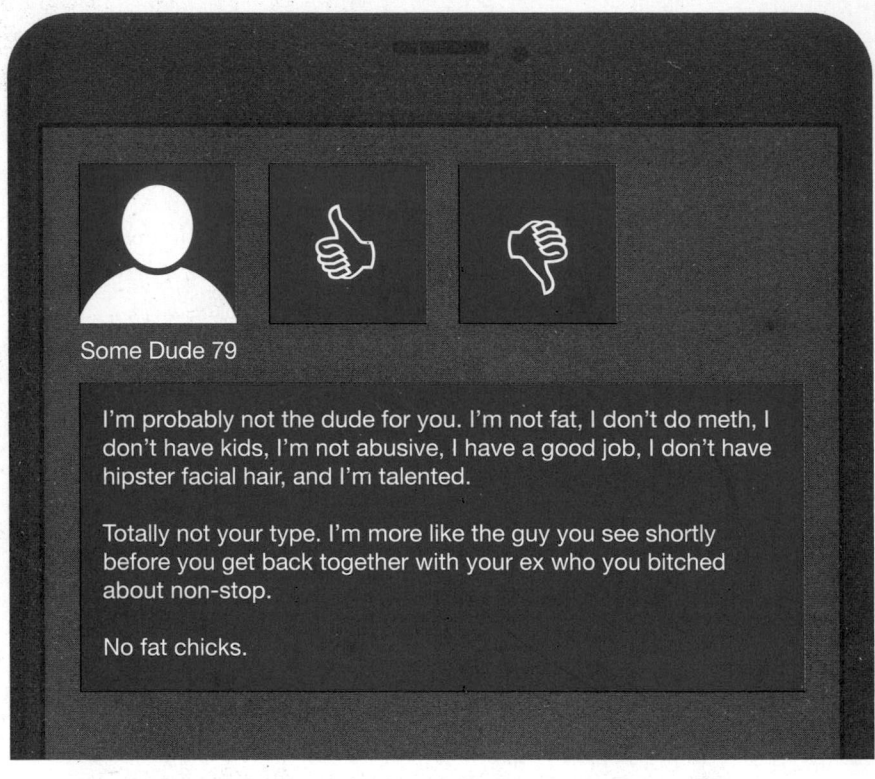

Some Dude 79

I'm probably not the dude for you. I'm not fat, I don't do meth, I don't have kids, I'm not abusive, I have a good job, I don't have hipster facial hair, and I'm talented.

Totally not your type. I'm more like the guy you see shortly before you get back together with your ex who you bitched about non-stop.

No fat chicks.

"Please feel sorry for me! But also, no fat chicks!"

3. Michael Mansplainer

Michael Mansplainer is here to save the day! Did you major in astrophysics? Well, guess what? Michael's here to explain it to you! Thank god for this genius. If it weren't for him, you never would have understood the properties of dark matter, which happens to be the subject of your master's thesis!

A mansplainer saves the day again:

Hey there Sam

You're a metalsmith?

Yes sir

Make me a knife

No that's a bladesmith
Not what I do

You would make a million dollars a year if you made and sold quality outdoor knives as a pretty girl. A million cute girls make jewelry. None of them make outdoors knives. Guys would buy from you left and right. You wouldn't be able to make them fast enough to keep up w demand.

Especially if you came up w a legit name for the brand. Not girly, bc guys won't buy it. But something that lets them know you made it

Sweetblade or SweetEdge etc

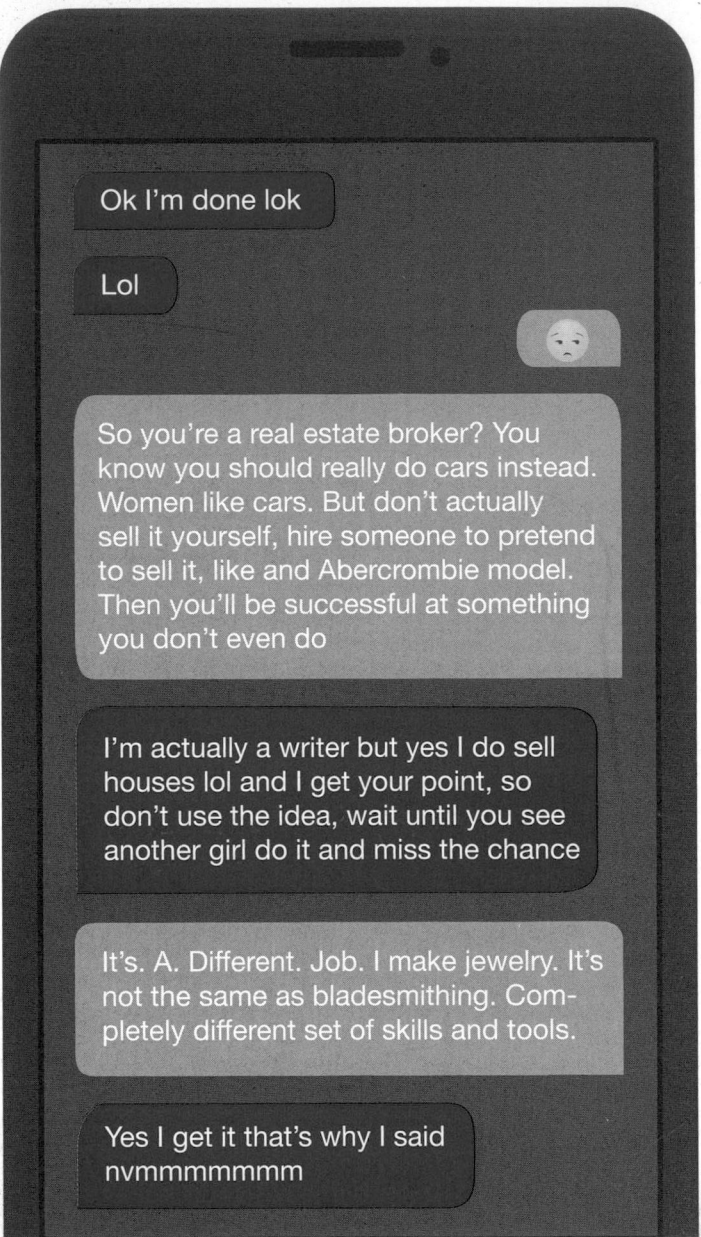

4. Male Feminist Mitch

If there's one thing I've learned about men thus far, it's DO NOT TRUST A MAN WHO SAYS HE'S A FEMINIST JUST BECAUSE HE SAYS HE'S A FEMINIST. The #MeToo movement has underscored that no one should be trusted, especially when men who previously seemed to be feminist and woke are accused of sexual misconduct or assault. It seems that some men are using the feminist label in order to get us to sleep with them.

I'm not saying don't trust any man who says he's a feminist, but probably don't automatically give them a free pass. If you ask if he's a feminist in casual conversation, and he says yes, great. But I always side-eye any man's profile that proclaims his wokeness with the feminist label without being asked. Real feminist allies are aware that it's more than just claiming the name, it's doing the work, listening to women, and giving up power. I believe men can be feminists (I know not everyone agrees), but they need to prove it in their actions. Don't just take them at their word.

I matched with "Mitch" on Tinder in 2015. He seemed really sweet. His profile said that he had moved to LA recently, he was a dog walker, and he loved beer, pizza, and doughnuts. He said he was "a feminist, music nerd, record collector, concert-goer, and urban adventurer." He liked coffee and tattoos and was from the Midwest. When I matched with him, I was all 😍😍. These are all interests of mine as well.

I sent him the first message. "I'm into everything about your profile. Are you trolling me?"

"No," he said. "I'm not smart enough to troll anyone."

"LOL," I responded. "I was attempting to make a joke."

"Oh," he replied. "I'm not funny either."

And that should've been my clue that we probably wouldn't get along. Any guy who doesn't get my sense of humor probably won't understand me as a human being. Regardless, I gave him the benefit of the doubt and brushed it off. I then attempted to banter about music, and suggested that we meet up the next day.

"No," he said. "Let's do it tonight. You're young, I'm a troublemaker."

"Oh I see," I said. "What do you suggest we do?"

"I've got a billion ideas. I've been wanting to drive around Beverly Hills late at night, or cruise around Laurel Canyon or Mulholland Drive and see all the winding roads with big mansions. Ride bikes. Make drinks and listen to records. I can go on..."

These all sounded great to me. I love it when a guy can suggest creative date ideas instead of the usual drinks or coffee.

We continued talking, and I asked what music he was into.

"Indie, shoegaze, electronic, ambient, experimental, new age, postrock."

"Cool," I said.

Then I looked up from my phone for a few minutes and continued watching a movie with my friend. I was entertaining the idea of possibly meeting up with him later that night when suddenly I got a phone call from him.

"WHO DO YOU THINK YOU ARE?!" he yelled. "I was trying to explain something and you cut me off."

He continued to berate me. I couldn't tell what he was talking about. He wouldn't let me get a word in. It all happened so fast, I can't even remember what he said or what he was talking about. I just know that it scared me. We had just been talking so nicely and now I was getting yelled at for no reason. Eventually, he addressed me as "Marissa."

"Marissa?" I asked. "Who do you think you're talking to? This is Alexandra."

He kept yelling. "You said your name was something else!"

"No, this is Alexandra. I don't know who you think you're talking to, but I think you have the wrong number."

I hung up. I had no idea what to think, but it made me uncomfortable.

Two seconds later he called me back.

"Wow," he said. "I thought I was talking to someone else. I just sold my business and I was getting really frustrated with the people who I sold it to. Sorry about that."

"Yeah," I said. "I didn't know what to think. I didn't know why you were yelling at me. I thought I was talking to a crazy person. That was pretty insane."

And the second I said that, he flew off the handle again. He continued to yell at me in the same way he had been yelling at the first woman. He told me that if I insulted him, that meant he had the right to insult me.

"I'm a feminist and I believe in treating women the same way men are treated. Do you see why it was insulting, what you just said?"

"I'm sorry," I said. "I didn't mean it like that."

"Well I was trying to apologize and you had to kick sand in my face. Let me tell you a story."

"No," I said. "I think we're done here and I don't want to meet you anymore. I have to go. Goodbye."

He called me back immediately. I didn't pick up.

"Please call me back at least let me be civil. one simple phone call to end on good terms and we're done," he texted me.

He called me three more times and I ignored them. But the fourth time, I picked up. This guy was unhinged, and frankly, I just wanted to be sure he wasn't going to murder me.

"Please let me tell you a story," he said. "Let me just tell you this one thing, and then I'll leave you alone."

"Fine," I said.

"January 23 was the day that I snapped," he said. "I'm a dog walker, and I was walking a dog when a man came up and asked to pet the dog. But he didn't wait. He just put his hand out. The dog bit his sleeve and ripped it. The man was angry. I said I would bring it to a tailor and have it fixed or pay for the damage. I started walking to my car and the guy followed me. He thought I was running away but I said I would give him my information. He kept getting in my face, and I told him to stop, but he wouldn't. So finally, I snapped and head-butted him in the face. I broke his nose. I just got out of there. He didn't know who I was or have my contact information. So I ran, and I'm on the run from the cops. So you can see why I'm pretty tense."

He brought up that I had "insulted" him and that I should apologize because "You never know when someone is going to snap."

I said, "I'm sorry. I didn't mean to offend you. I'm going to go to bed now. Goodbye."

He was still trying to talk over me, and even went so far to say that I am "the reason women have a bad reputation." The phone call lasted twenty-two minutes. I'm not really sure why I let him berate me for so long, but I wanted to know he wasn't actually going to come after me or find out where I lived.

Luckily, he didn't know much information about me, and I ended up blocking his number. I was relieved that I hadn't met up with him, or told him any identifying details about myself. I learned that it's important to screen dates thoroughly before you meet them, even if they're your type and have all the same interests and call themselves "feminists."

5. Filthy Frank

There's a certain type of guy who often pops up in your inbox out of nowhere to deliver a full-on, explicitly detailed description of what he'd like to do to you. It's basically the equivalent of that creepy dude who walks up behind you on the street and whispers something gross in your ear. Filthy Frank wants you to know that his sexual fantasies are about you, whether you like it or not. Your opinion on them doesn't matter, as long as he gets to infiltrate your life with his demented imagination.

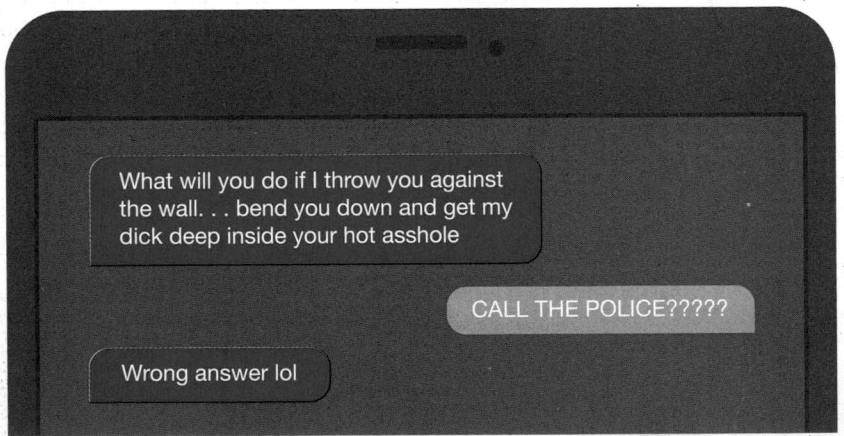

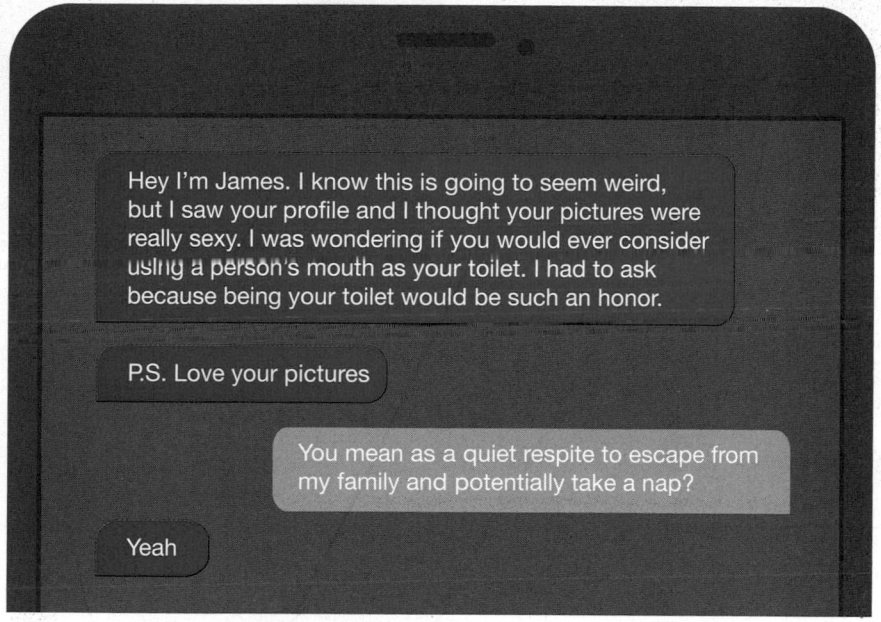

Hey I'm James. I know this is going to seem weird, but I saw your profile and I thought your pictures were really sexy. I was wondering if you would ever consider using a person's mouth as your toilet. I had to ask because being your toilet would be such an honor.

P.S. Love your pictures

You mean as a quiet respite to escape from my family and potentially take a nap?

Yeah

6. Pickup Artist Peter

Pickup artists (PUAs) are socially inept nerds who come up with a set of usually problematic techniques to sleep with as many women as possible. PUAs have been a festering group since the 1980s, but they really picked up steam when Neil Strauss's *The Game: Penetrating the Secret Society of Pickup Artists* was published in 2005. Since then, Strauss has denounced his book, which was seen as a bible for pickup artists, saying, "It was really a book about scared men who were afraid of women. . . . It was never meant to be an advocacy of a lifestyle, even though it's come to symbolize one."[4]

But pickup artist communities are still flourishing online. They've just switched up their techniques and ditched the name. There might be a few PUAs who still go to clubs to pick up women, but many have taken to online dating instead, and you can be sure you'll run into one on any dating app.

Pickup artists think that by using their own pseudo-psychology they can hypnotize or trick women into sleeping with them. Basically, push these secret "buttons" and no woman will be able to resist your charms. A lot of times, you'll be able to tell a pickup artist because they believe in made-up or debunked science, like the theory of "alpha males."

This dude on the dating site Plenty of Fish has obviously fallen for the PUA theory that alpha males exist, and that he is one of them. Then he tries to impress the woman with his "facts."

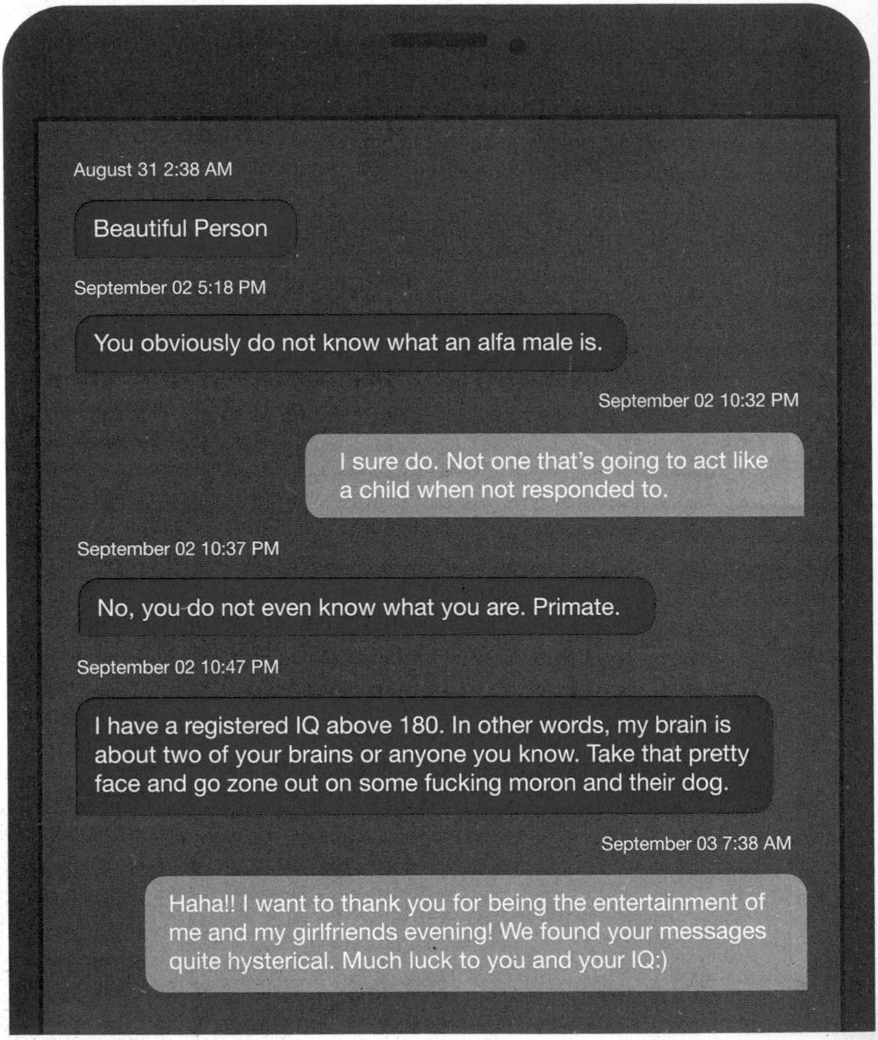

August 31 2:38 AM

Beautiful Person

September 02 5:18 PM

You obviously do not know what an alfa male is.

September 02 10:32 PM

I sure do. Not one that's going to act like a child when not responded to.

September 02 10:37 PM

No, you do not even know what you are. Primate.

September 02 10:47 PM

I have a registered IQ above 180. In other words, my brain is about two of your brains or anyone you know. Take that pretty face and go zone out on some fucking moron and their dog.

September 03 7:38 AM

Haha!! I want to thank you for being the entertainment of me and my girlfriends evening! We found your messages quite hysterical. Much luck to you and your IQ:)

PUAs are always trying to justify their ideas with bogus theories, allegedly grounded in biology.

In the following submission, we see what kind of logic is inside PUA guys. The submitter said, "This dude got butt hurt when I wouldn't let him come over to my house after communicating for hmm. . . . 30 mins or less. Then I stopped responding & this is what I got."

So you didn't answer me, guess there's no plans on your end. Let me break down tinder for you. Guys literally like every picture. I have an app that does it for me. You then narrow down your matches and unmatch the real beat girls. Then there's different categories within the remaining fuckable ones. You have your dimes, which are totally worth taking out and dropping some dough on well because they're fucking hot. Then there's the middle ground these are the girls that you don't mind grabbing a drink with because if you run into someone you may know it won't be too embarrassing. Then you have the girls that are called the bench. They might be a little overweight, which you can tell when all the pictures are at angles and there's not a single body shot. These are the girls you say the outrageous shit too hoping that you just might get your penis wet without having to take anyone out on Tuesday night. So please, don't let it go to your head.

There's nothing like a reprehensible dude showing his true colors by revealing his dating "strategy" to make you want to weep for humanity. It really illustrates his blatant hatred for women, as well as his utter delight in completely dehumanizing them.

7. Trevor the Troll

No matter who you are, you've probably dealt with a troll at some point on the internet: a (usually anonymous) individual who spews abhorrent opinions for the sole purpose of making you feel bad. They say offensive things just to get a response—any response.

HE'S PROBABLY A TROLL IF HE:

- Opens with an insult or only matches with you to tell you what's wrong with your profile
- Doesn't have a profile picture and/or didn't fill out his profile
- Has a ridiculous tagline like "All women are cunts."

This is a pretty standard troll example—someone who created a profile just to create chaos:

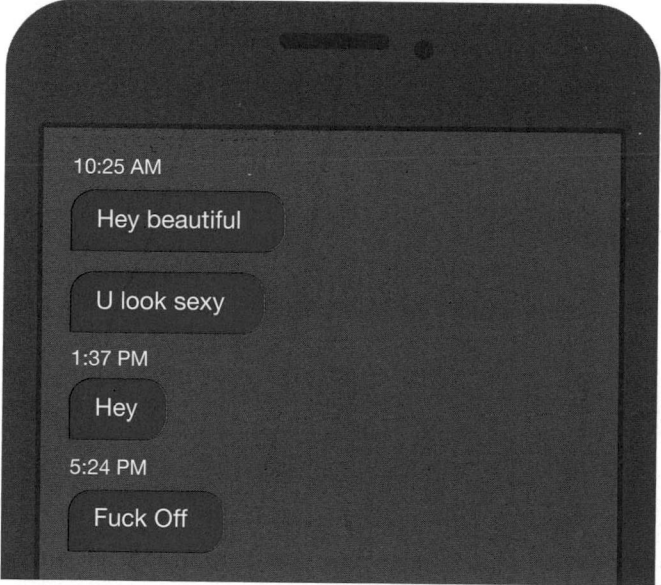

To Bye Felipe:

Never talked nor responded to the guy. What a weirdo! Also his profile picture was of Robert Pattinson hahaha #byefelipe.

8. Trump-Supporter Tanner

Trump-Supporter Tanner is definitely a white guy, "preppy" in nature, probably wearing a polo or a T-shirt with a suit jacket. Khakis. Boat shoes. His profile mentions hating "PC culture." If you're lucky, one of their pictures will feature the iconic red Make America Great Again hat, making it easy to swipe left or block them right away.

Be careful if you include that you're a feminist in your profile, as a Trump-Supporter Tanner won't be able to resist trying to educate you.

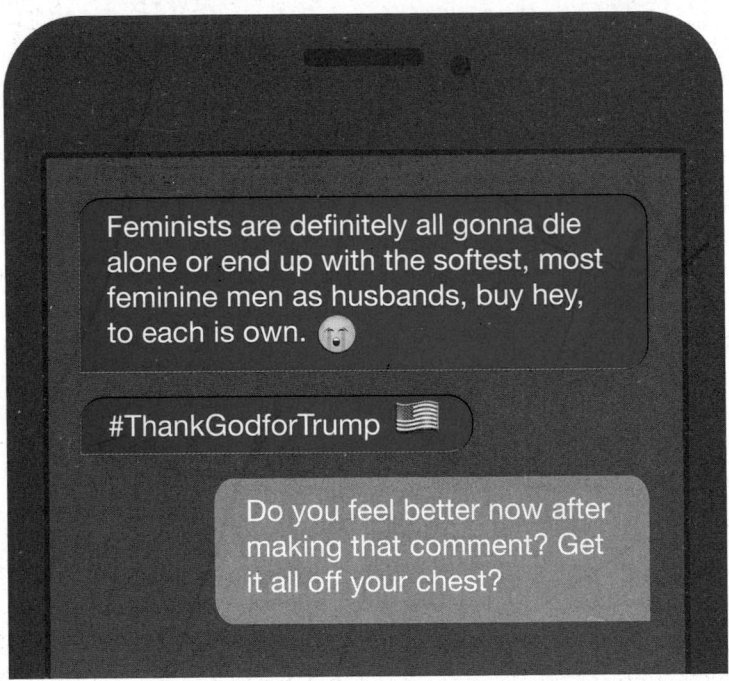

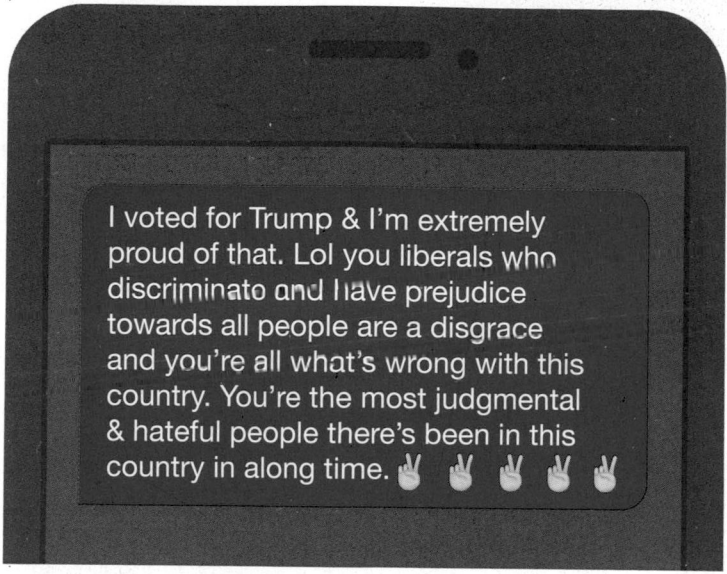

They simply want to go out of their way to insult you for no other reason than they are sad and despicable people.

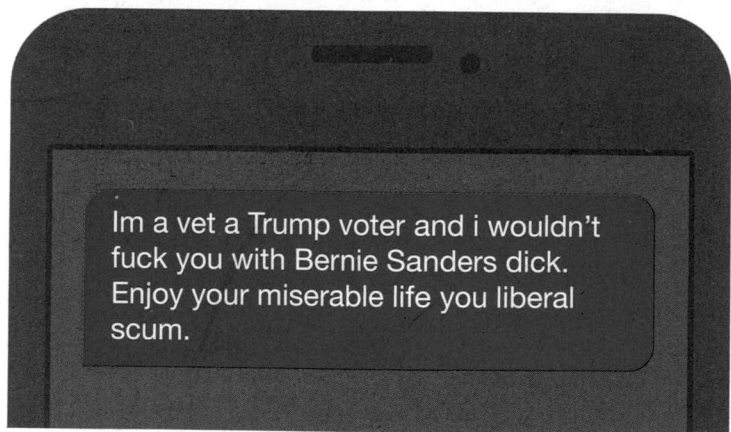

Block and report them!

9. White Supremacist Wayne

With the rise of blatant racists elected to the highest offices in the United States, so too have risen the outspoken Nazis of the alt-right. Christopher Cantwell, a prominent white supremacist at the Charlottesville, Virginia rally, was later found to have had active OkCupid, Tinder, and Match.com profiles. Within minutes of discovering this, OkCupid banned Cantwell, and Tinder and Match soon followed suit. While OkCupid and other dating sites have pledged to ban those in hate groups, you never know when one's going to slip through.

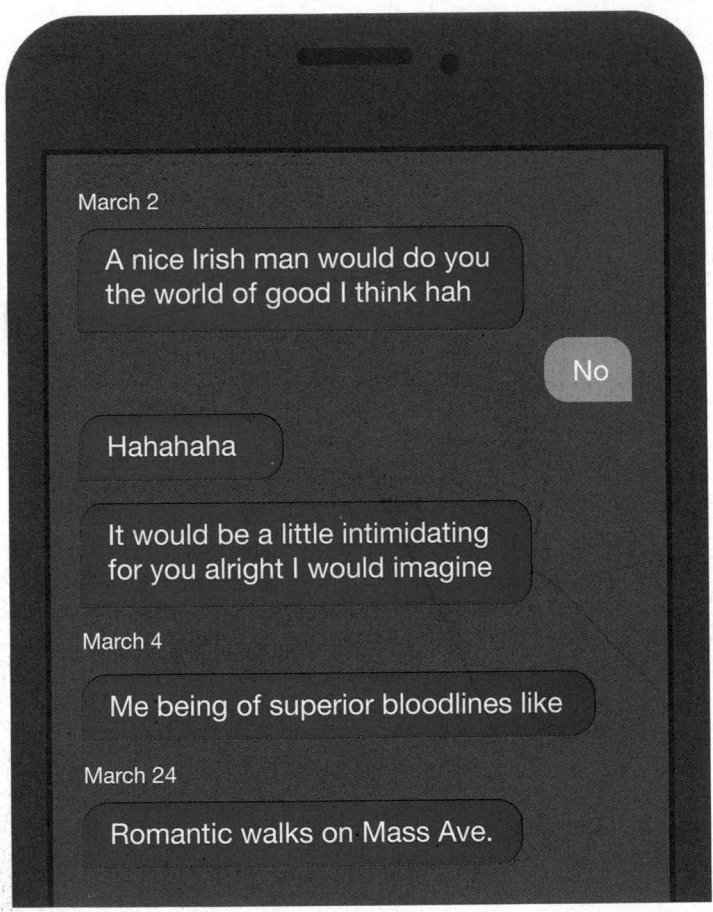

"Superior bloodlines"? Really makes you long for the days when racists were afraid.

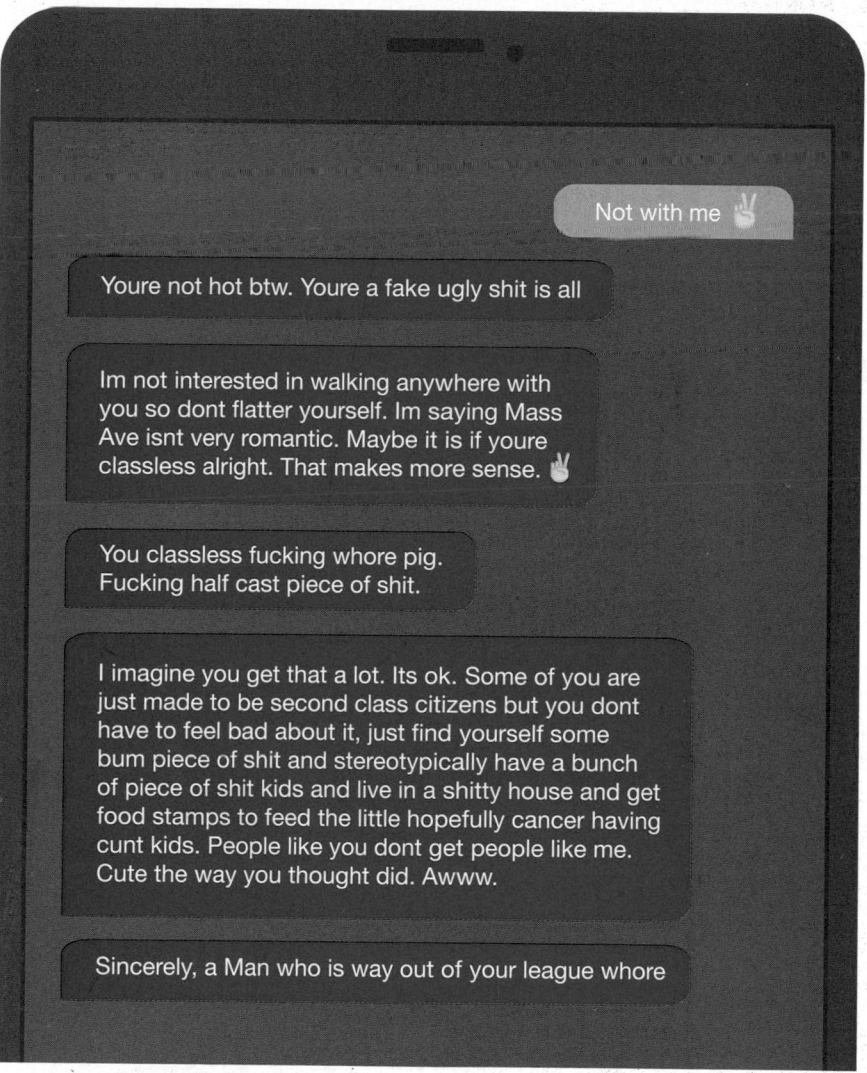

> Not with me ✌️

Youre not hot btw. Youre a fake ugly shit is all

Im not interested in walking anywhere with you so dont flatter yourself. Im saying Mass Ave isnt very romantic. Maybe it is if youre classless alright. That makes more sense. ✌️

You classless fucking whore pig. Fucking half cast piece of shit.

I imagine you get that a lot. Its ok. Some of you are just made to be second class citizens but you dont have to feel bad about it, just find yourself some bum piece of shit and stereotypically have a bunch of piece of shit kids and live in a shitty house and get food stamps to feed the little hopefully cancer having cunt kids. People like you dont get people like me. Cute the way you thought did. Awww.

Sincerely, a Man who is way out of your league whore

I repeat: BLOCK AND REPORT!

10. Patrick Bateman

This is a particularly terrifying type of guy who may seem great at first, but then he does something extremely creepy that makes you question your personal safety, like Patrick Bateman, the wealthy businessman character who is also secretly a serial killer from the Brett Easton Ellis novel and subsequent film, *American Psycho*. Patrick Batemans are usually very attractive and charming in the beginning, which makes it even harder to predict that they will turn on you.

Remember the original Felipe? The one who lashed out at me personally for not wanting to chat? Well, I'm pretty sure he is actually a legitimate sociopath. I have now heard from five other women who have been victimized by this man. In his dating profile, he describes himself as "tall, dark and handsome," but is secretive about photos because of his "profession as a lawyer." He seems to have a pretty predictable pattern of repeatedly sending women obvious copy-and-pasted form letters. When they don't respond or they reject him, he flies off the handle. This particular man was the inspiration for creating Bye Felipe. One of the creepiest things about this guy is that after he sends you an aggressive message and you inevitably report and block him, he comes back with another profile with a similar username and continues to message you as if nothing happened. He has sent me messages from five accounts, which I blocked immediately, but I still never know when he's going to make another one and ask if I "want to chat."

After the Bye Felipe Instagram account became popular, stories about this same guy came trickling in from other women.

"One of your Buzzfeed posts looked familiar, and it turns out it was a pushy guy from OkCupid that wouldn't leave me alone!"

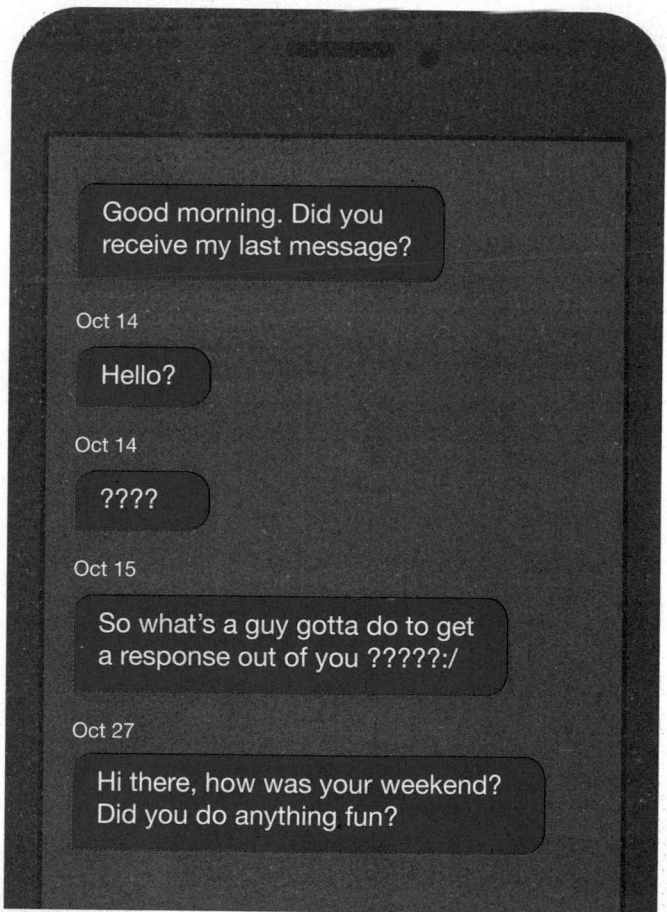

Good morning. Did you receive my last message?

Oct 14

Hello?

Oct 14

????

Oct 15

So what's a guy gotta do to get a response out of you ?????:/

Oct 27

Hi there, how was your weekend? Did you do anything fun?

Then, from a second woman: "He keeps creating new profiles and contacting me regardless of how I've blocked him EVERY TIME!"

A third woman said, "He sent me the same message about ten or fifteen times and I never responded and eventually blocked him, which caused him to create a new account and send the same message from there. So, I blocked him again and the same thing happened—six more times. I'm a very nice person and also terrified of scary men like this, but I eventually stood up for myself and he FLIPPED OUT. I was terrified walking around LA, even though it's so huge, because this man is a legit psycho."

Then, a fourth who had previously dismissed him sent me screenshots of her telling him she wasn't interested anymore after chatting with him for a few weeks.

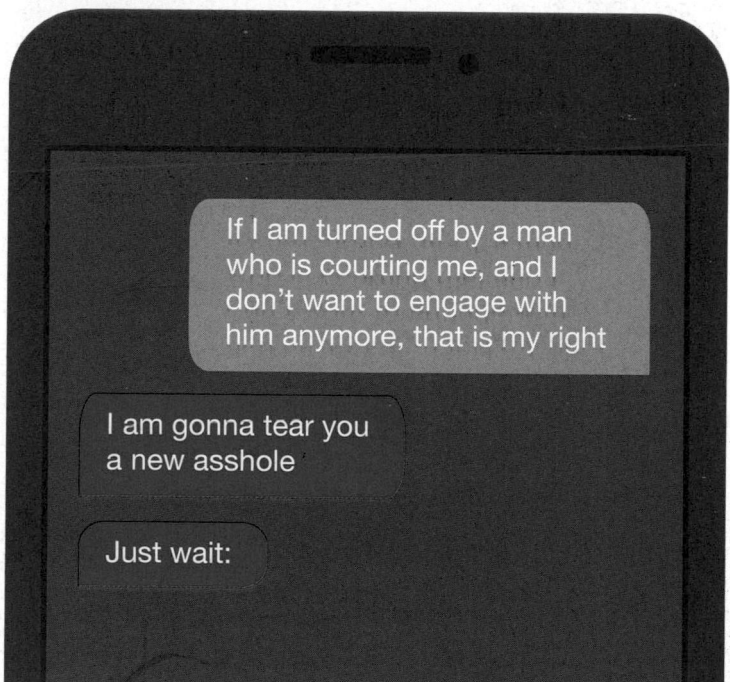

> If I am turned off by a man who is courting me, and I don't want to engage with him anymore, that is my right

> I am gonna tear you a new asshole

> Just wait:

He subsequently messaged her from another account:

This submitter told me she was looking into reporting him to the Bar Association.

Finally, the cherry on top of the shit sundae this man has created: I received this submission from a fifth woman.

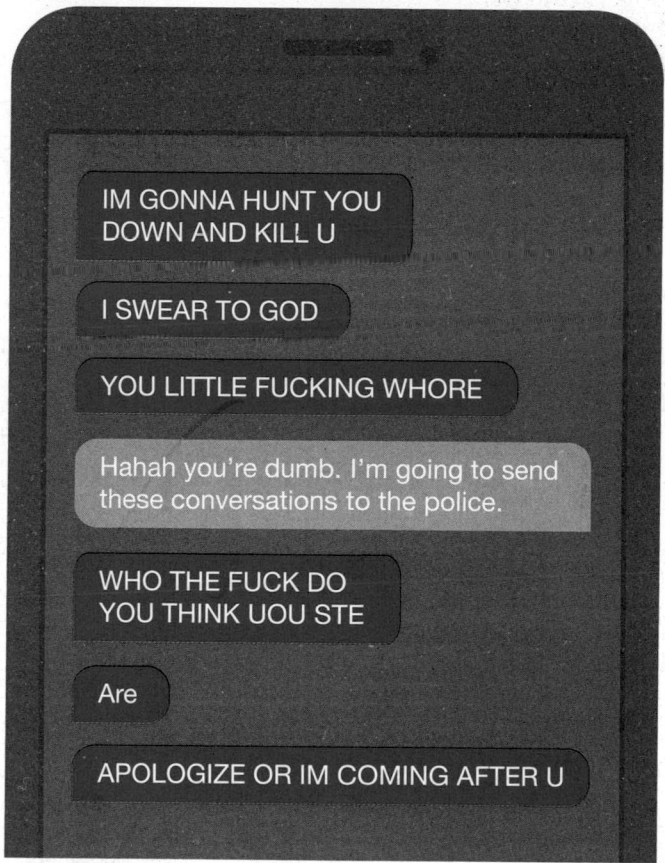

The last submitter said she was intending to report him to the police.

In *American Psycho*, Patrick Bateman treats everything in his life as a commodity, including women. In a quote from the novel, Bateman says, "Though it does sporadically penetrate how unacceptable some of what I'm doing actually is, I just remind myself that this thing, this girl, this meat, is nothing . . ." This sentiment seems to ring true for almost every guy featured on Bye Felipe. They don't think of women as human beings, but as objects they can own, consume, and dispose of at any time. Are they all serial killers? Obviously not, but they all seem to have the base belief that they hold authority over women.

CHAPTER 2

Swipe Left
to Avoid a
Terrible Fate

Online dating is just more dangerous for women than it is for cis men. A lot of guys don't realize that the stakes are infinitely higher for women who are engaged in online dating. When you ask men what they're scared about when going on dates arranged online, it's not that they're worried about their physical safety, it's about whether or not they'll have wasted their time with a person to whom they're not attracted. Wow, dudes, must be hard.

A COMPARISON OF BIGGEST FEARS ABOUT ONLINE DATING

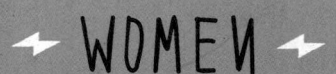

⚡ WOMEN ⚡	⚡ MEN ⚡
• being insulted when not interested	• woman doesn't look like her pics
• being harassed	• woman weighs more than expected
• being stalked	• woman doesn't respond
• being raped	• woman not interested
• being kidnapped	
• being murdered	
• revenge porn	

That's why it's so important for women to take precautions before meeting someone in person. Of course, no one wants to waste time on a date when they could have avoided it, but our main concern is simply not getting murdered.

This chapter will explore a few ways to minimize and possibly even eliminate your interactions with assholes/serial killers. Knowing the enemy helps you get a sense of the red flags to look for. I'll also cover the safest ways to build your profile. Once you're online, you must keep your Felipe Fence up at all times. What is a Felipe Fence? It's a set of standard rules you follow that will significantly reduce the odds of coming in contact with, and experiencing a Bye Felipe situation. If he doesn't meet your Felipe Fence standard or has more than two red flags, cut him loose swiftly and ruthlessly so you can move on to the next one. We'll get to rejection techniques as well, and I'll show you how to make a clean break.

First things first. When you're making your profile, follow my official dating rules for safety and fun.

1. USE UNIQUE PHOTOS: When you create your profile, it's safer to take all new photos that you only use for dating profiles—photos that are not on Facebook or anywhere else. Why? A little thing called "Google reverse image search." Go to images.google.com and drag your current profile picture into the search bar. Try not to crap yourself when you see all the personal information that comes up. Bonus: Use this same tactic to research him before your date. (Especially if you think he's a catfish!)

2. LIMIT HOW MUCH YOU SHARE ABOUT YOURSELF (AT FIRST): Do a search engine check on yourself. Make sure a stranger wouldn't be able to find personal details about you without your telling them, like your address or phone number. Don't link your Instagram account to your dating account unless it's locked down too. Don't use your last name in your username.

3. GOOGLE THE SHIT OUT OF HIM: Get your private investigator pants on and look for anything weird online before you go on your first date. Don't know his last name? It's usually incredibly easy to find. All you need are two pieces of information about him. Dudes are usually not too concerned about online stalkers, so all their information is just out there. You can usually figure out where he's from or where he went to school just from small talk. What does he do? Oftentimes, you can find out who he is before even talking if he lists where he works on his profile. Facebook makes it ridiculously easy to find people. Say his name is Tim and he went to NYU, but lives in Silverlake, Los Angeles. All you have to do is search "Tim NYU" and narrow the results to only show people who live in Los Angeles. I've also had great results with Google searching a first name + his phone number. If he has his number connected to his Facebook account, he might also show up in your "people you may know" section.

About a year ago, I noticed that this section of my account was a Who's Who of dudes I'd gone on one date with and never spoken to again. It was basically a straight-up list of one-night stands. Can you say CREEPY? This is because Facebook connects to your saved contacts in your phone and brings up profiles associated with them. You may be able to disable this from coming up in your privacy settings and prevent yourself from showing up by not synching your phone contacts to Facebook.

And That's Why You Always Do a Google

My friend Rae had a particularly close call in 2016 when she was talking to a man, "Daniel," from OkCupid. They had talked on the phone a few times and were finally going to meet up, but Rae wanted to know his full name first. She always researches anyone she's going to meet by looking them up on Google and Facebook.

"Before I went to meet up with him, obviously, I wanted to know who the hell he was and that's how everything kind of came out," she said.

Daniel was particularly hesitant to give her his full name, but he eventually did over the phone. Typing it into Google, Rae found some alarming news articles about him. He had been arrested and charged for binding, gagging, and assaulting a sex worker who he thought had stolen money from him.

Rae contacted OkCupid and told them about Daniel and sent links to the articles about him. OkCupid responded by thanking her for bringing it to their attention, and that they didn't want someone like that on their site. They deleted and banned the username, email and IP address associated with him. Rae blocked his phone number and, thankfully, never heard from him again.

My friend Mary also met a fellow on OkCupid and found out later that she should have researched him more.

"This was 2012 and I barely had my first smartphone and wasn't as *on* Facebook as I am now," she said. "I went out with a guy for almost a month after "matching" on OkCupid. We slept together. I went to his office Xmas party and met his roommates, who were very nice, but one of them had a girlfriend and she was VERY NOT NICE to me. I didn't understand why at the time. I thought maybe she had beef with him, so I brushed it aside."

Mary said she asked him on her podcast to promote his band's upcoming show.

"When I went on Facebook to post about our new episode, I looked up the band's page so I could add the link and then decided to friend him," she said. "His profile picture was of him and a very cute girl."

Mary gave him the benefit of the doubt and figured maybe they were broken up.

"After I friend requested him, he must have blocked me because I couldn't find his profile afterwards," she said.

And then Mary put the pieces together. She remembered that during the podcast, one of his band mates mentioned a woman letting them practice at her parents' house for two years. When her podcast co-host asked who the woman was, one of them slapped Joe on the back and said, "Joe's meal ticket once she finishes grad school!"

Apparently, Joe was engaged to the woman and thought Mary wouldn't find out because his fiancé was attending grad school on the east coast.

"His room was shockingly clean because I found out later he had put all of her stuff in a bin in the closet so he could sleep with other girls while she was gone," Mary said.

Since Joe had blocked Mary, she couldn't contact his fiancé to let her know about what was going on, and once the band realized they all blocked her too.

Sometimes, a dude's profile can show no red flags and he'll even seem normal when messaging, but you never know when he might be an under-the-radar conservative. (Sorry, this book is not for Republicans. Go read Ayn Rand or something.)

My friend Lauren Kenner was texting a guy from Bumble and decided to check his Twitter feed. "Dude retweets Trump AND Tomi Lahren and called DT a 'smart, effective president.' I just feel like I Matrix-dodged a bullet."

"Were there any warning signs?" I asked. "Was he wearing khakis?"

"No clues! He worked on [a liberal comedian's TV show] for four years and had photos of it!"

Lesson: It's always good to do a double-check on their political values. How is it even possible to be aroused by someone who actively participates in stripping you of your bodily autonomy, not to mention the slimy racist and classist policies they support. It's unfortunate if you're one of those socially-liberal, fiscally-conservative people being lumped in with the KKK. But it's just that anyone associated in any way with the sentient burnt Cheeto in charge makes our lady boners shrivel up like the dried out old pinto bean you find on the seat of your car from that time you ate street tacos at 3 a.m.

INTERESTING FACTS I'VE UNCOVERED WHEN I GOOGLED DUDES BEFORE THE DATE

- He had been arrested and charged as a rare book thief. *I still went on the date.*

- He was a comedian and his jokes were sexist and *not* funny. *I canceled.*

- He had a girlfriend. *Canceled.*

- He once had white boy dreads (a.k.a. nope ropes). *CANCELED.*

- He liked U2. *No thanks.*

- He was a libertarian who posted Ayn Rand quotes on Facebook. *Nope.*

Don't Go Overboard, Though

There is a caveat with the "Google him" rule, however: you shouldn't go *too* deep on the research. Just make sure he is who he says he is and there's nothing else suspicious about him. You don't want to learn too much about someone before you meet them, lest you become a little too obsessed. And then you're on the date, and you're asking him questions you already know the answers to, and you feel weird because you've already seen his ex-girlfriend's mom's vacation pictures. (This has happened to me.) Or, you might boot someone that you could have gotten along with for an insignificant reason. Like if you find out he likes Sublime, but maybe it's only in an ironic way. (I dismiss people based on musical taste all the time.

Maybe I should be less snobby.) Keep it short; just make sure he's not a murderer, and then get off his Facebook page!

4. GIVE HIM A BURNER NUMBER:
A lot of times, dudes want to switch from apps to texting. In this case, if you're not quite comfortable giving them your real number yet, use an app like Burner, which lets you create as many phone numbers as you want. Another option is getting a Google Voice number. That way, if he turns out to be secretly aggro, it's an extra layer of security between you. The best thing about these apps is that you can still text, call, and send picture messages, but the dude won't know your real number until he earns your trust. If it turns out you don't want to continue communicating with him, Burner even has a feature called Ghostbot that automatically deescalates communication for you by sending innocuous texts on your behalf. The response times vary, just as they would if you were sending them. It's so easy! Let the Ghostbot do the ghosting for you!

5. CONSIDER TALKING ON THE PHONE BEFORE YOU MEET: I'm not going to tell you that you *have* to talk on the phone with someone before you go on a date with them. I have always had a phobia of talking to strangers on the phone. But at least consider it. This is especially helpful if you're not looking to waste time going on dates with incompatible people, because you can usually tell right away if you'll get along on the phone. You can even ask them about your deal-breakers and get that out of the way.

6. IF YOU HAVE FRIENDS IN COMMON, ASK THEM ABOUT HIM: Many apps will show if you have Facebook friends in common. Usually you can find out what type of person they are by asking your friend. Don't always assume they are good people just because you have a friend in common. A few times, I've asked about a guy I matched with and my friend has said, "Oh, no. Stay away. He's the *worst*."

7. TELL SOMEONE WHERE YOU'RE GOING: Let your roommate or a friend know you're going on a first date and when you expect to be home. Text your BFF and check in with her when you go to the bathroom. There are even apps that let you share your GPS location with certain friends or family and create easy ways to alert and share information with the police with the tap of a button. As new apps are always being developed, search "women's safety apps" to find the latest.

8. DON'T LET HIM WALK YOU HOME: One time, I met an actor on OkCupid. I don't know why I went on this date, because I wasn't really feeling it in the first place, but I agreed to meet him for a drink at a bar by my house. The moment I walked into the bar, I immediately knew I wasn't attracted to him. But I was already there and decided to give him a chance, so I had a beer with him. It was fine, we didn't have much in common, but he seemed OK. I said I was tired and had to work the next morning. We left the bar, and he insisted on walking me home. OK, fine. I let him. We get to my door, and I try to say goodbye, but he asks if he can use my bathroom.

"Umm . . . yeah I guess," I said.

So, I let him in, he goes to the bathroom, comes out, and there's an awkward silence.

"Do you have any tea?" he asks.

My eyes just about rolled out of my head and down the street. I did have tea, but most definitely wasn't about to give him any.

"No, I don't," I said. "I'm really tired. I have to go to bed."

"Oh, OK. You don't have any tea?"

"No, I don't have any." I stared at him blankly while internally screaming.

"OK, I guess I'll go then. Good night."

It looked like he was going to go in for a hug, but I went to hold the door for him. Finally, he was out of my house. I couldn't believe that he'd weaseled himself in in the first place. I felt overly annoyed and angry at myself that I'd let him. My intuition didn't tell me that he was dangerous, but who knows? I had only talked to this guy for a little over an hour. If he did turn out to be dangerous, asking to use my bathroom would have been a great line to get into my house. Thankfully, I knew that my roommate was home and would hear me if there was a problem. I was grudgingly being polite to avoid awkwardness, but he made it more awkward by not taking the hint that I wasn't interested and lingering in my doorway. If I had been more on the ball that night, I could have told him, "No you can't use my bathroom, my plumbing is actually backed up, and we have a plumber coming in the morning." This reminded me that it definitely takes more effort to look out for your own safety, and it's important to always be vigilant about your boundaries.

RED FLAGS CODE:
DANGEROUS DUDES

- Narcissistic phrases in their profiles. This is sometimes hard to distinguish since everyone has a lot of "I" or "Me" statements, but follow your gut. If they're going on and on about how good-looking they are (and it's not a joke), back away.
- They say they "don't want drama" or "hate playing games." This usually means exactly the opposite. They actually LOVE drama because it probably follows them everywhere.
- Their profile pictures are poorly composed images of random body parts, but not their face. Or one blurry, dark photo.
- They only have one profile picture, and they're not smiling in the photo. Or their mouth is smiling but their eyes aren't. You know, the creeper smile.
- Possessive language. Take for example, this email submission: "This dude sent me this after he asked me to wear a skirt on 1st date and I decided to wear jeans instead!"

Leaving home now. The whole skirt thing was not working for me tonight so don't be disappointed

Dude ur kidding right????

I asked u for ONE tiny pathetic little thing and expressed how much I would appreciate it. . . and THIS is how u treat me? Hehe... well...thanks for showing ur worth.

You are controlling and crazy. Go fuck yourself!

no u moron...

it has to do with HOW u treat me. . . and ur bullshit that I got upset with

the fact that u act this way and what u write . . hehe how PATHETIC! u are a DISGRACE to mankind PLZ go jump of bridge do us all a favor ..u ugly PIECE OF SHIT. u are NOTHING buy garbage and ALWAYS will be a loser

at LEAST show some class and don't text back .....my GOOOD u are DISGUSTING!

- Has a list of no's: "No fatties," "No sluts," "No women with opinions or brains."
- Is paranoid.
- Any signs of aggressive or controlling behavior.
- Copy-and-pasted messages looking for casual sex.

One of the most annoying things about online dating is that men usually have no clue about what women go through. They'll ask you to come over to their house right away, go for a hike in a nonpopulated area, or ask you to meet them at a bar in a shady part of town without a thought that it puts you in an unsafe position. I've had this same conversation SO many times.

DUDE: Just come to my place and we'll listen to some records.

ME: How about a drink first?

DUDE: We'll miss watching the sunset though.

ME: Yeah, well I'm not coming to your house before we meet in public. Do you know how many people would kill me if I end up coming over and you're a murderer?

DUDE: I swear I won't murder you!

ME: Likely story from a possible murderer . . .

Men never have to live their lives in constant fear of being physically assaulted from their date, so it's hard for them to fathom that you might not be too keen on putting yourself in easy-access rape situations. They're like, "LOL, I would never kill anyone. That's ridiculous." So they suggest plans before putting themselves in our position. I wouldn't necessarily consider this a serious red flag because a lot of men are just absentminded and don't think about it. But if he continues to push it, stand your ground and suggest other ideas. You probably already do this, but I always think about what people would say about me if I was hurt in a hypothetical situation. I shouldn't have to do this, but I can't stand the thought of people at my funeral going, "Well, did you hear how she was murdered? They met on Tinder and she just went to his house. They didn't even go on a date first! It's kind of her own fault."

HOT TIP:

I've received the best responses to dating profiles when I've been completely honest about what I'm looking for and not just trying to look "cool" or what I think is going to attract the most guys. I always upload accurate photos and state why I'm there. These profiles often receive the best responses.

UNMATCH HIM IF:

- He mentions a bad breakup on his profile or early on.
  Don't bother. He's not over it.
- All his pictures are trying too hard. Muscle flexing. All selfies.
  Just no.
- He takes too long to respond and only has one-word answers.
  He's probably not that interested. Worthy dudes will tell you details through chat and have thoughtful responses.
- He just rambles on about himself and asks you zero questions.

Dealing with Trolls

There might not yet be a way to completely avoid trolls when you're dating online, but there are a few ways you can limit your exposure. First, if you're using a dating platform where both of you have to like or approve each other before you can talk, it's best to be picky. If you're using an app where anyone can message you, use those message filters. For example, OkCupid has a setting where only people who fit the criteria of what you're looking for and have a certain match percentage will show up in your main inbox. Everyone else will go to the filtered inbox.

FILTER OUT RACISTS WITH OKCUPID'S QUESTIONS

On OkCupid, everyone answers questions in order to be matched with compatible people through their algorithm. These questions are often a handy tool for quickly checking for gross character flaws. Whenever I'm screening potential dates on OkCupid, I always check out their answers to the following questions, just to make sure.

- "Would you consider dating someone who has vocalized a strong negative bias toward a certain race of people?"
- "Is interracial marriage a bad idea?"
- "Do you use racial slurs when you are around friends or family whom you trust?"
- "Do you believe that there exists a statistical correlation between race and intelligence?"

Anyone who answers wrong gets nixed. Also, if you see anything wildly offensive in a profile, report it! OkCupid and many other dating apps have publicly stated that anyone who has hate speech or racist speech on their profile will be kicked off their sites.

Rob, 28
Sales Rep

DATING PROFILE TRANSLATIONS

"Tall enough for you to wear heels."
I'm boring.

Featured song is by the Chainsmokers.
I am a basic white dude.

"[Different country] guy in [your city] needing a tour guide!"
Probably a good lay.

"Good vibes only."
I'm basic AF.

"NO DRAMA."
I'm not over my ex and I will gaslight the shit out of you if you try to call me out.

"Why are women so crazy?"
I made my exes crazy by emotionally manipulating them, but take zero responsibility for it.

"Sapiosexual."
I am awful. I'm trying this thing where I date intelligent people, but only hot ones.

"Travel. Foodie. Gym."
There is nothing interesting about me.

"No pen pals. NO texting buddies."
I will want to meet you, like, tonight, and I will get annoyed if you're busy.

Has the word "Females" anywhere in his profile.
I don't think of women as people.

34

⊗ Man

⊙ 13 miles away

I really wish the females will go back to being women & not bitches these days. I'm angry because of you females I'm 34 years old & I've never been allowed to because you females are too damn difficult stuck up arrogant shallow, to just let me date-hook up or actually meet in person a slim attractive beautiful white, asian or just outside of black girlfriend that I can actually talk to hang out with-fuck make love date go do things with consistently. I'm tired of the games that these apps are

My Anthem

 Hero (feat. Josey Scott)

Josey Scott, Chad Kroeger

"If you don't look like your photos, you're buying the drinks until you do."
I am a deeply unfunny and unoriginal douchebag.

"CEO at selfmade."
Unemployed.

"I'm just gonna be blunt—I started my company young and sold half of it
recently . . . I'm blessed but still humble.—Yes that's my Ferrari—Confident
not cocky. Driven, ambitious and spiritual. I like nice things and to treat
the person I'm with to nice things as well . . .
I'm a douche-canoe, but might buy you stuff if you're hot enough.

"Hi, I'm Mark in Sherman Oaks. I moved here 12 years ago from
Massachusetts. I work in real estate and television. Nice photos!"
I didn't read your profile and I send this message to every woman on this site.

"Hello, I just wanted to stop by and say hello since I read your profile
and noticed we have a lot in common. I'm Dan by the way. So, how's your
weekend going?"
I didn't read your profile. We actually have nothing in common.

"Comedian."
Clinically depressed.

"I'm funny."
I am not funny.

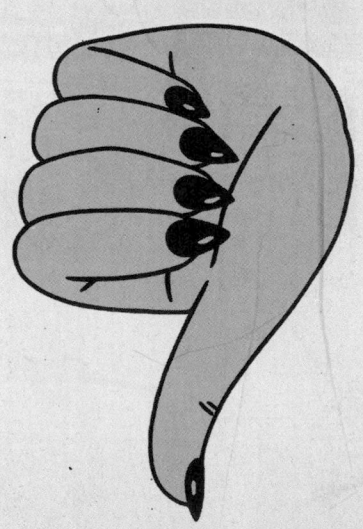

"Fluent in sarcasm."
I want you to think I'm smart. I am not.

"Alpha."
I'm an asshole.

"Just ask."
I'm not clever or creative enough to think of a tagline.

"Looking for a partner in crime."
I'm unimaginably boring.

"Just here for fun times."
I will try to make out with you in the first twenty minutes and I'll definitely
try to put it in without a condom.

"I own my own company."
I will talk at you for the better part of the date and not ask any questions.

All pictures are gym selfies.
I have no personality.

Main picture is a white guy surrounded by children in a developing country.
"Look at me white savior-ing these kids!"

Main picture is with a celebrity.
This is the most interesting thing about me.

All his pictures are of him in his band.
I name-drop all the famous people I know.

"DJ"
Douche

"Actor"
Waiter

ONLINE DATING BINGO

Mark with an X each item that you have encountered. Did you get a bingo? You win! How about a blackout? You win too! What's the prize? An increasingly dismal outlook on humanity! CONGRATS!

ONLINE DATING BINGO

PROFILE PIC IS JUST A LANDSCAPE	"JUST LOOKING FOR FUN"	MAKING THE SAME FACE IN EVERY PHOTO	ALL PICTURES ARE GROUP PHOTOS AND YOU CAN'T TELL WHICH ONE IS HIM	POSING WITH A DEAD ANIMAL
PICS WITH A BABY: "THAT'S NOT MY KID!"	POSING WITH A GUN	PROFILE PICS ARE ALL MEMES	GUY WHO SEEMS PERFECT AND GHOSTS YOU BEFORE YOU MEET	"WANDERLUST"
SHIRTLESS GYM SELFIE IN DIRTY MIRROR	DEFINITELY DIDN'T READ YOUR PROFILE BEFORE MESSAGING YOU	FREE SPACE	PROFILE PIC IS A JOKE HE STOLE	"HERE FOR HOOKUPS"
WAY TOO HOT TO BE A REAL PERSON	"420 FRIENDLY"	GENERIC COPY-AND-PASTED MESSAGE	MAIN PROFILE PIC IS JUST A PENIS	WEARING SUNGLASSES OR OBSCURING HIS FACE IN ALL PHOTOS
GUY STANDING BY AN EXPENSIVE CAR WITH A TERRIBLE HAIRCUT	FIRST MESSAGE IS COMPLIMENTING YOU ON YOUR APPEARANCE	"LOOKING FOR A PARTNER IN CRIME"	STRING OF CITIES, STATES, OR COUNTRIES THEY'VE LIVED IN	ONLY LISTS INSTAGRAM HANDLE AND HEIGHT

FuckBoy Flags

Depending on where you look on the internet, you'll find a few definitions of the word "fuckboy" (alternatively, fuckboi or fuccboi). It was previously used as a general insult in hip-hop songs and as a prison slang term, but the term evolved among women on the internet in recent years to refer to a special kind of asshole in the dating world. They used it to describe a guy who manipulates women under false pretenses just to sleep with them. Or an entitled man who refuses to put in any effort. One thing is clear, though: fuckboys are the worst!

Sometimes you can see a fuckboy from a mile away because he'll be at the bar dressed in trendy clothes that *just* cross the threshold of being considered ridiculous, eyeing every girl who walks in and trying to talk to them. Or he'll find you on social media and slide into your DMs, almost immediately trying to change the subject to sex. Then, there's the fuckboy who is harder to spot. He's a specific type of asshole who you may think is a genuine person at first, but soon reveals that he doesn't care about you as a person, and is actually only interested in sex. You might sleep with him once if he's charming, but he will ghost you immediately. Finally, there's the fuckboy who's the worst of all. He could be anyone. He'll take his time getting to know you, act like he's respecting you, text you all the time, make you let your guard down . . . only to disappoint you later. You'll hang out for weeks, but when he gets a whiff that you might be interested in something more serious, he goes cold. But by that time, you'll have caught feelings and be extremely conflicted, because how can you be sad about losing someone you weren't even officially "dating"?

-U UP?

Spoken Like a True Fuckboy Just Being Honest

> Not true. . . . of course I want to get n ur pants but I'm not a scumbag I do want more to eventually come out of it. ALL men want the sex and I'm sure u noticed that but I do truly want more...

> But I want the relationship first. Sorry.

> Lol no man will wait. . . all men want it . . . if they wait it's because there already getting it somewhere and u will just get cheated on . .. js

Be extra careful of the third type of fuckboy. He passed the tests. He's cute, you have things in common, he can hold a conversation, it doesn't seem like he's a bad guy. You may even go on more than one date with him (because he's usually hot as hell). Fuckboys aren't necessarily Felipes, but they might be worse because they have the power to make you let your guard down and emotionally destroy you. The following breeds of fuckboys will suck the life out of you and waste your time. If a guy shows signs of any of the following, cut him off posthaste!

MANCHILD MAX: Manchild Max is nearing, or past, forty and has no intention of getting his life together. He barely has a job, lives in a shoebox apartment, is probably an actor or musician, but has not made anything notable, and he might have a drinking problem. I once dated a forty-three-year-old actor who slept on the worst bedsheets you can possibly imagine. They were old, and made of polyester with scratchy pills covering them. It felt like sleeping on children's old race-car sheets, only without the car designs. They were so bad, I took a picture of them in the morning and sent it to my friends while running out of there vowing to never sleep at his place again. You can always tell a manchild because he talks about how he loves being single and is super-proud of his (poorly decorated) bachelor pad. Also, any whiff of genuine interest will send him scurrying for cover.

NONCOMMITTAL NATE: This guy is absolutely terrified of commitment. (This describes the majority of men you'll find on dating sites.) Attachment theory states that people who display the "avoidant" attachment style see close intimate relationships as infringing on their independence, so they frequently try to push people away.[5] But they thrive on attention, so they're always hitting you up at random intervals. If you ever try to text an avoidant Noncommittal Nate, he'll respond two days later. The other types of attachment styles are "anxious," which is basically a stage-5 clinger, and "secure," which is a normal and healthy person who isn't afraid of intimacy. Statistically, you're probably going to run into more avoidant types on dating apps and in general. There are just more of them out there in the world because the clingers and secures are usually already in relationships. The noncommittals are bouncing around from person to person, always being single. Beware the Noncommittal Nate mantra: "I don't like labels." Just believe him. If you are looking for a relationship, get out of there ASAP!

JUST-DUMPED DAVE: This guy is another VERY common type you will find on Tinder. It's often filled with sad dudes who pretend they're over a recent breakup, but aren't. He's fresh out of a relationship and looking to get his mind off the person who just ripped his heart out of his chest and stomped on it. You'll find Just-Dumped Daves in various stages of grieving. If he's just out of a long-term relationship, he doesn't really know how to date yet. He'll immediately hold your hand and be overly sweet because he doesn't understand how to be single. DO NOT FALL FOR IT. While a Just-Dumped Dave may seem exceedingly well-behaved, the law of breakups dictates that women get over it within weeks after the breakup is final, while men seem fine right after breakups but, in fact, only start to process their emotions many months or even years after the fact. I've had the thought myself, "He's so great though. I'll just wait for him to get over this breakup." DON'T. Unless you're looking for a casual hookup, just end it right there before he has a chance to leech onto you emotionally and then nonchalantly tell you that he's not over his ex a year after you've been dating.

EMOTIONALLY UNAVAILABLE EMMET: This guy was probably a great catch once upon a time. He's really sweet and cute, but a girl hurt him about ten years ago, so he acts like his heart is made of stone. He describes himself as having "been through the wringer," but he's not fresh out of a breakup. He just has a lot of baggage and refuses to deal with it, or expects someone else to take care of him. He wants a mommy. OK, Emmet, we've all been hurt. Everyone's been heartbroken before, but people get over it. Part of you feels bad for him and wants to help, but the other part wonders why it's your responsibility to fix him. It's not. Don't fix him. If he can't get it together and go to a therapist, it's not your job to be the stand-in mental health practitioner.

SOFTBOY SCOTT: BEWARE the softboy, perhaps the evilest of all the fuckboys. Softboy Scott knows exactly what a fuckboy is, and acknowledges that those guys are assholes. He's self-aware, sensitive, respectful. He talks about how most men aren't appreciative of women's emotional labor. But he also wants to cuddle. He's learned from the mistakes of fuckboys and knows just the right things to say so you'll let your guard down. Once you hook up with him, though, he'll disappear, never to text you back again.

TEN SIGNS THAT HE'S A FUCKBOY

1. Can make literally anything into something sexual.

2. Selfish, but swears he's not.

3. Always stringing you along with an apology and an "I miss you."

4. Won't respond to questions he doesn't want to answer.

5. Says exactly what you want to hear, but doesn't actually do what he says.

6. Completely disappears for three days, but will always have a vague excuse, like "I wasn't looking at my phone."

7. Has never asked you how you're doing.

8. Makes vague plans so that he can blow you off without feeling bad.

9. Has never taken you on an actual date.

10. Is always on his phone when he's with you.

CLASSIC FUCKBOY PHRASES
AND THEIR MEANINGS

Texts "U up?" at 3 a.m.
I'm trying to fuck.

"But what would you do if I were there?;) haha."
I'm trying to fuck.

"Haha and then what?;)."
I'm trying to fuck.

Combinations of the following emojis:
I'm trying to fuck.

"I'm not ready for a relationship/I don't believe in labels."
I'm trying to fuck and I don't want you to get attached.

"We should hang soon."
Maybe I'll want to fuck in the future, but only when it's convenient for me.

"Let me know when you're free."
I'm too lazy to make plans.

"Stay in touch!"
I'll probably ghost you if you text me again.

"I don't know what I want right now."
You can't make me have feelings for you.

What all of these fuckboys have in common is that they will string you along and even tell you that they're not looking for anything serious, but they're still looking for all of the perks of being your boyfriend. They all have something charming about them that's so sweet, it's like candy. But they'll tell you exactly what they are, either with their words or by their actions; you just have to listen. You have to read between the lines sometimes, but a classic fuckboy move is "breadcrumbing"—sending out flirtatious yet noncommittal texts as a lazy way of seeing if you want to hook up. Maybe it's a flirty gif. "Thinking about you 😊." If this is the case, your chances aren't good. The dating app Hinge found that 68 percent of women they polled on the app had been breadcrumbed or strung along. However, only 4 percent ended up in a relationship with the person. Fuckboys are alllllllways sending maintenance texts to keep you on the back burner. They want to know you're still interested in them, but only as an ego boost. "We should hang soon." "How's your day?" "What's up?" Don't fall for it! If he's not trying to see you in person, he's wasting your time!

SHOULD I ATTEMPT TO MAKE THIS FUCKBOY MY BOYFRIEND?

QUESTION: I met this guy on Tinder, and we went on the most romantic date. He took me to dinner, and then we walked on the beach. He seemed great! We really hit it off—the conversation flowed, and he kept telling me how amazing my eyes are and how beautiful he thinks I am. We made out and fooled around a bit. I was head over heels. We were texting constantly and he kept saying the sweetest things. We made plans to get drinks that weekend. The day of the second date, he said he had to rain-check because he had to work. Then he started answering my texts after an hour or two. One night, he was trying to sext at 2 a.m. but wouldn't come over. I thought he had to work. I looked at his Instagram, and he's always updating it, but he still hasn't made plans with me. For some reason, I'm still thinking about the first night though. He seemed really special, and he's the first guy I've liked in so long. Is there any way I can lock this down? I kinda want to see where things go, but I get the sense he's a player. What can I do to make sure I'm not just a hookup for him? How do I get him to commit?

ANSWER: Guuuuuurl, RUN. I know there are books and articles galore about how to get this type of guy to commit, and "tricks" and things to say to make him interested, but DO NOT. It's not worth it. Let's go over it. He rain-checked and didn't make plans to reschedule. Then he started not answering your texts, wanted to sext at 2 a.m., and he still hasn't made plans. He's not acting like he was in the beginning. *He is not interested.*

Believe me, I get that it's sooooo hard to get over someone when they tease you with a wonderful first meeting and they compliment you in just the right ways. I'm always a sucker for flattery. He is charming AF! But guess what? Judge him by his actions, not his words. Guys like to make plans ALL DAY but you need to pay attention to whether they actually follow through on them or not. Don't hold onto that one good night.

He is not worth your time or effort. You've let him know you're interested. If he wanted to hang out with you, he would figure out a way to make it happen! I know it seems nearly impossible to let it go when he made it seem like he cared about you in the beginning. Maybe you have a ton of things in common, maybe he's really good at nice gestures, maybe your first date was downright magical. BUT, if he's being rude and curving you, that is your answer about how he feels. You are probably fantasizing about how good you two would be together, but he's a fuckboy— of course he's charming. He will text you at 4 a.m. and somehow make you want to bend to his every whim. He's been perfecting these charm skills on all the other women who came before you, and now he's an expert at manipulation. You have done your due diligence in letting him know you're into him. Now it's time for him to reciprocate.

It's always so hard to see it clearly when you're currently experiencing it because you have so many emotions invested. That's why a good way to get some clarity is to tell a friend and get their opinion, or pretend that your friend told you about this guy. What would you say to your friend? If it's that your friend should dump him and move on, there's your answer. We often put up with bullshit that we would never tell a friend to deal with.

If he is not respecting you, cut him off. I'm sure he's super-hot and you want to make excuses for him, but if he is not giving the same amount of effort you are putting in, leave him in the dust.

THE FIRST GUY I EVER MET ON TINDER

Sometimes, you take all the precautions, or most of them, but you never really know.

The first guy I ever met on Tinder was cute. He was pretty much my jam. Attractive, seemed intelligent, an artist . . . sign me up. We chatted a bit, and he seemed like a sweet guy. I normally don't like to chat toooooo much before a date because I like to just meet to see if there's any chemistry, and I like to just have the small talk in person. I didn't know too much about him, other than he had just graduated from art school, and he seemed like a chill dude.

We met up at a bar not too far from his neighborhood, and as we started talking, I discovered we had some pretty crazy things in common.

- We both grew up in Minnesota.
- He went to undergrad at the same school where one of my oldest and best friends studied.
- He double-majored in the same subject as said friend.
- He knew this friend and had gone to parties at her house.

Yeah, small world. But this is remarkable. Because he was the first person I ever met from Tinder in Los Angeles, I had no prior knowledge of his history, and what are the chances that he also grew up in Minnesota and knew my best friend from childhood?

The date went pretty well, in my opinion. He was really cute, and we had lots to talk about. We had similar music and movie tastes and an affinity for art. A drink at the first bar led to a drink at another bar down the street, then a drink at a third bar, where we sat in a booth in the back and crept closer to each other, exchanging flirty smiles.

He walked me back to my car, and we made out before I got in to drive back home. I giddily texted my best friend from home that I met a guy on Tinder who she knew. I needed all the deets.

"I feel like he did something violent once," she said. "But I can't remember what it was."

"Hmm. Maybe it was that he got in a fistfight with his roommate? He told me a story about how they fought about dirty dishes and it was never the same afterward," I said.

"Yeah, maybe that was it," she replied.

Two days later, she texted me. "I remembered what it was. My friend reminded me. HE THREW POOP AT HIS EX-GIRLFRIEND."

I was shocked. First of all, was it his own poop? Someone else's poop? Animal poop? There's somehow a difference between handling your own poop and digging cat poop out of a litter box. My friend has since clarified that it was his own. How could I have gone on a date with someone so clearly unhinged? Although it wasn't directed at me, I still couldn't help but judge. While I will admit I am relying on hearsay, it's still disturbing to learn about his former hostile behavior. I never found out why he might have thrown the poo. Did she do something REALLY bad to provoke it, or did he just lose it?

The lesson here is that, sometimes, even though you can be very cautious and date safely, sometimes you can't completely avoid a violent guy. If you find that you have friends in common with him (which are usually listed on Tinder), definitely ask your mutual friends about his character. While this particular guy's hostility was not directed at me, I was glad to have found out about his tendencies before I was on the receiving end of a flying pile of poo.

CHAPTER 3

this is what a meninist looks like

Why Are Men?

There are millions of reasons women regularly turn their faces up to the sky, waving their clenched fists above their heads and yell to the heavens in frustration, "WHY ARE MEN?" Some reasons apply to the average clueless fuckboy they're dating, and some apply to the stranger troll who shows up in their inboxes demanding attention.

TEN QUESTIONS THAT MAKE YOU SAY, "WHY ARE MEN?"

1. Why do men hit on us and then insult us?

2. Why do men expect us to be interested when they open with a completely inappropriate and offensive sexual question?

3. Why do men pressure women into watching them masturbate?

4. Why do men expose themselves to us without asking?

5. Why do men act interested and then ghost?

6. Why do men date someone for three years with no intention of committing to them?

7. Why do men explain subjects to us when we are experts on those subjects?

8. Why do men act entitled to our bodies and attention?

9. Why do men assume every woman is attracted to them?

10. Why do men think that we owe them sex when we're polite to them?

The answers to the question "WHY ARE MEN?" are as infinite as the stars. But mainly? It's because of *patriarchy*. The shitty parts of patriarchy, like toxic masculinity, rape culture, objectification of women, racism, classism, etc., totally fuck up men's brains. But men also suffer from a myriad of personal problems that make them act like assholes, like low self-esteem, emotional immaturity, and commitment issues.

But first, what is patriarchy? Are you ready for a crash course in some snowflake-social-justice-warrior bullshit? Good, because I minored in women's studies in college, and I'm about to do you a learn.

PATRIARCHY: n. Control by men of a disproportionately large share of power.

Duh, we live in a patriarchy, folks! In the United States, men control the government, most religions, much of society, and a shit-ton of the ideas about how men and women should act. Living in a patriarchy means men are seen as leaders and rulers, and women are seen as "less than," weaker, and "other." Examples of this make up basically every post on @ByeFelipe.

Toxic masculinity—that's any of the destructive aspects of "traditional masculinity," or what we think about what it means to be a "real man." Real men are strong and not weak. They should never ask for help. Real men are violent. They don't show emotion unless it's anger. They are the sexual aggressors and always want sex. Sound familiar? Oh, yeah, it sounds like this dude:

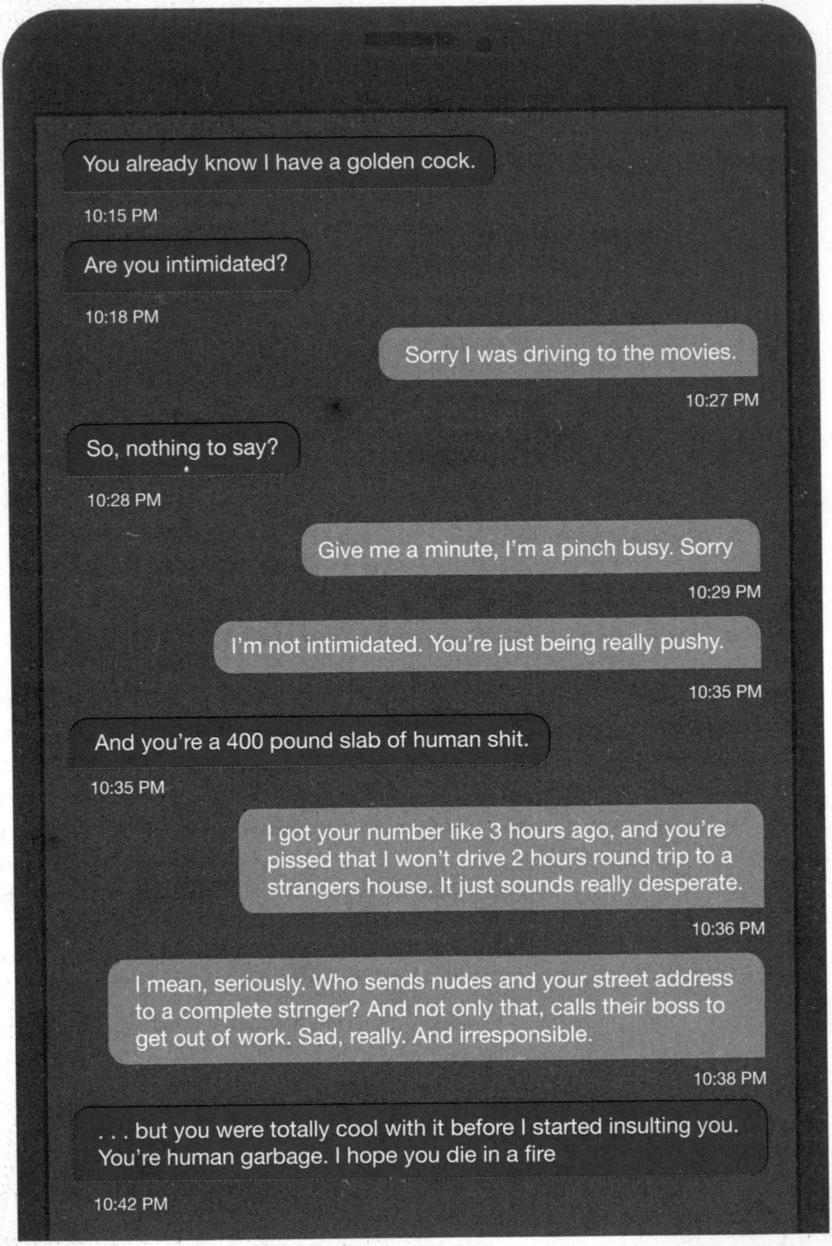

You already know I have a golden cock.

10:15 PM

Are you intimidated?

10:18 PM

Sorry I was driving to the movies.

10:27 PM

So, nothing to say?

10:28 PM

Give me a minute, I'm a pinch busy. Sorry

10:29 PM

I'm not intimidated. You're just being really pushy.

10:35 PM

And you're a 400 pound slab of human shit.

10:35 PM

I got your number like 3 hours ago, and you're pissed that I won't drive 2 hours round trip to a strangers house. It just sounds really desperate.

10:36 PM

I mean, seriously. Who sends nudes and your street address to a complete strnger? And not only that, calls their boss to get out of work. Sad, really. And irresponsible.

10:38 PM

. . . but you were totally cool with it before I started insulting you. You're human garbage. I hope you die in a fire

10:42 PM

Let's be clear: Masculinity, in and of itself, is not bad. It is only the toxic parts that we as feminists are trying to eradicate. No one is telling men that they need to give up being dudes. Men can still be masculine, we just want to redefine "masculine" as treating women equally and with respect! Men can still be helpful, be gentleman, be devoted to their jobs, and provide for their families. But, hey, here's an idea: How about we also let men do whatever they want as long as they're not hurting anyone?

One thing that sucks is that both men and women reinforce traditional/toxic masculinity by shaming men for doing anything that could be seen as "girly": crying, taking an interest in stuff like fashion or makeup, showing vulnerability, and asking for help. On a Reddit thread asking men what they would do if it wasn't so "feminine" or "socially unacceptable," men revealed they'd start quilting, knitting, wearing skirts and dresses, smelling flowery, and teaching preschool.[6] Wouldn't it be cool if dudes were allowed to do whatever the fuck they wanted, like wear skirts, start knitting, or, I don't know, listen to women? Men aren't often raised to feel comfortable expressing emotions unless those emotions are anger and violence. Sadness? Vulnerability? Sensitivity? NOPE, TOO BAD. "Real men don't get sad." So of course, when dudes do feel these emotions, they don't come out as tears, but as frustration and anger. Hmm, maybe that's why so many men have violent outbursts when we say no.

Toxic masculinity is behind pretty much all forms of harassment toward women, whether it's on the street, online, or in the workplace. It's about asserting power. I'd guess that men catcall for the same reasons they harass women online. And why do men catcall? According to one study looking at video game players, dudes who were "losers" of the game were more likely to catcall because they felt their social hierarchy statuses were threatened. Another study found that men take out their feelings of inadequacy on women by intimidating them on the street, according to researchers at Promundo.[7] However, when asked, up to 90 percent of the men said the reason they sexually harassed women was just for fun and excitement. GET THESE MEN SOME HOBBIES, PLEASE!

Toxic masculinity also allows men to act as if they're entitled to our bodies. They often think we owe them sex all the time for some reason. There's an OkCupid question that asks, "Do you feel there are any circumstances in which a person is obligated to have sex with you?" Just check out a couple of profiles, and you'll see that a surprising number of men answer yes, even though this is 100 percent absolutely, definitively, unquestionably, and completely wrong. There is literally no circumstance in which a person is obligated to have sex with you, dudes!

Toxic masculinity gives men an empathy problem. They have no interest in understanding women or caring about their realities.

HEALTHY MASCULINITY: *Hey, wouldn't you have better relationships with women if you took one second to try to understand their problems?*

TOXIC MASCULINITY: *REAL MEN don't care about women's problems!*

Why Are FuckBoys?

Fuckboys are always making me question my sanity. What are they thinking? What planet did they come from? How did they get to be so fucked up?

There's a lot to unpack in this example of an obvious fuckboy. The original poster said she had been texting this guy she met on Tinder, who "started all sweet," then quickly asked her to come over to hook up at 8:30 in the morning. The woman declined, and the next thing he sent was a dick pic. The following is what happened next:

> That's not worth the ride. Really?

> Your loss...

> I'm sure that you're awesome in bed I'm just not in the mood for sex

> **Fair enough... if you aren't in the mood... I respect it.**
>
> **I wish we could cuddle and lay next to each other**
>
> **I would make you feel beautiful. I know that's what you want**

> I want to go on real dates
>
> Is what I want

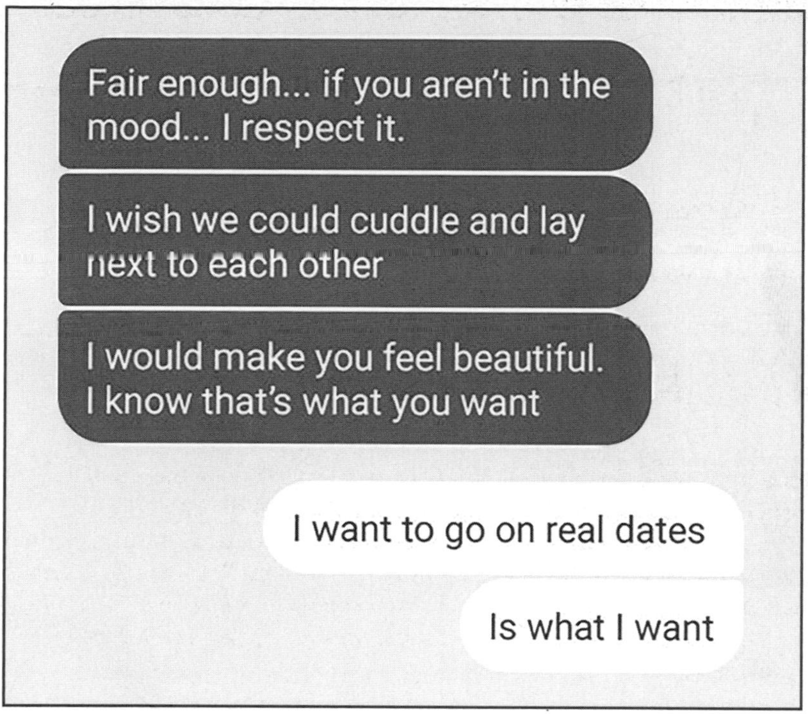

First of all, she's awfully polite for having just received an unsolicited dick pic, even reassuring him that it's not his fault, he's probably "awesome in bed," but the problem is with her not being in the mood.

He seems to take it OK at first, but then he disregards what she just said she wanted, and explains to her what he thinks she wants. "I would make you feel beautiful. I know that's what you want."

OH, HELL NO. This dude thinks that the reason women sleep with them is to feel beautiful? Oh, honey, no. Women sleep with you to have fun or to forge a human connection. But assuming that we don't feel beautiful unless we're boning a dude? WRONG. He assumes that all women have low self-esteem and that the cure for it is his dick.

She tries to set him straight. They're obviously on Tinder looking for different things: "I want to go on dates, is what I want." She's still polite, but correcting him about her standards.

> You went from fun and hot to way too dramatic. Sorry....

> Good luck Meg.

> I'm gonna go get naked with my friend Connie. I'll send you some pictures of how to relax. You really should stop overthinking everything. You'll end up alone.

3 min

It is here that we discover this man's deeply disturbing thought process, which is also, I'd like to point out, a metaphor for the sad state of dating in 2018. Going on a real date, this man thinks, is "way too dramatic." WHAT?!?! I have so many questions about this dude's thought process.

Going on dates is "dramatic"? Where did he get the idea that he could ask a woman he's never met to come to his house to hook up like he's ordering a pizza for delivery? When a woman doesn't want to jump on his dick first thing in the morning she's "overthinking it"?

And his attempt at making her jealous of a clearly made-up woman named "Connie"—or more likely the name of his hand . . . Did he think that would be an effective way to get her to come over? Because it makes me want to throw him into an active volcano.

This fuckboy's level of laziness is unparalleled. How did men come to be this inept, rude, and entitled?

I have a theory that the concentration of fuckboys on Tinder is much higher than that of the general population because many fuckboys have had their hearts broken. Usually, the first thing people tell their friends after they go through a breakup is to go on Tinder and forget about their ex. But this creates a massive influx of selfish, emotionally unavailable assholes who have personal vendettas against their exes. They make it their mission to jam the first person they can find in order to stop thinking about the person responsible for turning their heart to stone. Hurt people are hurt people, ya know what I'm sayin'?

Why Are Trolls?

A significant number of the submissions I see on a daily basis are from women dealing with trolls. These are men who come at you and call you ugly in their first message. They aren't even attempting to hit on you; they just receive pleasure from causing pain to others. They are sadists. No, really, trolls are more likely to have some form of personality disorder, as noted in a 2014 research study on the psychology of internet trolls, titled "Trolls Just Want to Have Fun."[8] Researchers found that people who troll are more likely to score higher on the "Dark Tetrad" personality traits:

DARK TETRAD

- Sadism—getting pleasure from causing pain to others
- Narcissism—extreme self-centeredness
- Psychopathy—a complete lack of conscience, empathy, or remorse
- Machiavellianism—an amoral willingness to manipulate others for personal gain

Of these four personality traits, sadism and Machiavellianism were the most closely related to trolling behavior.[9] Basically, the more pain they cause, the better they feel. Trolls were also more likely to be disagreeable. Another interesting fact was that, according to the study authors, men are more likely to have Dark Tetrad qualities than women are by about 10 to 15 percent.

Wait a minute, don't these traits sound familiar? They kind of sound like every fuckboy I've ever met: a selfish, manipulative, pain-causing dude with an empathy deficit. It makes sense, because the Dark Triad traits (narcissism, psychopathy, and Machiavellianism) are also associated with a measure of superficial charm.[10] Fuckboys tend to think very highly of themselves, dress well, and generally know how to get people to like them, which is why they can be so attractive. They're bad boys. But what separates the trolls from the fuckboys? I'd be willing to guess it's the level of sadism. Take the sadism away, and you have a fuckboy. Turn up the sadism, and you have a troll. Either way, all these personality traits are pretty difficult to change because people are genetically predisposed to them. Dealing with trolls can be upsetting and annoying, but the next time you get trolled, remind yourself not to take it personally because it's probably the result of something they can't change. And don't let yourself get bent out of shape, just ignore them: DON'T FEED THE TROLLS.

The bright side: Maybe this means the world is not as full of misogyny and hate as we previously thought.

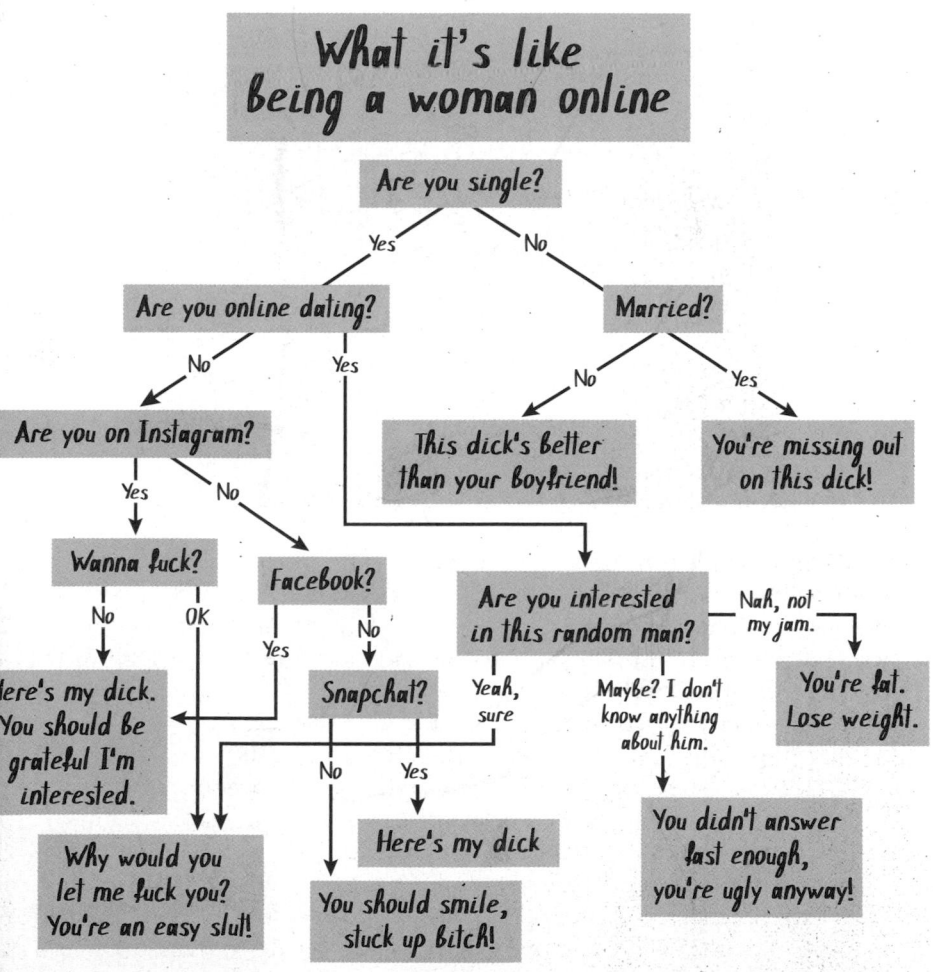

Why Are Nice Guys™?

Almost everyone has met a Nice Guy.™ Note that I'm trademarking this term to differentiate it from the real nice guys. Nice Guys™ are dudes who call themselves "nice," implying that they are caring, sensitive, and polite, but who are only using these qualities to attempt to get someone to sleep with them. In reality, they are not "nice," but think they are entitled to sex in exchange for their "good deeds." They think that because they collected a certain number of stamps on their Acting Like a Decent Human Being Loyalty Program Card, they can cash them in for a sexual favor of their choice.

This Nice Guy™ on Plenty of Fish has a full-on conversation with himself about how great he is.

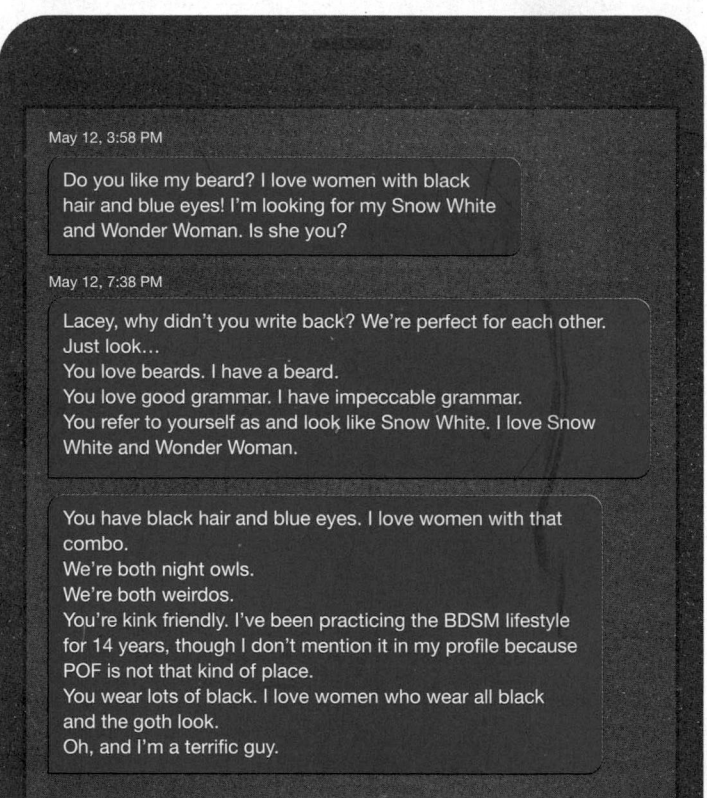

May 12, 3:58 PM

Do you like my beard? I love women with black hair and blue eyes! I'm looking for my Snow White and Wonder Woman. Is she you?

May 12, 7:38 PM

Lacey, why didn't you write back? We're perfect for each other. Just look…
You love beards. I have a beard.
You love good grammar. I have impeccable grammar.
You refer to yourself as and look like Snow White. I love Snow White and Wonder Woman.

You have black hair and blue eyes. I love women with that combo.
We're both night owls.
We're both weirdos.
You're kink friendly. I've been practicing the BDSM lifestyle for 14 years, though I don't mention it in my profile because POF is not that kind of place.
You wear lots of black. I love women who wear all black and the goth look.
Oh, and I'm a terrific guy.

Until he turns.

> You're a piece of white trash with your tacky tattoos. You're no Snow White. One was pure and beautiful. And you have the grammar of a grade schooler. You're an embarrassment to written English.

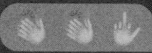

> I was never interested in you. Yes, you have the hair and eyes I want, but that's it. This was a test and you failed miserably. You see, you women love to respond to negativity but not positivity. You ask for something specific in a man, like a beard in your case, but when that bearded man writes you a message, you ignore him. I've concluded from the test results that all women, not just you, are incompetent and are only trying to waste guys' time, making online dating a complete waste of everybody's time.

> Lacey, how could you possibly not be interested or attracted to such a fine male specimen? I'm a dream guy. I could give you everything you desire in a relationship. I'm a terrific vanilla guy who's into kink and loves women with black hair, blue eyes, and wear plenty of black. It's called courtesy. You were looking for a bearded man, so I wrote you. You don't know how lucky you are to receive a message from me – and you complain? I told you I didn't mean that harsh comment. It was test to see if you'd reply to negativity or positivity, and you failed. I would certainly tell you that to your face if I meant it. You're not bright, and after this short communication, not somebody, I want to love. Enjoy all the preverts and losers. You're absolutely perfect each other. You women are despicable.

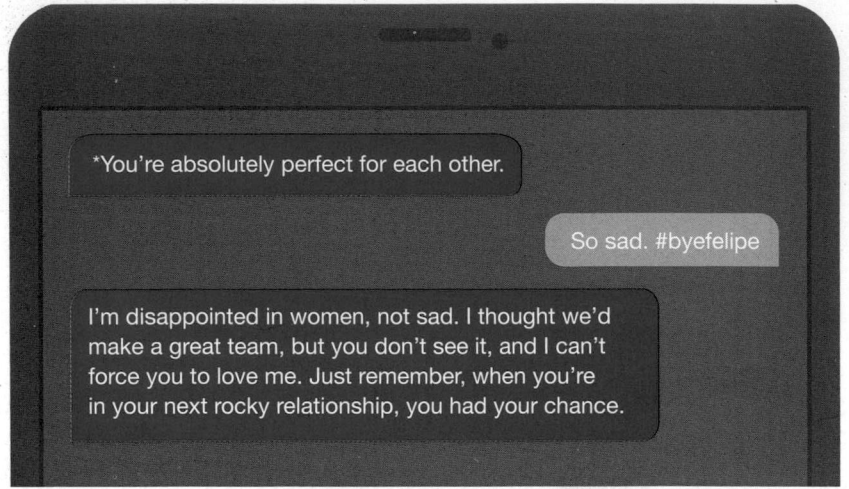

Nice Guys™ operate under the mantra of "Nice guys finish last. Women only like assholes." They think that they should "get a chance" at a date if they are not outwardly rotten. They complain about the "friend zone," and expect a prize when they say, "You're not fat, you're beautiful to me," or that they're "not like most guys," they "could have taken advantage of you when you were drunk at that party," but they didn't. Nice Guys™ are typically very immature.

Nice Guys'™ problems usually stem from the fact that they usually aren't living the life they want to live. They aren't getting interest from women, and instead of realizing that maybe they should work on and improve themselves, the easier thing to do is blame women and society. They won't admit that they are holding *themselves* back.

As they are usually young and inexperienced, Nice Guys™ will eventually evolve, and they can go one of two ways:

1. Realizing that women are people and snapping out of their Nice Guy™ ways, or

2. Getting sucked into bogus online self-help groups such as Pickup Artists, Men's Rights Activists, meninism, The Red Pill, or any number of underground 4Chan communities.

Nice Guys™ are ripe for being radicalized by groups that give them hope and say that they'll help them get women to like them, when, in reality, the core principle of the group is hating women. But they don't care that these groups are not "nice," because they just want to belong.

Why Are Pickup Artists?

In 2005, Neil Strauss published *The Game: Penetrating the Secret Society of Pickup Artists*, which triggered an avalanche of courses and classes, designed to teach men tricks to get women to sleep with them. *The Game* exploded in popularity, and there was even an absurd reality TV show about it. Pickup artists had a good ten-year run, but started to disappear when Tinder was invented. Honestly, no one really calls themselves pickup artists (PUAs) anymore. It's passé. However, the teachings live on and have mutated into other communities. Dudes figured out that they needed to change it up after women caught on to the gimmicks like "negging" (subtly giving a backhanded compliment to a woman so she subconsciously tries to seek their approval), so now they call their courses "social engineering" seminars. I have a sneaking suspicion that former PUAs and men who have gone to these seminars are the senders of a large percentage of unsolicited dick pics. Why? Let me connect the dots.

Perhaps one of the last vestiges of classic pickup artistry today is a company called Real Social Dynamics (RSD). Started by former PUA Julien Blanc, RSD teaches courses (for thousands of dollars) on how to intimidate and control women with aggressive physical and "psychological" techniques. In 2014, Blanc released a YouTube video from one of his seminars in which he encouraged men to seduce women who don't speak English by touching them without their consent. The video features footage of him in Tokyo grabbing women and shoving their faces into his crotch while saying "Pikachu." (Wow! He's not only a sexual harasser, he's a racist too!)

"In Tokyo, if you're a white male, you can do what you want," Blanc said in the video.[11]

Hmm, sounds familiar. Like I've heard it somewhere before ...

Name the source of this quote:

"When you're a star, they let you do it . You can do anything."

Answer: Donald Trump

Blanc is actively training men to become narcissistic sexual harassers, so we shouldn't be surprised when those men send unsolicited dick pics and commit other heinous acts. We see the horrifying effects of this PUA culture when men who take this kind of training commit rape and brag about it in their online forums. Three men involved with another pickup artist company, called Efficient Pickup, were sentenced to eight years in prison (the maximum) for raping an unconscious woman in San Diego in 2013.[12] But just because PUA courses are out of fashion now doesn't mean their sleazy students have gone away.

Of Course, He Calls Them Females

The "red pill" is a reference to the 1999 film *The Matrix*. Taking the "red pill" means you "wake up" and realize "the truth," that women are the enemy and feminism is the source of all your problems. It's definitely NOT that you are deeply insecure and are totally unfamiliar with social norms.

PUA communities laid the groundwork for the Reddit group The Red Pill, with 200,000 subscribers, described as a "discussion of sexual strategy in a culture increasingly lacking a positive identity for men." This newer PUA iteration attracts the same types of guys: young, inexperienced—many have never had sex. In "swallowing the Red Pill," these (often depressed and troubled) men are said to have learned "the truth." "Truths" they are taught include: Anything they see in the media about relationships is #fakenews, feminism is evil, sexism doesn't exist, and women have easy lives while men are oppressed. And, of course, The Red Pill relies on pseudosocial psychology that boils down modern dating to fake evolutionary theory. Like any good cult, they cherry-pick the facts they believe and rely on "science" that they made up in their own heads. This means that they always refer to women as "females." (Another attempt at dehumanizing them.) TRP pushes the notion that men are the real victims in society, further supporting the culture of resentment toward women. Those who fall for it become increasingly bitter and angry.

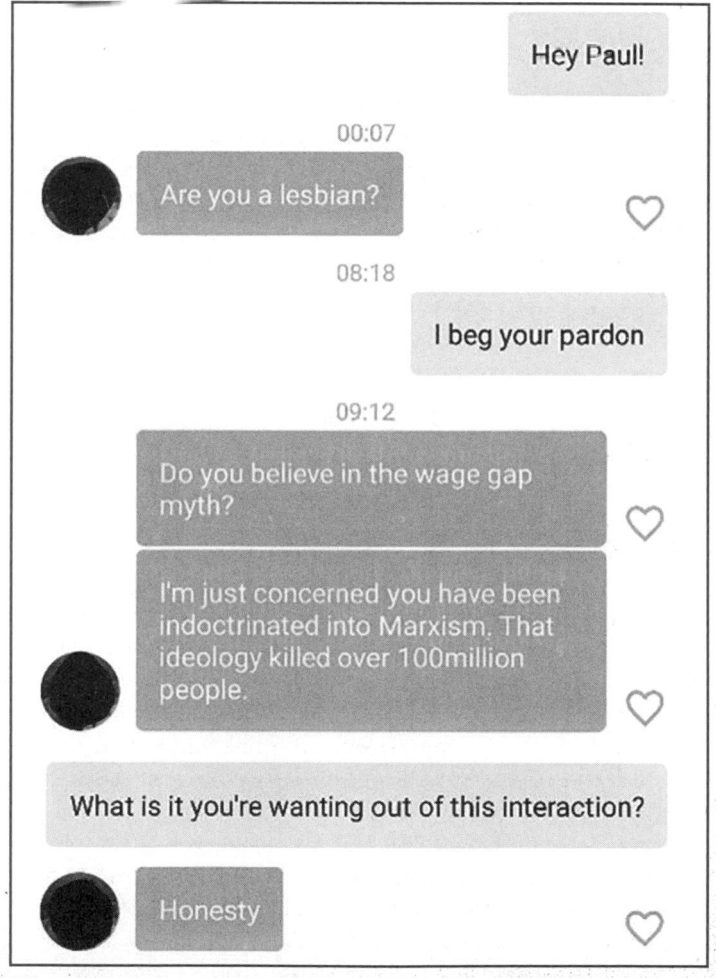

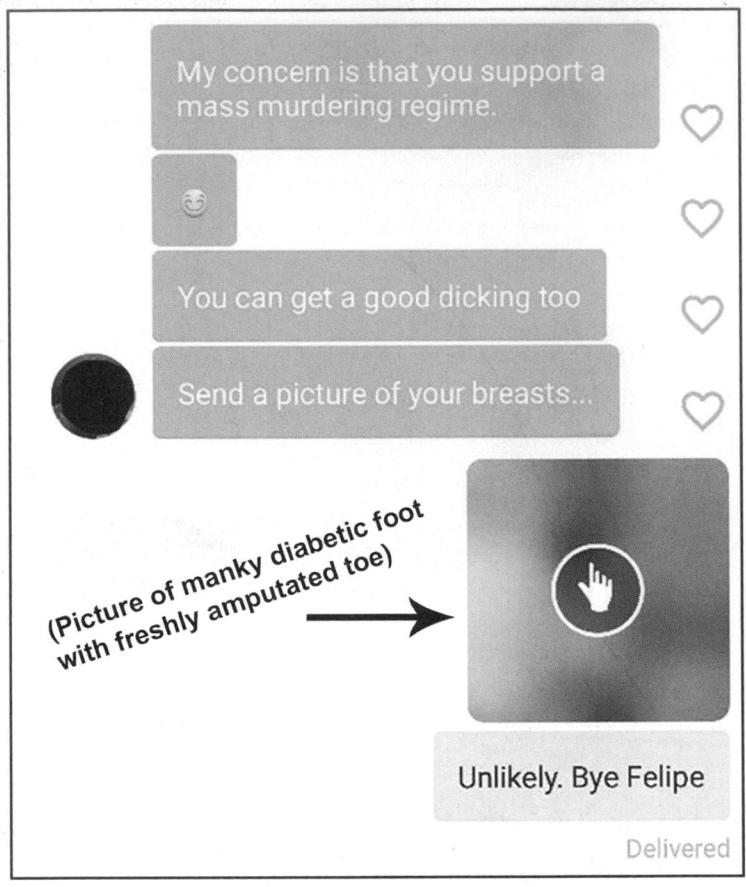

The Red Pill hammers home one of the central tenets that underlies Bye Felipe interactions: "Rejection is not rejection." In one of the most popular posts, titled "HOW TO GET LAID LIKE A WARLORD: 37 Rules of Approaching Model-Tier Girls," men learn to overcome rejection by not acknowledging it. Apparently, they believe that women are sneaky and conniving, always "shit-testing" men. The post proclaims, "When a woman insults you, belittles you, mocks you, or says something provocative to get a reaction—these are all examples of active tests."[13]

Oh no, it couldn't possibly mean be that she just DOESN'T LIKE YOU. These Red Pill lessons about not listening to women is why you get men who can't take no for an answer. These groups tell guys that if they get rejected, it's because they're "too high value," and women are nervous around them, but secretly like them. (Cough—*Entitlement*—cough.)

You can identify manosphere dudes because they're always trying to reduce women to their reproductive ability. They use, again, made-up "facts" to try to make us feel bad. It always makes me want to yawn.

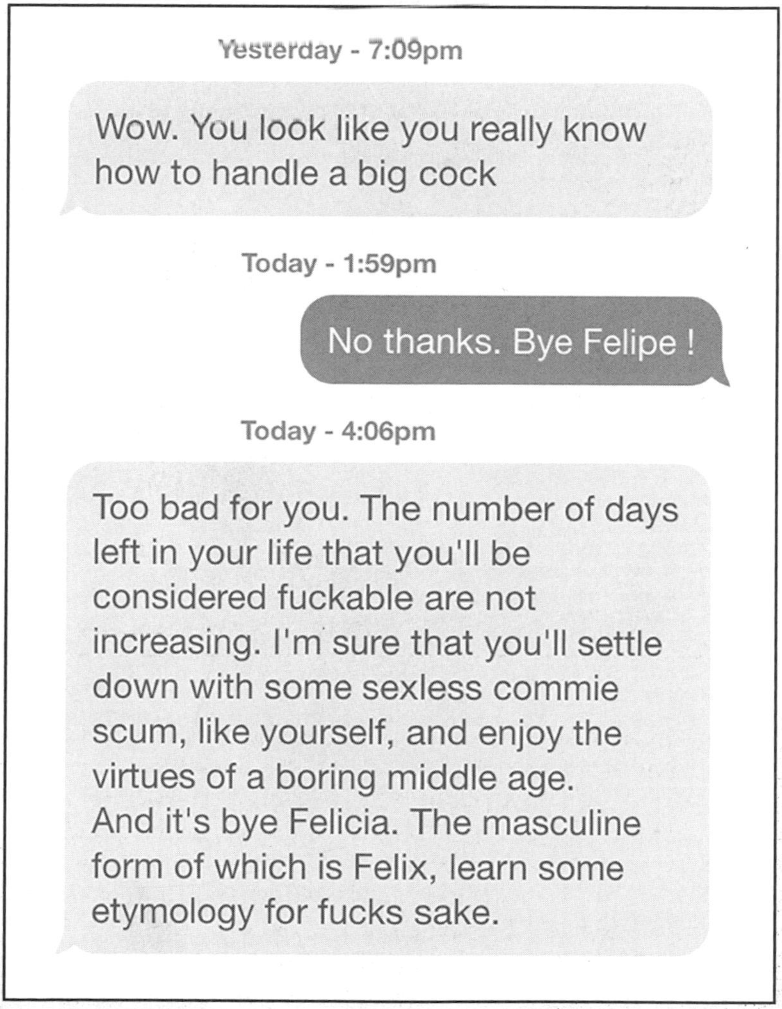

Yesterday - 7:09pm

Wow. You look like you really know how to handle a big cock

Today - 1:59pm

No thanks. Bye Felipe !

Today - 4:06pm

Too bad for you. The number of days left in your life that you'll be considered fuckable are not increasing. I'm sure that you'll settle down with some sexless commie scum, like yourself, and enjoy the virtues of a boring middle age. And it's bye Felicia. The masculine form of which is Felix, learn some etymology for fucks sake.

Manosphere men just blatantly hate women. But at least they don't try to hide it.

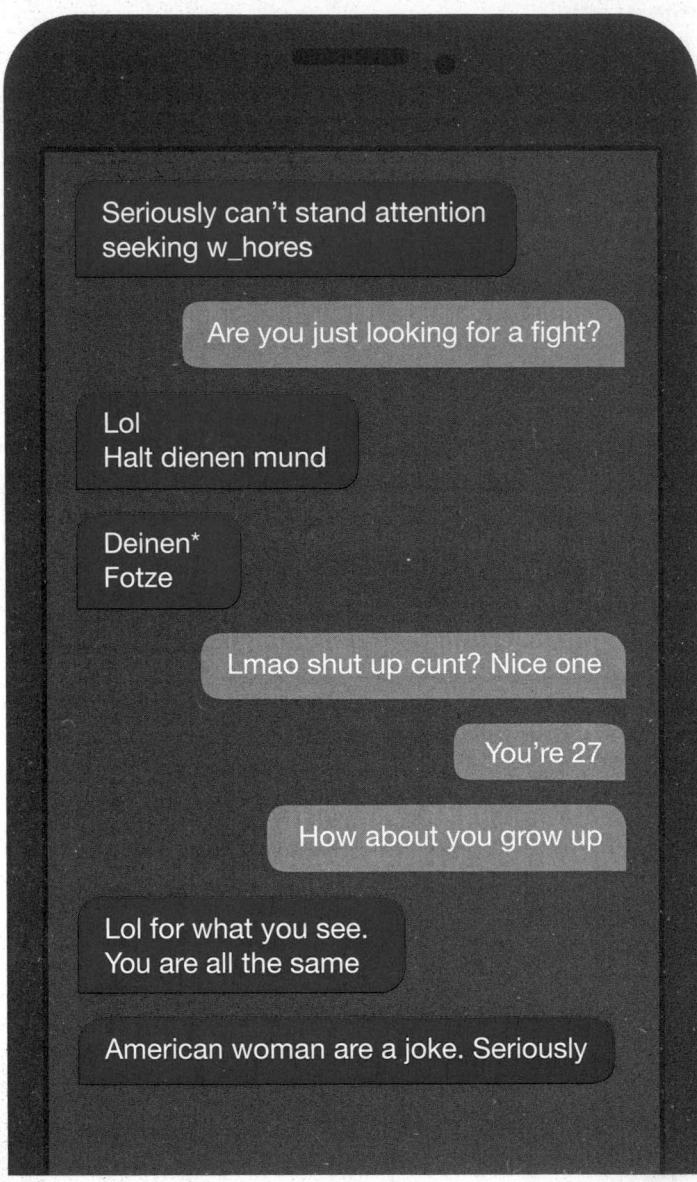

Seriously can't stand attention seeking w_hores

Are you just looking for a fight?

Lol
Halt dienen mund

Deinen*
Fotze

Lmao shut up cunt? Nice one

You're 27

How about you grow up

Lol for what you see.
You are all the same

American woman are a joke. Seriously

Lmao you hate women that much

Only those in this country. Self assorted. Expccting everything for them as if you riding the highest horse. Very pathetic

Take 5 secs to realize
You are not a sh_it princess

You're a 27 year old man talking like you're a 16 year old boy
How about you go complain to some other almost 30 yeat old guy who also hates women as much as you. Okay? You don't know shit about me so don't act like a 16 year old boy trying to put down women

Lmao you know talking to a women like this will get you no where with one.

Haha triggered?

Nope just giving advice to someone who obviously needs it

Oh, I'm not done yet. There are even *worse* PUA spin-off groups that have taken off in the last few years. It has been confirmed that the alt-right and racist groups recruit men from The Red Pill.[14] They have admitted targeting sub-Reddit groups for "loser/virgin/lonely/angry" young men. Hating people of color just seems like a logical place for men who hate women to go. Former PUA blogger and current garbage diarrhea man hereinafter referred to as Douche V—went from writing nonsense like "5 Reasons to Date a Girl with an Eating Disorder"[15] to being a poster boy for the alt-right. His previous writings included sex-themed travel guides that tell men how to get laid in places like Eastern Europe, where the women are "compliant" because "feminism has not made strong inroads."[16]

Douche V symbolizes the rise of the blatant misogyny and racism we now see in the news every day. But he also shows us how the original ideas of Nice Guys™ and pickup artists have evolved. He invented his own term for how "real men" should be and called it "neomasculinity," which he defines as combining "traditional beliefs, masculinity, and animal biology into one ideological system." Sounds science-y, except for the fact that none of it is based on actual science. He basically just preaches antifeminism and encourages men to be actively sexist in order to get laid.

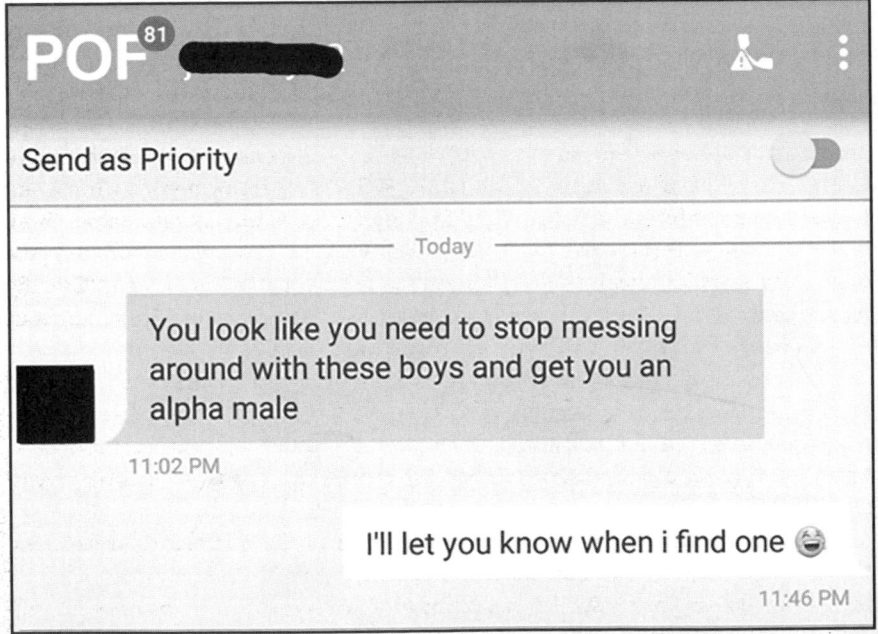

In his article "Feminism Killed the Nice Guy," he repeats the "nice guys finish last" mantra, but extrapolates that in order to get laid, men must not respect women, not believe that the genders are equal, and not listen to women about anything. "You must believe that you are superior and deserve more than [women]. With the addition of game practice, you will then be sexually rewarded for those beliefs."[17]

How many men actually believe his bullshit? Since the 2016 election, Douche V's site traffic jumped from around 150,000 monthly visitors to over 500,000 in the span of a few months.[18] It's hard to say how many true followers he has because most "neomasculinists" have a fear of being outed. But you can bet that these Douche followers are also at least a few of the guys who end up on Bye Felipe. His entire mission is to whip men into an army of angry, bitter dickheads whose only goal is to dehumanize and sleep with as many women as possible.

Incel Hell

Another Reddit group in the manosphere is an especially depressing subgroup called "incels," which stands for involuntary celibate, or dudes who are failing at finding a romantic relationship and are extremely pessimistic about it. Members of the Reddit incels group reject Red Pill ideas about self-help and claim to be "a support group for people who lack romantic relationships and sex." They say the group is just a place to vent, and that they don't actually act like they do on the forum in real life. "Some of the ideas expressed are definitely extreme but we allow them because having a forum to vent is vital for a person's overall mental health. Think of it like a safety release valve for negative emotions." In a constant revolving circle of negative spiraling, incels refer to themselves as "subhuman" and having "literally no redeemable traits," and then complain about not getting laid and fantasize about a world where women can't read and are owned like property.

On their FAQ page, incels claim they feel they are not entitled to love, sex, or relationships. They also claim not to hate women, but pretty much every post proves otherwise. Oftentimes, commenters who aren't incels—so-called "normies"—try to give them advice, but they're so stubbornly pessimistic that they reject all attempts.

I'm not sure that incels are a large source of Bye Felipe material, because the thought of talking to a woman usually makes them break out in a sweat, but I do think they contribute to the general culture of misogyny on the internet. Should we feel sorry for incels? I have no doubt they've been treated horribly and bullied their entire lives. A lot of them claim that they were not bitter or angry growing up, but since women and society rejected them, their self-worth has been completely shattered. They are frustrated and lonely. But they take no responsibility for their own mental well-being.

I suspect that many of these guys join manosphere groups because they suffer from social anxiety or social phobia, and the groups are a way to deal with their condition instead of going to a therapist or physician. A 2015 study found that people suffering from depression experience pain from social rejection for a longer period of time since their brains produce fewer "natural opioids," which reduce pain and stress.[19] So, it's natural that these men would try to find solace on the internet. The only problem is, most of the self-help resources they can find online are complete garbage. It's insanely easy to stumble on YouTube videos made by these bitter, hateful men, spewing completely heinous advice.

A second group in opposition to The Red Pill and incels has also emerged. Called The Black Pill, it is basically the extreme nihilistic version of these groups. They think that reality is rigged against them and that because they are "subhuman," they are destined to fail, no matter what. They resent The Red Pill for offering them false hope of ever having a romantic relationship.

Please, Go Your Own Way

Finally, the latest branch of Red Pill–esque groups is Men Going Their Own Way, or #MGTOW. It claims to be "more of a philosophy on how to live life instead of a movement" and is described as a group of men who have opted out of relationships. They say they're not bitter men who can't get a date, because a lot of them have been married and had children. It's just that they felt that they got screwed over by a woman at some point—maybe they got a divorce or got cheated on—and decided not to deal with women anymore. The most hilarious thing about MGTOW is that they think they're somehow getting revenge on women.

According to the MGTOW Reddit page, "If MGTOW's growth is alarming to you then you're going to have to change what causes them to go MGTOW. Which means change the divorce courts, the attack on masculinity, the institution of marriage, social expectations on men, etc. Things such as shaming them, calling them "man-boys," having white-knights [men who stand up for feminism] attack them, and other methods will do nothing to stop this growth."[20]

Excuse me while I stifle my laughter. Believe me, MGTOW is *not* alarming AT ALL. In fact, Men Going Their Own Way, I thank you, sincerely, from all of womankind. (I'm not being sarcastic.) MGTOW claim that members of their group won't catcall, won't stare at you at the gym, won't ask for your number. "In fact, a MGTOW won't even bother to look in your direction." But watch out, because, according to them, it's a "double edged sword." They're also not going to buy you drinks or dinner or take you for a ride in their sports cars. (Boo hoo.) The best part is that they refuse to flirt! "Especially in a society where a guy is one false rape accusation or sexual harassment case away from a jail sentence."

THANK ODIN! This is exactly what we as women have been striving for this entire time: that emotionally unavailable, stingy, obnoxious men leave us alone, once and for all. We don't want your drinks, dinner, cars, or repugnant personalities. Thank you, from the bottom of my heart, for saving thousands of women from making the frustrating mistake of going on pointless dates with your members.

The funniest part about the manosphere is that all the groups hate each other. Elliot Roger, the twenty-two-year-old murderer who killed six people in 2014 because he was angry that women wouldn't sleep with him was the epitome of a Nice Guy™. He was also active in a group called PUAHate.com, which revolved around anti-pickup artist discussions. Douche V claims to hate Men's Rights Activists. Incels generally hate Red Pills. And these are just a few examples of the thousands of revolting extremist breeding grounds online. It doesn't really matter which of the toxic manosphere communities these men end up in because the under-lying ideology of all of them is exactly the same: objectifying, manipulating, and dominating women.

Racism + Sexism

In addition to misogyny, we also need to think about how racism and sexism dovetail with each other to figure out the answer to "Why are men?" Our culture is still racist as hell! Women of color have to battle both sexism and racism: The term for this is "misogynoir." (Not to mention class, sexual orientation, ethnicity, etc.) They experience sexism differently from white women, and it's often hard to separate the sexism part from the racism part. There is no universal women's experience because some women face more discrimination because of their race. Women of color often face specific racial biases on dating apps and are hyper-sexualized and fetishized.

Many times, women of color are targets of specific racist sexism, like the following:

Yet another example of men buying into the stereotype that the only women who are desirable are white. These types of men think they're doing us such a giant favor for being interested in someone who is outside of what white supremacy regards as "the norm." BARF!

Racism and sexism also permeate the culture from the top down, starting with straight white men and affecting other marginalized groups. How white men treat men of color, in turn, affects how men of color treat women. These histories of racism cannot be separated from white power structures.

MANOSPHERE LINGO GLOSSARY

ALPHA: A guy with a controlling and dominant personality. Believes that all women are attracted to assholes or bad boys. (Never mind that the wolf study this term came from was proven false and the idea that it exists in human social science has not been proven.)

AWALT: "All women are like that," meaning "females" are hardwired to behave a certain way.

BETA: What Red Pill dudes call Nice Guys™.

BLACK PILL: The extreme nihilist version of The Red Pill. They think that reality is rigged against them and that because they are "subhuman," they are destined to fail, no matter what.

BLUE PILL: A normal person who thinks women are people and hasn't taken the Red Pill.

CHAD: A typical jacked hot guy douche who probably bullied Red Pill dudes in college.

FEMINIST: Red Pillers think feminists want superiority over men. They believe that women are privileged in society, and use this as a reason to demonize them.

FHO: Female Humanoid Organism—woman, female, or girl. A term used by incels ironically to troll women.

HYPERGAMY: Red Pillers have a theory "called hypergamy," that women instinctively "seek out the best alpha available," and that they sleep with as many of them as possible. Obviously a projection, since Red Pillers actively try to sleep with as many "hot" women as possible, yet slut shame them at the same time.

INCEL: Involuntary Celibate. A man who wants to get laid, but can't.

MANOSPHERE: Any blogs, message boards, or sites run by Men's Rights Activists, Men Going Their Own Way, Pickup Artists, or Red Pill groups.

MGTOW: Men Going Their Own Way; dudes who felt they got screwed over once (i.e., got divorced or had to pay child support) and now refuse to have relationships with women.

ORBITER: The new word for a guy who was "friend-zoned." Typical signs of orbiter status: likes and comments on new Facebook photos. Go-to guy when girl has problem with boyfriend. Also known as emotional tampon.

SHIT TEST: Something a woman says that makes men think she's testing them for "alpha traits."

STACEY: A hot woman.

WHITE KNIGHT: A man who stands up for women.

What all these conversations in the manosphere actually do is validate the crisis of masculinity. Men are the biggest policers of masculinity, to their own detriment, and taking one glance at any of these groups reinforces that fact. Patriarchal ideals are bad for men *and* women—this is something feminists have been talking about this entire time. It sounds weird to say, but feminists actually have something in common with PUAs, MRAs, and incels: We all have a problem with the fact that men get bullied for not being the ideal masculine man. Men and women are both responsible for telling them, "Man up!" "Grow a pair!" "Stop being a pussy!" But the manosphere isn't identifying the root of the problem correctly, which is that the unattainable masculine ideal, the seed of all of their problems, is rooted in patriarchal society.

I'll admit, I have done my fair share of mocking and insulting these guys, but I always try not to shame them for physical appearance or things they can't help. My mocking is always based on their hypocrisy or inability to make sense—their laughable attempts at insults. What we have to remember is that ad hominem attacks make people double down on their arguments and find groups who agree with them. Once they find that community, they get support and are surrounded by people who "get it." It doesn't matter to these guys that their nonsensical ideas have hurt themselves and other people, because they just want to belong somewhere. These guys are victims of patriarchy and gender roles. They are surrounded by messages that their number one priority should be sex, and they get these messages from everywhere: movies, TV, friends, family, pop culture in general. Telling them that they're gross and will die alone only confirms their twisted worldview because that's what they already believe about themselves.

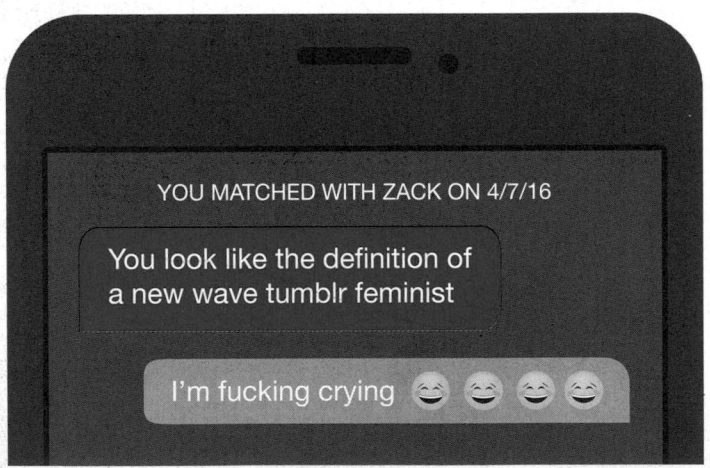

YOU MATCHED WITH ZACK ON 4/7/16

You look like the definition of a new wave tumblr feminist

I'm fucking crying 😄 😄 😄 😄

> Like instead of unmatching, you spent the time to send that fucking message? 😂 😂 😂

> I'm weak.

I did I don't match with potential meme girls often

Are you going to start telling me about your next Sjw warrior campaign and how in a white male so everything is my fault?

> I can't with this 😄 😄

What do feminists yell out during mf intercourse? Omg I'm about to finish you're TRIGGERING me

> Dude, like my question is why are you talking to me about this? It just seems like you have a lot of personal issues with women and maybe tinder isn't the best place for you.

If the manosphere is so concerned about their fragile egos being so irreparably damaged by masculinity bullying, you would think they'd be fighting for the rights of all men to define their own masculinity however they want. But instead, they hold on to all the toxic parts of masculinity and force everyone to conform. (I have a secret fantasy where one day I wake up in the alternate reality/parallel universe where Hillary won and men's rights folks realize that we're all just arguing for the same things, but, alas, I'm still here in the Trump upside-down.)

When we try to talk to people about the concept of privilege and tell them that they have it when they don't feel they have it, no other argument about feminism makes sense in their minds. The concept of privilege is hard to understand when you're a straight cis white man (level 10/10 privilege, according to feminism) and you still aren't successful. They can't grasp the basic fact that men have inherent privilege over women because they've been told it should be easy for them, that they had advantages, and yet they're still failing.

If we can't even agree on the same premise of privilege—that it's easier for some people to succeed based on race, class, gender, ability—there's no way any of us will be able to reason with them or change their minds. They post articles about "why we aren't living in a patriarchy" that feature facts about men being disadvantaged, such as, "Men are more likely to commit suicide than women." But this just proves the problems of living in a patriarchy. The manosphere claims they are against the feminization of men. They say that men should be traditionally masculine: not show emotion, not ask for help, not talk about their feelings. But what qualities typically lead to self-destruction?

They come up with all these examples about how men are losing and women are gaining, but they don't realize that the root cause is patriarchy, and that's what feminists are fighting against.

The manosphere in and of itself is an example of the thing it claims isn't real. It's simply repeating back to us what we already know: that we live in a patriarchy and that men have inherent power over women. They are parroting the messages patriarchal society tells them, but they truly believe those ideas are true and fair. And why wouldn't they agree when patriarchal culture puts them in a favorable position? They don't want to be equal—they want to be dominant—because at their core, they feel like failures.

All of this is to say that if these men have no empathy for women now, they won't be gaining it anytime soon. They are simply inept. Even I have a sliver of empathy for them, which sounds ludicrous. I can see how they would misguidedly form the conclusions that they do, but they are so completely wrong that there's no use in trying to reason with them. Some of these men are simply just despicable people, and there's nothing anyone can do about it.

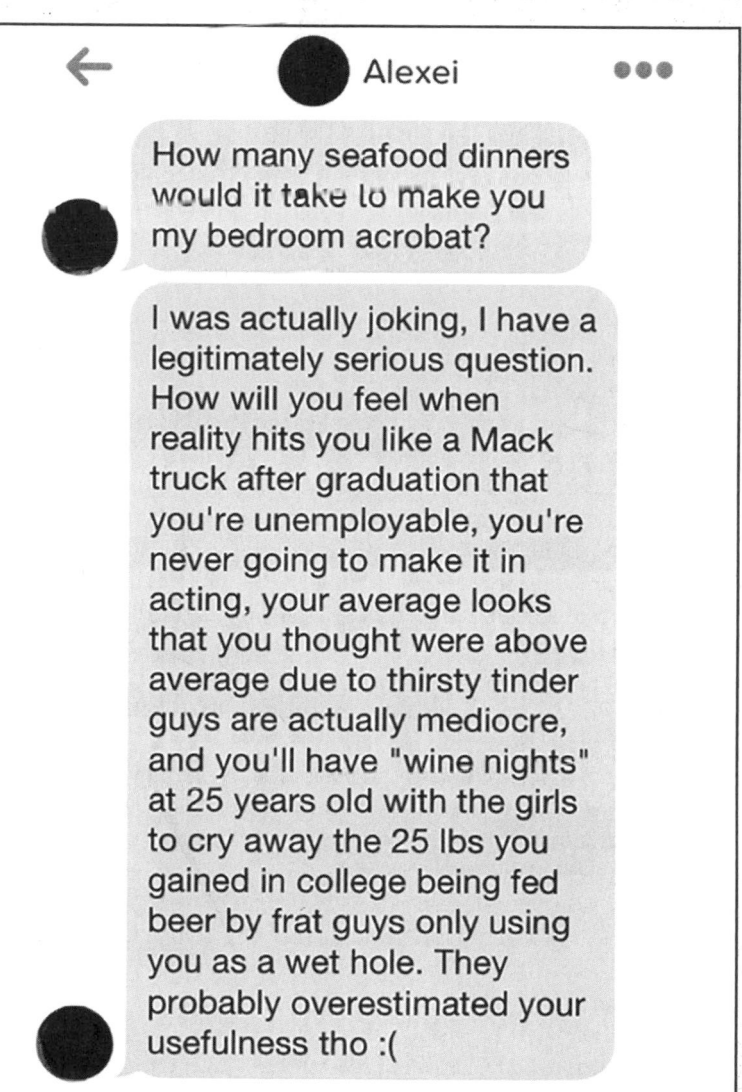

Alexei

How many seafood dinners would it take to make you my bedroom acrobat?

I was actually joking, I have a legitimately serious question. How will you feel when reality hits you like a Mack truck after graduation that you're unemployable, you're never going to make it in acting, your average looks that you thought were above average due to thirsty tinder guys are actually mediocre, and you'll have "wine nights" at 25 years old with the girls to cry away the 25 lbs you gained in college being fed beer by frat guys only using you as a wet hole. They probably overestimated your usefulness tho :(

There are men who defect from PUA, The Red Pill, and incels. Just look at Neil Strauss (of *The Game*). After spiraling and going to rehab for sex addiction, he has since moved past his pickup days and is now preaching for healthy relationships, commitment, and therapy with his latest book, *The Truth*. What happened? When he wrote *The Game*, he knew it was about low self-esteem and male insecurity. According to him, he went to therapy after cheating on the woman he loved and discovered that his problems stemmed from always needing to being in control, which doesn't lend itself to intimacy: "To me, the biggest shock of my life, was how . . . We all have narcissistic mothers. . . . What happens when you grow up with your identity being squashed by this mother who never sees you but only sees herself, is you grow up with a fear of being overpowered by the feminine again. . . . And then when you start to realize, OK, this has nothing to do with the world, it's just me, I've got to get over it—that's when everything kind of changes."[21]

WHAT DID HE THINK WAS GOING TO HAPPEN?

Hey, let's play a game called "What Did He Think Was Going to Happen?" This is where I give you a list of opening lines and you guess what he thought was going to happen.

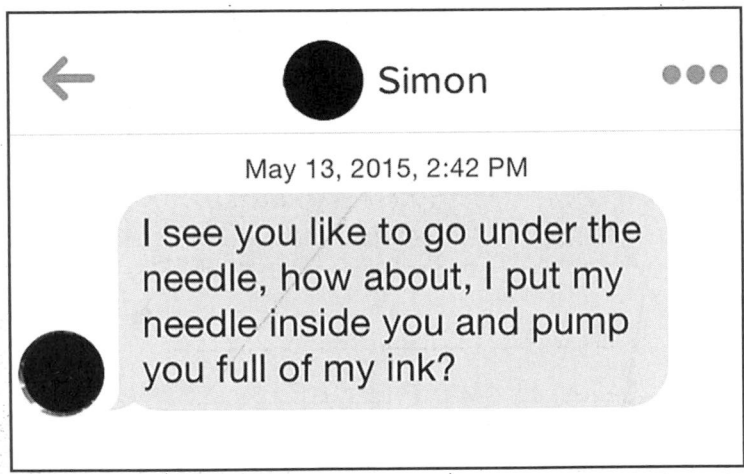

HAHAHAHA You're hilarious, that definitely didn't make me want to barf.

Just what I wanted!

> Do you want to get to know each other and then have a one night stand?

Today - 9:18pm

> Were you raised on a farm? Because you sure know how to raise a cock. You raised a thick cock just now.

Today - 10:17pm

> Forget the one night stand I'm not like that. It's more of the random straight forward message just to get the attention. Forget it though it's a joke okay. Peace out. I'm not interested either your too self absorbed.

How could I say no to this charming message?!?

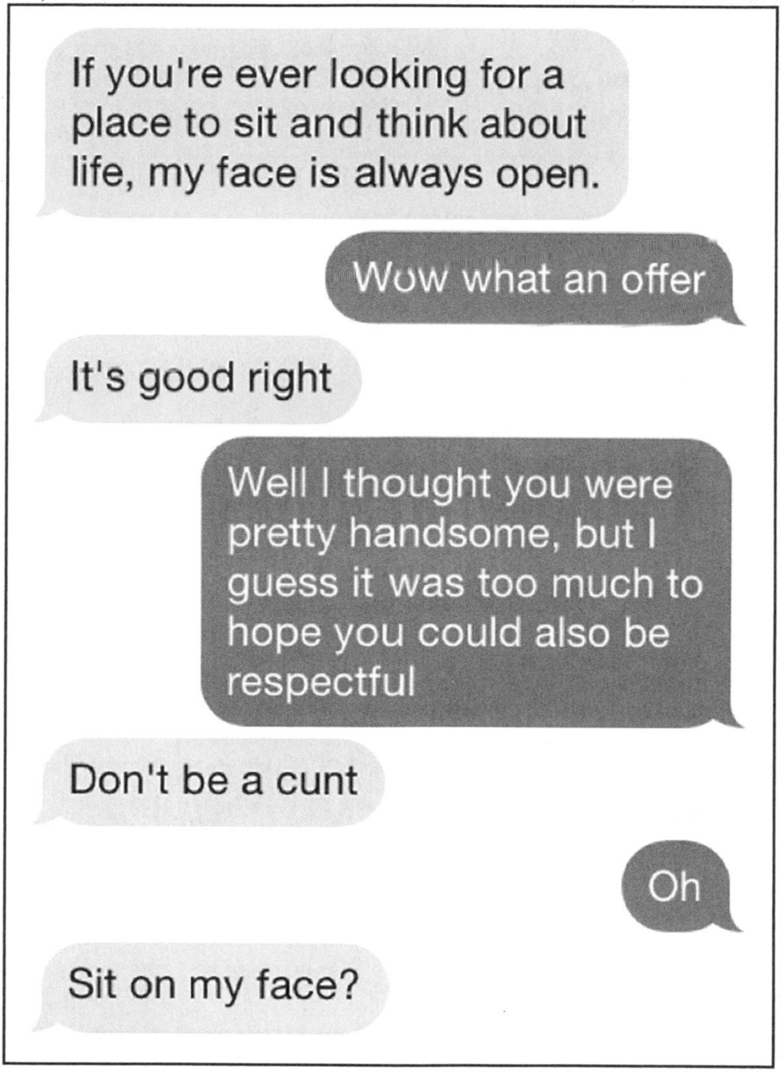

If you're ever looking for a place to sit and think about life, my face is always open.

Wow what an offer

It's good right

Well I thought you were pretty handsome, but I guess it was too much to hope you could also be respectful

Don't be a cunt

Oh

Sit on my face?

OK, I'll be right over!

> Hey can I squeeze your boobs

Sure, as hard as you want!

> R u allergic to semen?

No, it's my favorite food!

 look your hot, if you don't talk to me I'll put your picture on craigslist on the men's seeking men section.

I LOVE being blackmailed!

CHAPTER 4

WTF Can We Do to Deal with Men?

Have we all come to the conclusion that a lot of men have serious problems? What *can* we do to deal with them? What are the best ways of deflecting the bullshit that continually gets flung at us online?

When men flip out after being rejected on the Bye Felipe Instagram account, there are always a couple of people in the comments who say, "She was rude. At least be polite." And then when I post one where they respond politely, the commenters say, "Why did she even respond?" This is the double bind that made me want to start Bye Felipe in the first place, because we're damned if we do respond and damned if we don't. There's no winning if you're a woman who isn't interested.

Let's compare. Here's what happens when we're polite:

Hey..! Your style totally works for you ...! looks beautiful

Today – 12:55pm

Hi thanks for the message but I'm not interested. All the best

Today – 1:57pm

Sorry sent to the wrong person .. Even I don't like fat bitches ..

"Just don't respond!" Hmm, OK, let's try that.

YOU MATCHED WITH ██████ ON 9/17/17

Well you're absolutely gorgeous Heather

 XOXO

Today 3:11 AM

Ha k, well fuck you too then

Today 10:07 AM

Let me take a wild guess! You're only into black guys I bet

Um, what???
OK, let's try again.

 Hi Samantha! I just signed up and liked your profile. What do you like to cook?

Today – 11:40am

 I'm putting more pics up. So you don't think I'm some scam artist. Im just starting over. It's my bday tmo. This girl talked to me for a week. Then disappeared :(

Today – 12:40pm

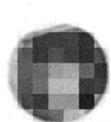 Fuck you then. You stupid fucking whore just like all of them on these sites. I hope you meet a guy that beats your fucking head in

Maybe we should educate them. They just don't know any better—they've made it this far in life to become adult men, but they've never learned how to interact in polite society. OH YEAH, THAT'S NOT OUR JOB. Unless you're getting paid for dating advice, don't take on an idiot charity case unless you're bored and maybe it sounds like a fun time. One submitter on Instagram wrote, "This guy DMed me yesterday asking why I'm on Tinder. He seemed kinda weird, but I gave him a shot, and he was far too aggressive about wanting my number and wanting to meet, and it just made me uneasy. I asked him for a few details about himself and when I politely declined him asking me out (repeatedly) this is what ensued."

So I really like your personality and am obviously physically attracted to you!

I say you give us the chance to hangout 1 time and have drinks and see how it goes? If we don't click then I'll admit you were right and won't try again. Deal?

I already said I'm not interested

And I'm basically out of town until like mid October

So that's how you are you can judge based off pictures

Why not give a guy a chance in person?

So we can do it when you get back then...

> Because you clearly can't read a situation

No it's not that I just am not a judge mental person and like to give everyone the benefit of the doubt

Why not meet you and have a drink and if we don't click then oh well no ones hurt lol

> Because I don't have the time to waste on someone I'm not interested

> in*

But how do you know we won't click and like hanging out? Who knows till we meet and get to talking…

My hunches are usually always correct

I think despite the age thing you'd be surprised Meredith

> Dude. I'm not interested.

> Like you hunches are clearly not correct because you don't know when to take no for an answer

Your right I don't and I think judgmental ppl are inconsiderate

Guess we're just different

I like to give everyone a chance and you don't hased off pictures

I consider men who do not respect consent to be inconsiderate.

I have said I am not interested multiple times now.

So I send you one pic and you come to that conclusion lol

Please respect my answer.

And bc I'm 2 years younger wow

No, your entire approach toward me has led me to that conclusion.

You don't respect consent.

You think you are entitled to a chance with every woman.

Nobody is entitled to that.

I don't respect self righteous judgmental women who think they're better than everyone else

If this interaction had been in person it would be extremely predatory.

Despite your amazing tits and nice eyes that makes you unattractive 🤮

Prolly fake anyways

Oh okay so because I am politely and respectfully telling you that I am not interested and telling you that I feel like you are being aggressive and predatory, suddenly that is my fault?

And that is unacceptable.

It's your fault that your judgmental based off age and pics

One second you say ok get to know me and then after the age thing you say sorry not interested

I have been nothing but nice and respectful. I am judging you based off of your inability to respect my wishes.

You do not respect my right to consent or my right to say no.

And that is unacceptable.

And you make it easy to judge you. I'm not asking you anymore

> Do not message me againX

> *again.

I'm pointing out your flaws

Your fake and stuck up

> You are a predator.

No I'm just honest

> Leave me alone or I will report you.

And you're a stuck up person who feels self entitled and like she's better than every body and you ain't trust me. Nothing special

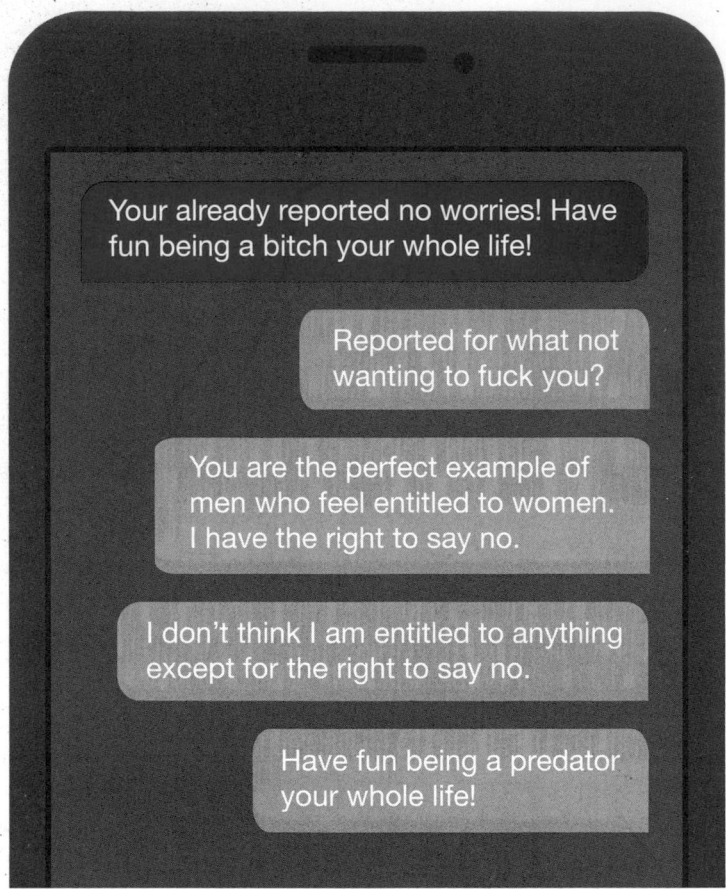

I believe the fundamental problem with some men lies in the fact that they don't generally care about our feelings, emotions, or struggles. They have an inability to see or be made aware of the pain they cause.

This is pretty obvious, but women, especially young women, are more than twice as likely to say they've been sexually harassed online compared to young men (21 percent versus 9 percent of eighteen- to twenty-nine-year-olds, according to a 2017 Pew study).[22] Online harassment affects our lives! When a random man online says he wants to rape you and sends you a dick pic, it kind of ruins your day. It's difficult to just let that slide and forget about it. Online threats impact our lives in a very real way. Surprising no one, women are also twice as likely as men to say their online harassment was "extremely upsetting" or "very upsetting" (35 percent versus 16 percent). Yet, the vast majority of young men—73 percent—say that people take offensive content online "too seriously." Seems like it would be easy for them to say when they don't often experience the psychological and emotional trauma of a malevolent stranger threatening their safety. Yes, the majority of online harassment isn't that big of a deal and can easily be ignored, but most straight men have the privilege of never having experienced genuine fear because of their gender and sexuality. They believe only their own realities.

Half of women say that offensive content online is too often excused, which means a lot of us don't feel that our struggles are being taken seriously. If men could understand what it's like to experience sexism as we do, they might begin to understand and even change. If only their reality were full of larger, angrier, dumber, and more violent people that often wanted to take sexual advantage of them. Unless extraterrestrial beings come to Earth to dominate and terrorize men, most dudes are not going to get it. However, some men do get it. When we point out our pain and make others aware of it, change is possible. Luckily, men don't have to actually experience sexism to understand it. They could just take a second and imagine what it's like, or listen to a woman for once.

Maybe if we could somehow show them what it's like to be a woman, how much we have experienced that has made us feel "less than," they would think twice about their behavior. This was one of my original goals for Bye Felipe, to give men a peek into what kinds of messages we get. I thought giving men a glimpse into our world could foster some empathy. Men need to possess a certain level of emotional intelligence in order to process empathy. That's why we shouldn't waste our time on dudes who don't accept our reality. And dudes who flip out on women when they aren't interested in them obviously have no emotional intelligence. So pick your battles.

What else have we learned so far? According to Felipes, women are just wrong. There's no way to be right if you are not interested in going on a date with him. I say, if we can't win either way, we can at least have some fun with it.

INCREASE THE THING

I've seen dudes bust into many an inbox like the Kool-Aid man smashing through walls to tell women about their unsolicited manpinions like: "Hey, I know you didn't ask, but I don't like that thing on your profile. Just thought I'd let you know."

This is when you say, "Hey thanks!!!! I don't give a fuck about what you think. I'm gonna keep doing that thing you don't like even more because I do like it. BYEEE."

My favorite example of this was when Christina Topacio had the perfect response to a man telling her she needed to lose weight. Christina chatted with a guy we'll call "Ben" on a dating site and became Facebook friends, but never met him because their schedules got busy. Six months later, he messaged her out of the blue:

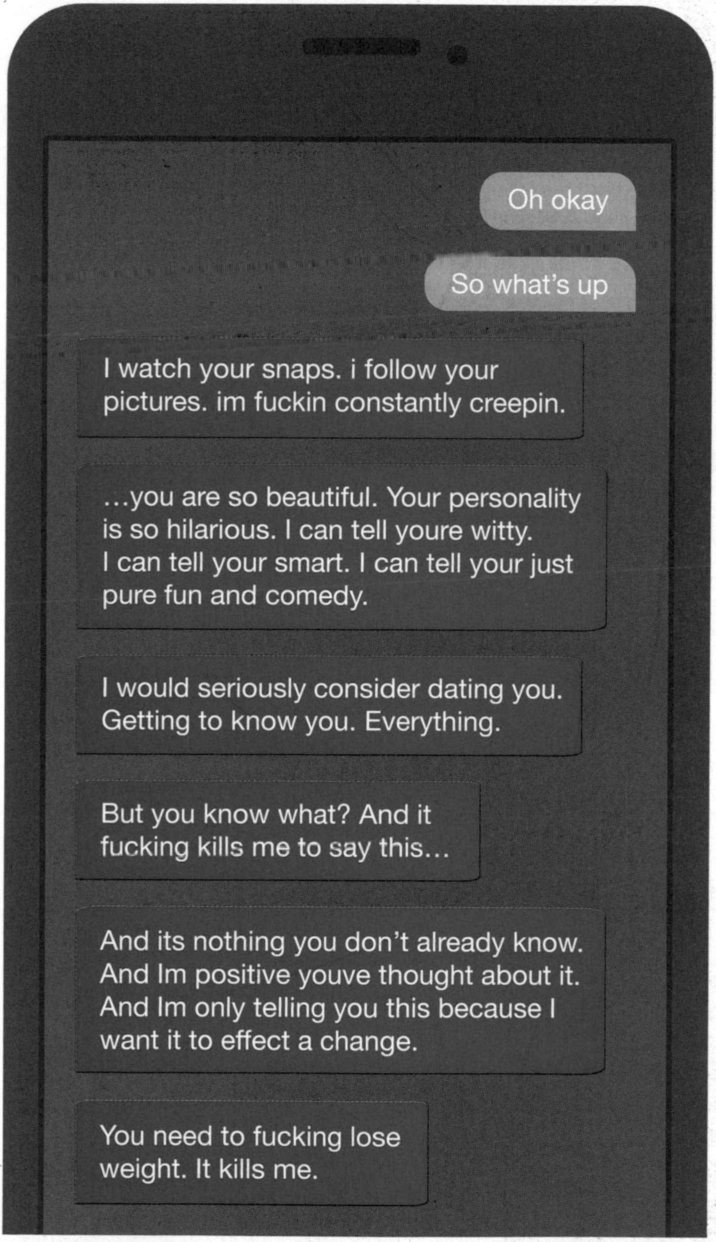

Oh okay

So what's up

I watch your snaps. i follow your pictures. im fuckin constantly creepin.

...you are so beautiful. Your personality is so hilarious. I can tell youre witty. I can tell your smart. I can tell your just pure fun and comedy.

I would seriously consider dating you. Getting to know you. Everything.

But you know what? And it fucking kills me to say this...

And its nothing you don't already know. And Im positive youve thought about it. And Im only telling you this because I want it to effect a change.

You need to fucking lose weight. It kills me.

Haha.

Whoa. Cool.

Well your opinion is your own. Thanks for your feedback. 🙄

Ok maybe NEED is the wrong word. And maybe Im a superficial asshole. But its literally the ONLY reason I haven't made something happen. And maybe Im a self important jerk off whos thinking my thoughts should matter but yah. There it is.

have a great one.

Night

10:06 PM

"I realized this didn't warrant an irrational response," Christina said. "If I lashed out, he would have proven some underlying point." So, cool-as-a-cucumber, she sent him a selfie of her eating a giant Chipotle burrito bowl. Then, she tweeted a screenshot of the conversation and Ben's reputation was pulverized by the internet. She lived happily ever after.

JUST TROLL HIM BACK

After about the hundredth time you receive an incoherent question about your sex life as an opener on your dating profile, the urge may come over you to argue with a 'roided-out douchebag. This meathead on OkCupid, whose profile picture just featured his bulging biceps, was a worthy target.

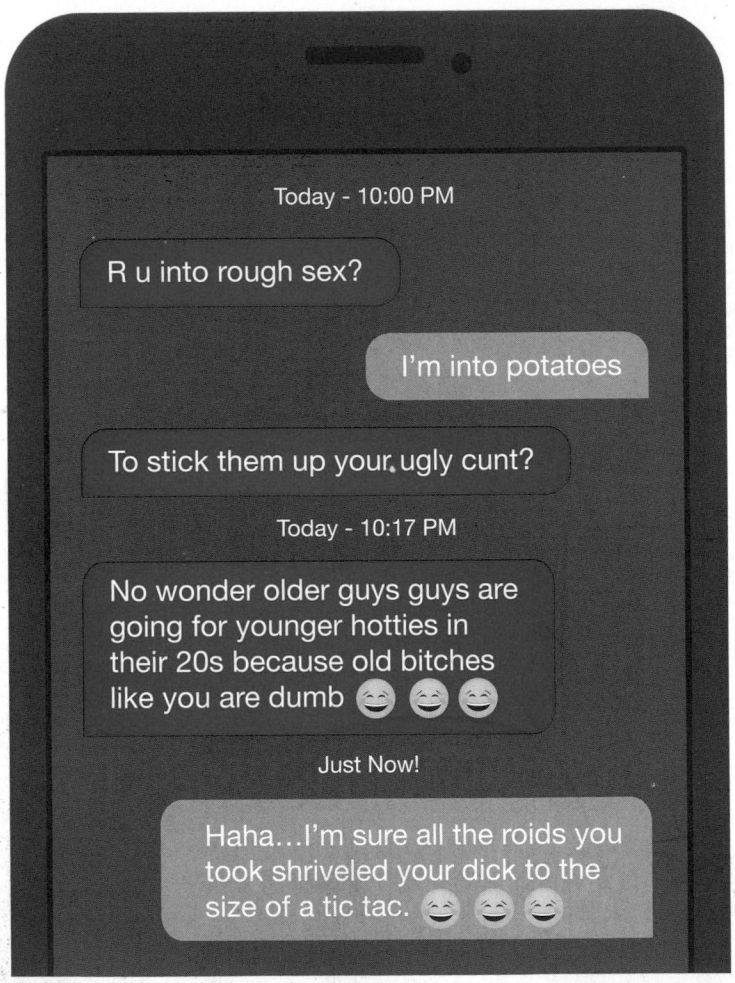

THE GODFATHER RESPONSE

The brilliantly creative writer Rax King (@raxkingisdead on Twitter) came up with the perfect answer for when a douchenoggin crudely asks for sex.

Can I have sex with you ?

Today – 1:26pm

I understand. You found paradise in America, you had a good trade, you made a good living. The police protected you and there were courts of law. You didn't need a friend like me. But, now you come to me, and you say: "Don Corleone, can I have sex with you?" But you don't ask with respect. You don't offer friendship. You don't even think to call me Godfather. Instead, you come into my house on the day my daughter is to be married, and you ask me if you can have sex with me. What have I ever done to make you treat me so disrespectfully?

OMG the way you are talking to me now!! You are scaring me now a lot. but I wanna make sure that you that I have never been in your house, and I have never met you before and we have never ever talked before? This is my first time. And yes I wanna get to know you Cuz I don't know a lot of people. And when I asked you about sex! Yes I wanna have sex because I didn't had enough. And to be honest maybe the way that I asked is rude. Sorry about that. But I have no way to ask for sex accept this way! Idk but forget about sec now. umm are you sure that I came to your house ? And met u or your Doughter ?? I don't think so!! But why are you saying this I've never been in your house

It's extra fun because he's never seen *The Godfather* and has no idea who Don Corleone is.

GIVE HIM A MAKEOVER

When a random man on Facebook asks for pics, just run his profile picture through a makeover app, add hair and makeup, and send it back. Instant sexy pic!

 Hey sexy
Send me a pic of your

Why did you put hair and make-up over my photo?

I don't want to talk to you anymore

SEND HIM WHAT HE WANTS—LITERALLY

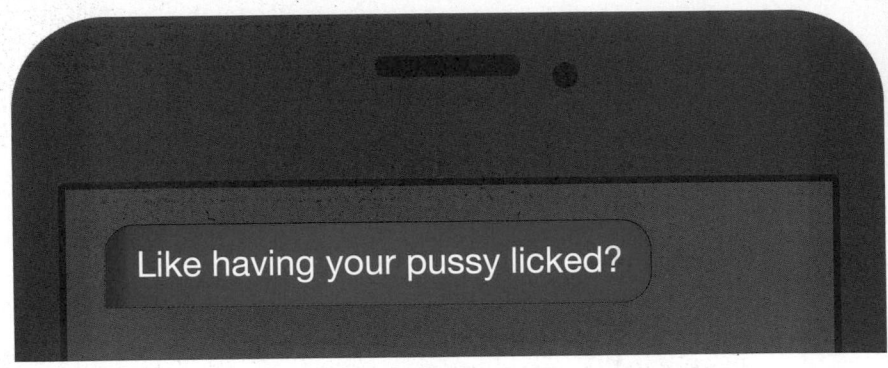

Why, yes, I *love* having my pussy licked. (Yes, I actually did lick my cat. His name is Tobias Fünke.)

TREAT HIM LIKE THE CHILD HE IS

Just know that when a grown man throws a tantrum, you're actually dealing with a child, so treat him like one.

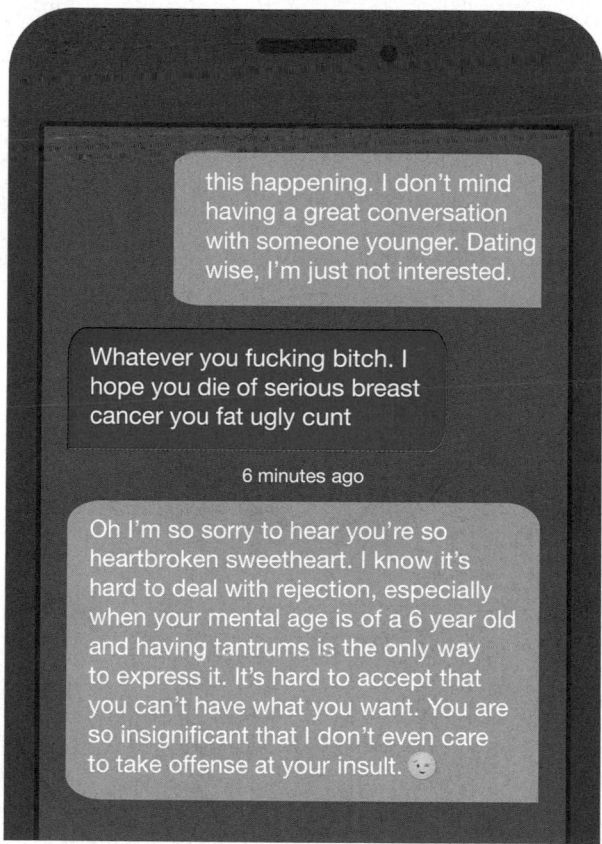

> this happening. I don't mind having a great conversation with someone younger. Dating wise, I'm just not interested.

> Whatever you fucking bitch. I hope you die of serious breast cancer you fat ugly cunt

6 minutes ago

> Oh I'm so sorry to hear you're so heartbroken sweetheart. I know it's hard to deal with rejection, especially when your mental age is of a 6 year old and having tantrums is the only way to express it. It's hard to accept that you can't have what you want. You are so insignificant that I don't even care to take offense at your insult. 😔

One of the best ways to neutralize toxic dudes is to think of them as babies! We don't take it personally when a baby has a tantrum. It's just his way of letting you know he's frustrated because he doesn't know how to communicate. Adult men have tantrums for the same reason. Treat men with low impulse control and poor communication skills exactly like the babies they are. Don't take it personally!

SPEAK FROM THE HEART

Just be honest and straightforward!

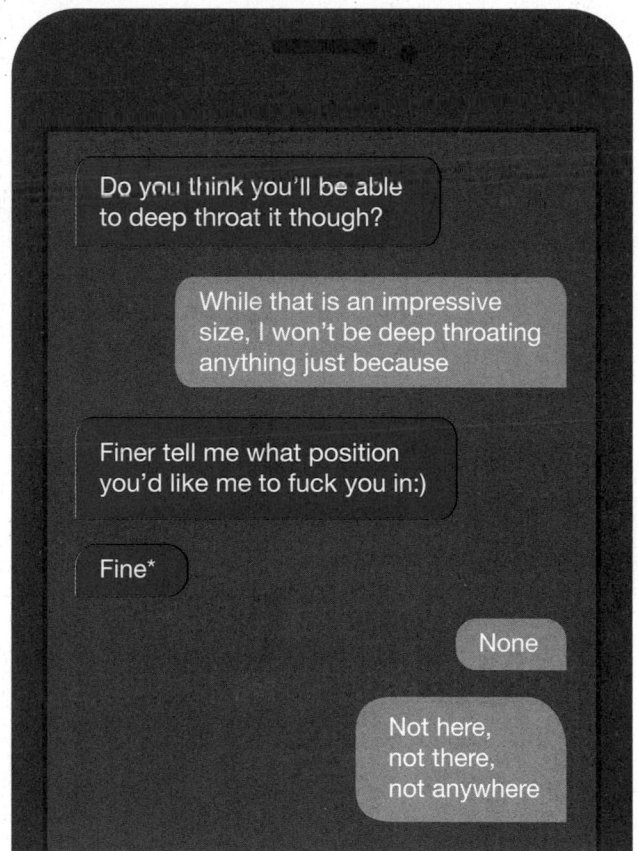

> I do not like green eggs and ham, I do not like them Sam I am

> Have you ever done anal ?

> John, may I be forward with you?

> Can you handle a girl that is very blunt?

> Of course

> Who the hell do you think you are that you're so damn good looking that you can ask someone these questions? I don't want your penis, I don't want you to fuck me, and I sure as shit will not be discussion anything anal with you!

> Delivered

GET PUNNY WITH IT

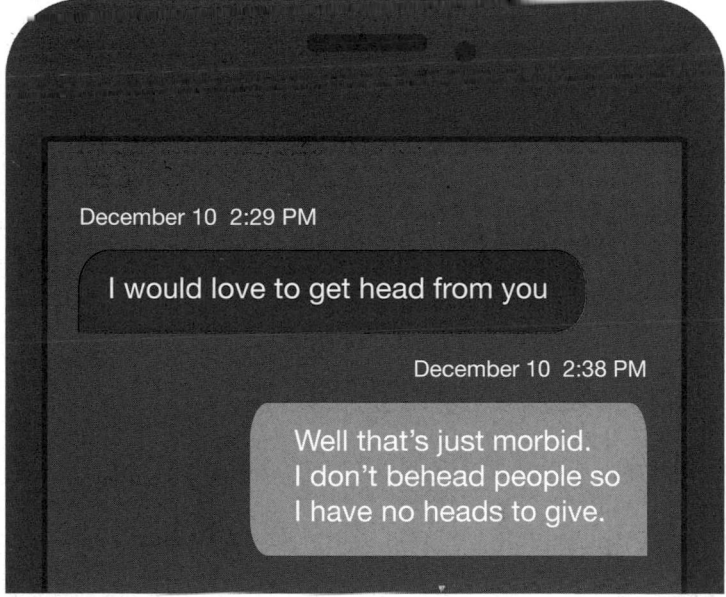

December 10 2:29 PM

I would love to get head from you

December 10 2:38 PM

Well that's just morbid.
I don't behead people so
I have no heads to give.

BLOCK AND REPORT

Most days, it's hard to have the strength to respond to anyone at all, which is when it's a good idea to just block and report him. In fact, it's almost always a good idea, especially with guys who feel entitled to talk to you. These dunderheads won't stop until you block them because they are woefully incapable of impulse control.

Here's an extreme example—the crap he was spewing was so bad I took the liberty of "bleeping" him in spots. I'm sure you'll be able to get the gist!

Hey sexy u change your mind yet?

No, Leave me alone.

Look. What im trying to say is id just really like to &%$@ the !#?% from your big fat preggo $!@& while u ride my big %?&@#!? @#&!. I'll %#?& your #?$+<)% too 😊

If you don't stop messaging me I'll be contacting local authorities.

You're disgusting. Take a fucking hint when a girl says no.

U should block me. Cus i rly cant help myself

Sry, your mean attitude is a rly big turn on for me

Oh you mean me saying no and to leave me alone is plain English? How nice, a girl rejecting you has encouraged you to sexually harass her with zero prompting.

Pretty much. Seriously tho u should block me.

I got a screw loose or something

How Creepy Is this?

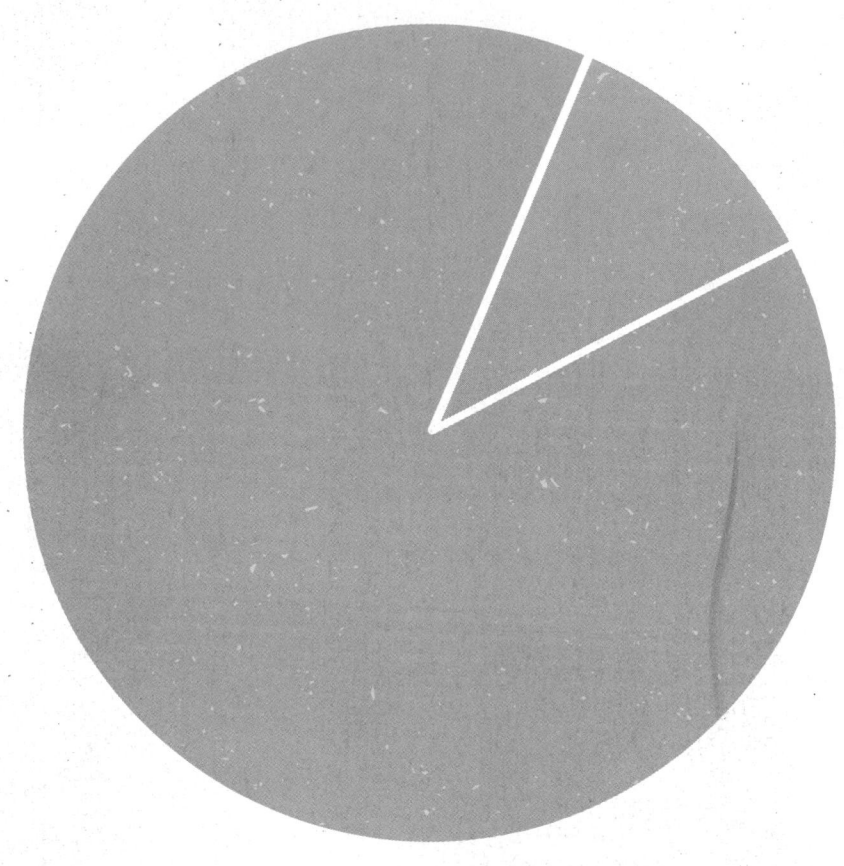

extremely

extremely but in gray

A common complaint I see is that the creep doesn't react well when he's blocked. You never really know if he's going to create another profile to continue harassing you or not. In a situation like this, find the dating site's customer support email or tweet at them. They should be able to block his IP address, and, if they can't, disable your account and find a different dating site.

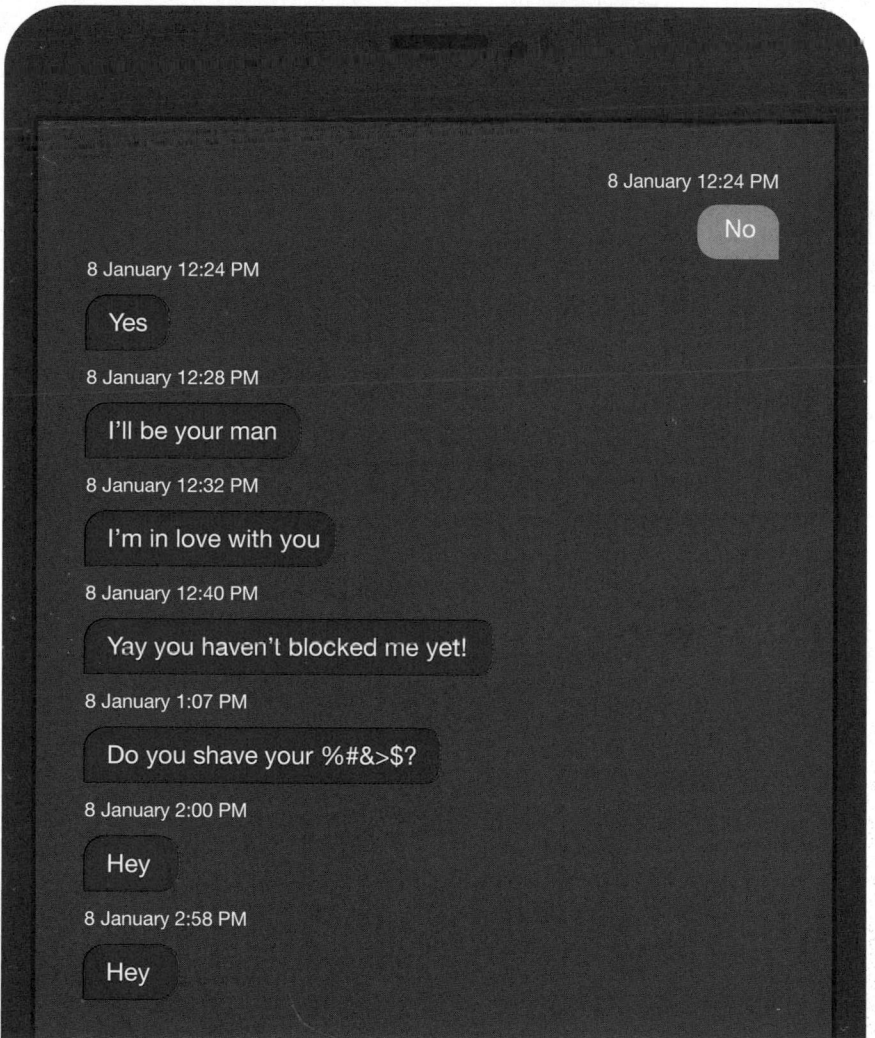

8 January 12:24 PM

No

8 January 12:24 PM

Yes

8 January 12:28 PM

I'll be your man

8 January 12:32 PM

I'm in love with you

8 January 12:40 PM

Yay you haven't blocked me yet!

8 January 1:07 PM

Do you shave your %#&>$?

8 January 2:00 PM

Hey

8 January 2:58 PM

Hey

8 January 5:56 PM

I could fill your &#@$> up with so much hot, sticky $#% it would blow your mind.

8 January 6:17 PM

I'd eat dinner off any part of your body

8 January 6:18 PM

My number is (redacted).

8 January 6:18 PM

I'd clean your #@!^ &?%>$ with my tongue

8 January 6:19 PM

If you were transparent, I'd make a snow globe out of you

8 January 6:21 PM

I'd collect your bath water in bottles and enjoy your sweet taste throughout the day

8 January 6:21 PM

I'd use your epic tits as my pillow for the night

8 January 6:23 PM

All of you, anywhere, anytime

8 January 6:24 PM

$500

Yikes! This Guy Might Be a Stalker

If a dude escalates the harassment and makes multiple accounts or finds you on social media, it's time to start monitoring the situation. My friend Lenora Claire has been forced to deal with a stalker who has sent her rape and death threats daily for years, and she's trying to change state and federal laws to help other victims. According to Lenora, because stalking laws have not been updated in decades, there's often little law enforcement can do if someone threatens your safety over the internet. In many cases, cops just tell you to get off the internet. I asked Lenora for some general tips about what to do if you think you might have a stalker on your hands.

If you begin to fear that your online harasser is escalating and intends to do you harm, it's important to start documenting all interaction as well as put the following precautions in place to secure your personal safety:

- Disable the location devices on your phone when you're not using it for navigation. You may not realize the digital footprint you leave when uploading content to your social media accounts, giving your stalker or harasser all kinds of information about your life and the places you frequent. It's also possible for someone to send you a link that, when clicked on, allows access to the GPS on your phone.
- Be very mindful if any links or emails feel suspicious. Continue to enjoy using social media, but do so responsibly. It's best not to check in places revealing your location, but if you must do this, make sure to do so after you have left.
- If you are being harassed over email, it is typically easy to verify an IP address. A Google search will give you instructions as to how. Unfortunately, social media sites will not turn over that information if your harasser is using multiple accounts unless made to do so by police, and this can take several months if police even feel it is worth pursuing, which is rarely the case.
- Inform your friends, loved ones, and neighbors of what is happening both

for emotional support and to have extra eyes looking out for you. There are multiple types of doorbell cams like Ring, which links to an app allowing you to view security footage via app on your phone.

- If the harassment has escalated to threats of violence, it's important consider compiling all evidence and filing a police report as well as obtaining a restraining order if you know the identity of the individual as well as a physical location of where to serve the protective order. It is generally the first step to finding any resolution with law enforcement. While in reality it is only a piece of paper and you should remain vigilant about your privacy and safety, it will legitimize your claims in the eyes of the law, making any further unwanted interaction a crime, and hopefully serve as a strict warning to deter their behavior.

PAY HIM BACK

One submitter, "Jane," sent me a nightmare text tirade she received after going on the most horrible date of her life with a *therapist*. On the date, Jane said, "The topic of women speaking up against sexual harassers came up, and he lost his shit. He began to rant about how it was a witch hunt and it would 'really hurt dating between men and women.' I then calmly replied that if it hindered my dating in any way but allowed women to feel safe in the workplace . . . then I'd be fine with that. He also said that a number of relationships he's been in started with a 'bit of push pull,' whatever the hell that means."

Jane tried to gently back out of the conversation and attempted to change the subject. "Trying to make small talk, I told him that my friend had mentioned that a number of customers had reportedly been roofied at the bar we were at. Then he BLEW up saying I was accusing him of possibly roofying me, and that's one of five things men don't want to hear on a date, and proceeded to tell me the other four, and when I tried to assure him that's not what I was saying at all he yelled, 'I am not done talking!'"

Jane tried to finish the rest of her drink to allow for a natural-ish exit.

"He was truly kind of frightening," she said.

Once she was done, she told him she was going to go. "He blew up again, saying, 'Of course you're going to fucking leave after finishing the drinks I paid for!' and stormed off like a child leaving the bar."

"Honestly, I was kind of in shock and laughed," Jane said. "The next day it hit me how truly scary it was and how troublesome it is that this man is a therapist and is in a position of power."

Then, he sent her the texts:

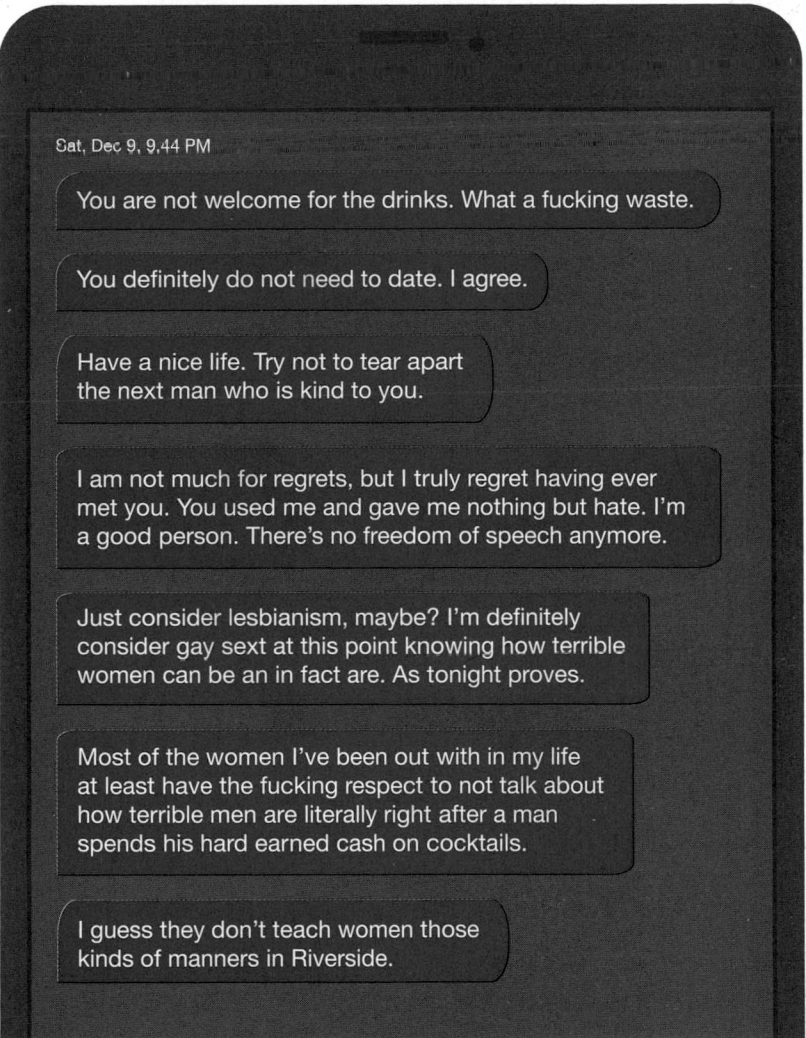

Sat, Dec 9, 9.44 PM

You are not welcome for the drinks. What a fucking waste.

You definitely do not need to date. I agree.

Have a nice life. Try not to tear apart the next man who is kind to you.

I am not much for regrets, but I truly regret having ever met you. You used me and gave me nothing but hate. I'm a good person. There's no freedom of speech anymore.

Just consider lesbianism, maybe? I'm definitely consider gay sext at this point knowing how terrible women can be an in fact are. As tonight proves.

Most of the women I've been out with in my life at least have the fucking respect to not talk about how terrible men are literally right after a man spends his hard earned cash on cocktails.

I guess they don't teach women those kinds of manners in Riverside.

Sat, Dec 9, 9:45 PM

You have taught me very important lessons that one cannot put a price tag on and I thank you dearly for that. You have confirmed my theories and hypotheses. Hypothesis is useful for the intellectually minded, I think. Not that a Master's degree and License to practice therapy in your Homestate means anything.

I'm just an evil man. I'll go be evil now, according to my nature. So unlike the selfishness of women who quote on their Facebook page that they "can't turn down a free glass of wine",

You are the problem. 👎

Imagine being that upset because someone didn't agree with your views for the price of two drinks! So, what did she do? She sent him his $20 back via Venmo.

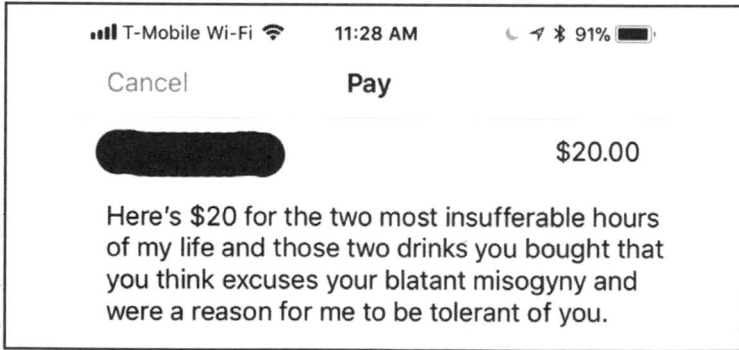

.ıll T-Mobile Wi-Fi 📶   11:28 AM   ◌ ✈ ✳ 91% 🔋

Cancel   **Pay**

$20.00

Here's $20 for the two most insufferable hours of my life and those two drinks you bought that you think excuses your blatant misogyny and were a reason for me to be tolerant of you.

She also discovered after the date, that he had previously been featured on Bye Felipe.

byefelipe Wow guys, we've got a therapist over here. Um, did you diagnose yourself as a psycho? #BYEFELIPE #ignored #hostile #men

The Bye Felipe submissions inbox is riddled with repeat offenders. I have had countless women send submissions from dudes who keep repeating their hostile behavior. I truly believe most of the problem stems from a small percentage of idiots who spread their hostility and anger far and wide. This is why it's SO important to always report the abuse. Speak up! No one can do anything about it if they don't know you have a problem. You could prevent a Felipe from doing the same thing to other women. Making the sites aware of the problem also encourages them to develop better policies to keep harassers off them and women safer.

USES FOR TINDER OTHER THAN FINDING DATES

Pretty much everyone is on Tinder at this point, and they're not all using it for dating. It doesn't take long to find dudes promoting their mixtapes and entrepreneurs "just looking to network." I've even seen hairdressers looking for clients. If everyone else is already doing it, why not get a little creative and think outside the box?

RIDESHARING: I was chatting with a guy from Tinder while simultaneously waiting in line to get into a certain popular '70s-themed bar in Hollywood. I was with three friends, it was raining, and the line wasn't moving. I already had plans to hang out with this particular dude later on, and when I told him about the situation, he suggested we go to another bar that was about a ten-minute drive away from where we were. "Want to come get us?" "OK fine lol." And he showed up minutes later to chauffeur us to the next bar. Success! Maybe Tinder is the new Uber.

ASK DUDES TO FIX STUFF: Living in LA, your car takes a beating. I let a friend borrow my 1999 Honda Civic and, unfortunately, someone hit the bumper while it was parked at her destination. I was driving it around with the bumper dented in, when I had an idea. "I wish I knew a guy who could fix car things," I thought. Normally my dad fixes my car, but since he was thousands of miles away, I'd probably need to pay someone a bunch of money to fix it. Hmm, where could I find someone to help me for a minimal amount of money? Tinder! I posted a (now defunct) "moment," offering to bake a pie for anyone who would hammer out the dent.

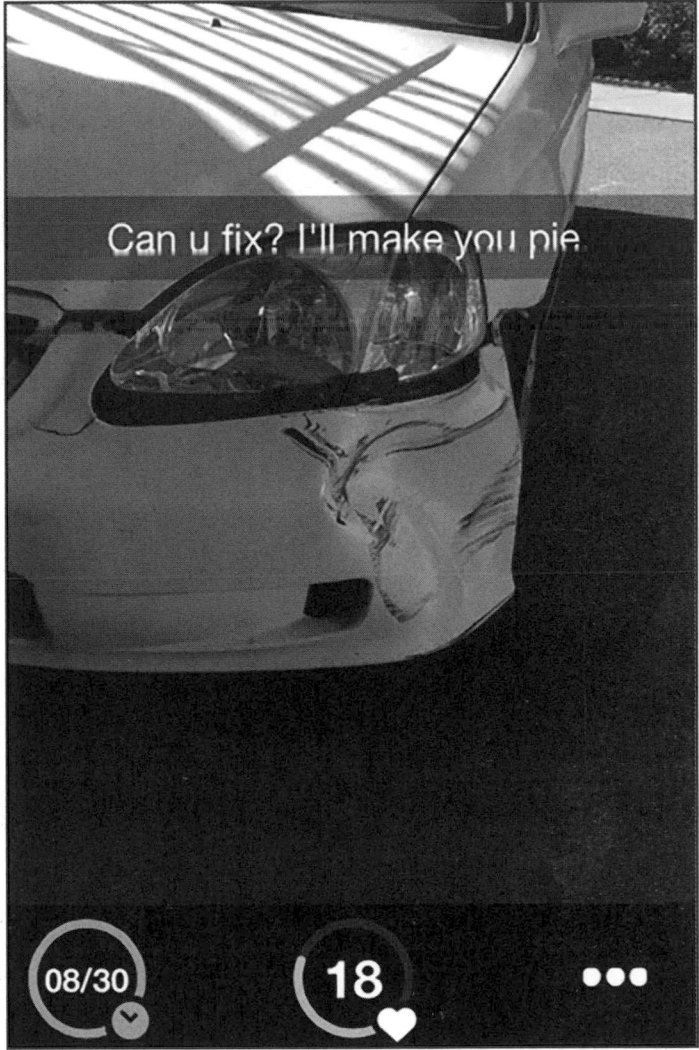

Can u fix? I'll make you pie

08/30

18

No one took me up on it, but I blame that on myself for not swiping right for enough "car guys" and also Los Angeles for having an extreme overpopulation of actors and comedians and an under-population of "car guys."

SELL STUFF: Who says Tinder can't be the new craigslist? In my OkCupid profile, I tried including a picture of a motorcycle I was trying to sell. I had a few dudes message me, saying they were interested in taking a look at it. It's a surprisingly effective way to market your vehicle for sale.

GET INTO SHOWS/CONCERTS/CLUBS: I used to get free tickets to concerts from my work frequently, so I'd offer them to my matches. I've been invited to sold-out screenings and events too.

GET A JOB: My friend Alex moved to LA and is currently "fucking his way to the top." He's already used Grindr to get an internship in his desired field.

USE IT WHEN TRAVELING TO FIND OUT WHERE THE COOLEST SPOTS ARE: I like to ask locals where the best restaurants and bars are if I'm in a new city,

JUST AS A CONFIDENCE BOOSTER: A 2017 study found that 44 percent of Tinder users said they use it for "confidence-boosting procrastination." Only 22 percent were "looking for a hookup," just 4 percent were "looking for a relationship," and 29 percent said for "other reasons."[23]

MAKE $5: The real hero we all needed is the woman who was kicked off Tinder for scamming a bunch of dudes for money. The 20-year-old college student's profile read "Send me $5, see what happens." Dudes would ask what the $5 was for, and she'd respond, "send it and find out," along with telling them how to pay her via PayPal. Once they'd send the money, she unmatched them. (However, after tweeting about her ingenious plan, Tinder caught on and removed her account because requesting money from other users violates their terms of service.)

The Dreaded Dick Pic

The thing about dick pics of the unsolicited variety is that this behavior is absolutely 100 percent harassment. Essentially, it's the equivalent of public flashing. Don't get me wrong, getting a dick pic from someone you already know and like, and who sends them with your consent, is great and fun. I loooove it when guys ask me if they can send a dick pic first. I always say yes because, LOL, I like to laugh.

It's the dick pics from strangers or dudes I haven't expressed that type of interest in that are problematic. After having seen hundreds, if not thousands, of unsolicited dick pics from the Bye Felipe submissions, I can honestly say I've seen every type you could imagine. Big ones, little ones, hard ones, soft ones, dick pics with objects for scale comparison, ones that make you want to barf, the list goes on and on. It's an epidemic. And for this reason, I was ecstatic when I heard about Whitney Bell and her unsolicited dick pic art show, "I Didn't Ask for This: A Lifetime of Dick Pics."

I stopped by Whitney's first show in Los Angeles in 2016, which featured two hundred framed photos of unsolicited dicks that Bell and her friends had received. I was blown away by the magnitude of the project. The gallery was set up like a home, complete with a bedroom, a living room, a kitchen, and a bathroom, and each scene was carefully arranged with dick pics displayed everywhere you looked.

Surprisingly, she got the idea for the show when she received a dick pic from someone she was seeing—it was one she wanted. She showed it to a friend who told her it was so beautiful: "It should be in a museum." Whitney celebrates dicks pics that are sent to willing recipients, but she has also seen the other side of dick pics, the unsolicited kind.

"I love a good dick. I just don't love harassment," she said.

I'm now proud to call Whitney a friend and sister in the battle against unwanted dick pics. She has continued the show, expanding it to use Bye Felipe examples among the dick pics and including workshops, panels, and speakers.

THE DICK PIC SENDER STARTER PACK

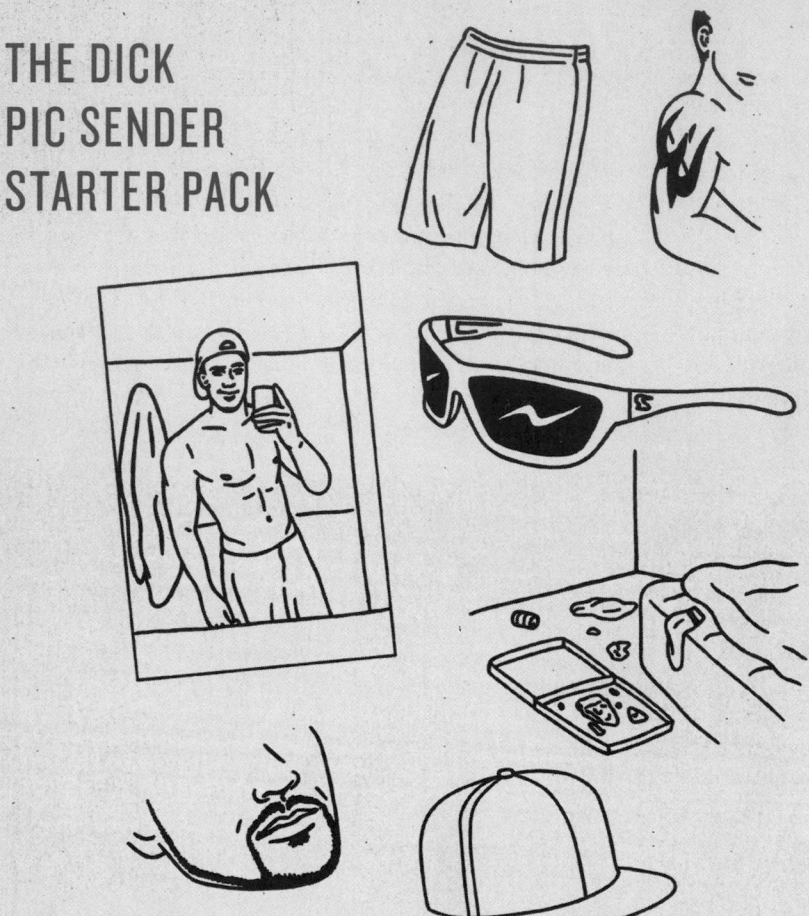

YOU KNOW HE'S GONNA SEND A DICK PIC IF YOU SEE HIM:

- Dressed in silky athletic shorts
- Pictured in a messy room that you can see in the background of his photos
- Wearing a sports baseball cap
- Wearing wraparound sunglasses
- Having bad facial hair
- Sporting the worst and most tacky tribal tattoos

WHY? Why do men send unsolicited dick pics?

People ask me this question all the time. I usually just say, "I don't know. Because of rape culture and they're creepy assholes who hate women." It's another form of sexual harassment, which is a power move, not about sex. They want to show us that they're in control. I think there are a ton of reasons guys send them.

Is it really that common? If you're a millennial woman in the United States, you've probably received a dick pic at some point, because, according to a 2017 online survey conducted by YouGov, an internet-based market research company, 53 percent of eighteen- to thirty-four-year-old women polled have received a dick pic of any kind, and of that group, 78 percent said they have received an unsolicited one. That means that about 41 percent of all millennial women have received a wiener picture they didn't ask for.

QUESTION: I've never received a dick pic. Ever. Is there something wrong with me?

ANSWER: You haven't received a dick pic *yet*. If you are still reading this, there's a good chance that you will in the future. They don't seem to be going out of fashion anytime soon. But no, there's nothing wrong with you. I'd consider you lucky. You are #blessed.

When you take into account women across all age groups, the percentage who have received a dick pic is lower: 29 percent. Of those, 60 percent had received an unsolicited dick pic. That means about 17 percent of all women have received an unsolicited dick pic.

When asking women, "Has a man ever sent you a dick pic of themselves?" here are the responses they received:

"HAVE YOU RECEIVED A DICK PICK?"

	All women	18–24	25–55	55+
Yes, I have	29%	53%	35%	8%
No, I have not	54%	33%	54%	70%
Don't know	1%	3%	1%	0%
Prefer not to say	15%	11%	11%	22%

"HAS A MAN EVER SENT YOU A DICK PIC OF HIMSELF WITHOUT YOU HAVING ASKED FOR ONE?"

	All women	18–24	25–55	55+
Yes, I have	60%	78%	69%	22%
No, I have not	7%	7%	9%	5%
Don't know	0%	1%	—	—
Prefer not to say	32%	22%	22%	73%

All this data sounded pretty correct to me. However, while researching the raw numbers about men's responses for this survey, I noticed something interesting. Buckle up, because I'm about to make some totally unscientific speculations. I'm not a mathematician, but I *am* fairly good at knowing when men are lying.

A WEIGHTED SAMPLE OF 1,143 MEN WERE ASKED "HAVE YOU EVER TAKEN A DICK PIC OF YOURSELF SELF AND SENT IT TO A WOMAN?"

17% said	"Yes, I have."
71% said	"No, I have not."
1% said	"Don't know." (. . . OK, but how can you not know??)
11% said	"Prefer not to say."

This question is asking about dick pics in general—both solicited and unsolicited. It's neither here nor there, because if these guys are sending them to women who want them, great! Cool, I hope they have fun and healthy sex lives. However, the responses "Prefer not to say" and "Don't know" gave me pause. It's a pretty simple question. Who would respond that way? Let's imagine you're a man taking this survey and you had sent a dick pic, but you didn't want to admit it. Maybe you were embarrassed about it or thought that your answers could somehow be tracked. I would wager a guess that you'd probably be more likely to answer, "Prefer not to say" or even just lie and say, "No.

Next, let's imagine you had never sent a dick pic. Why would you check "Prefer not to say" instead of "No"? Maybe the sending-dick-pics-is-cool gang was standing over your shoulder and judging you? Unlikely. And lastly, how can you *not know* if you've ever sent a dick pic? Maybe you thought you *might* have sent one when you were drunk last weekend, but you can't really remember . . . Well, that's fair, actually. Hence—and this is *purely speculative*—but I'm going to theorize that the *actual* percentage of men who have sent a dick pic is closer to around **28 percent** (17 percent admitters + 11 percent prefer-not-to-say liars). And that doesn't even count the liars who said no.

Another thing I learned is that millennial men are coo-coo bananas. Surprising no one, many more millennial men send dick pics than older men do. Here's how eighteen- to thirty-four-year-old men answered the same question, "Have you ever taken a dick pic of yourself and sent it to a woman?"

18- TO 34-YEAR-OLD MEN WERE ASKED "HAVE YOU EVER TAKEN A DICK PIC OF YOURSELF SELF AND SENT IT TO A WOMAN?"

27% said	"Yes, I have."
50% said	"No, I have not."
3% said	"Don't know." (Again, how could you not know???)
20% said	"Prefer not to say."

So, using the same logic as above, let's just theorize that about 47 percent of millennial men have *probably* sent a dick pic, 27 percent of whom are open about it, and 20 percent of whom didn't want to admit it. That's almost half! Only 50 percent said they definitely have never sent a dick pic, a little less than a third were like, "Yeah, I've sent a sausage pic, who cares?" and the rest were like, "I'll never tell!" I feel that those 20 percent are hiding something.

The survey goes on to ask the 17 percent of men (all ages) who said they had sent dick pics, "And have you ever taken a dick pic of yourself and sent it to a woman **without having been asked**?"

17% OF MEN (ALL AGES) WHO SAID THEY SENT DICK PICS, "HAVE YOU EVER SENT A DICK PIC TO A WOMAN WITHOUT BEING ASKED?"

22% said	"Yes, I have."
40% said	"No, I have not."
1% said	"Don't know."
37% said	"Prefer not to say."

To be fair, depending on how the men interpreted the question, I suppose it could be read in the context of a guy sending a dick pic to a girlfriend/wife or a woman who didn't technically *ask*, but who was expecting it, or at least wouldn't mind seeing it. But I think it's safe to assume that most people would understand this question to mean "sending it to a woman who didn't know it was coming." The key thing to pay attention to here is *consent*.

Before I even apply my theory, let me just point out that more men said, "Prefer not to say" than said "Yes, I send unsolicited dick pics," which sounds suspect AF. So, using my super-unscientific method, let's just guesstimate that of men who have *probably* sent a dick pic (28 percent), about 59 percent (22 percent yes + 37 percent prefer not to say) have probably sent an unsolicited one. I don't think it would be much of a stretch to say that **the majority of guys who have sent a dick pic have sent an *unsolicited* dick pic.** This comes out to about **16.5 percent of all men have probably sent an *unsolicited* dick pic**. And to cross-reference that number, remember that about 17 percent of all women said they'd received an unsolicited dick pic.

This guy REALLY wants you to say it's OK for him to send you a dick pic . . . At least he's asking first?

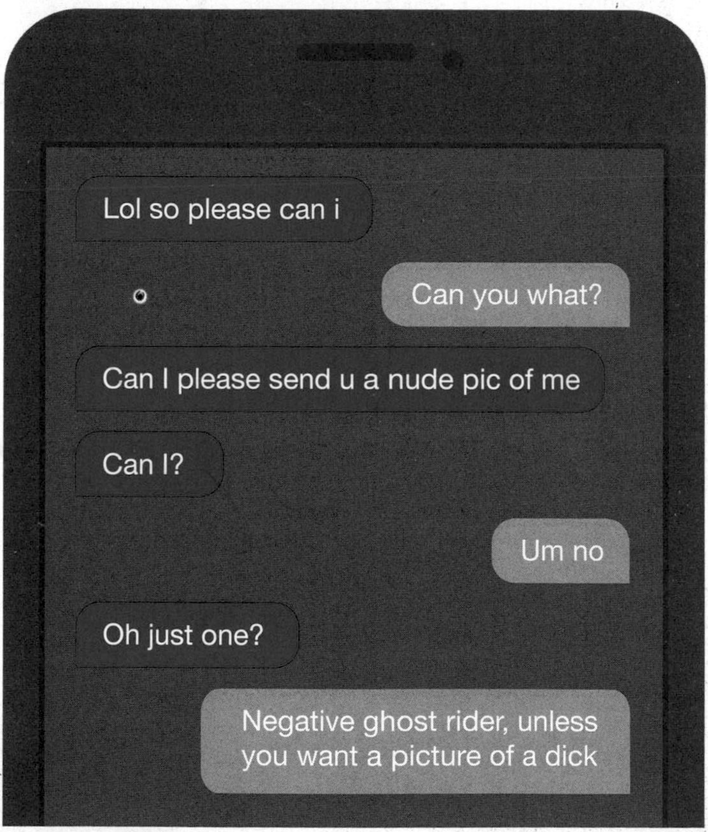

> Lol so please can i

> > Can you what?

> Can I please send u a nude pic of me

> Can I?

> > Um no

> Oh just one?

> > Negative ghost rider, unless you want a picture of a dick

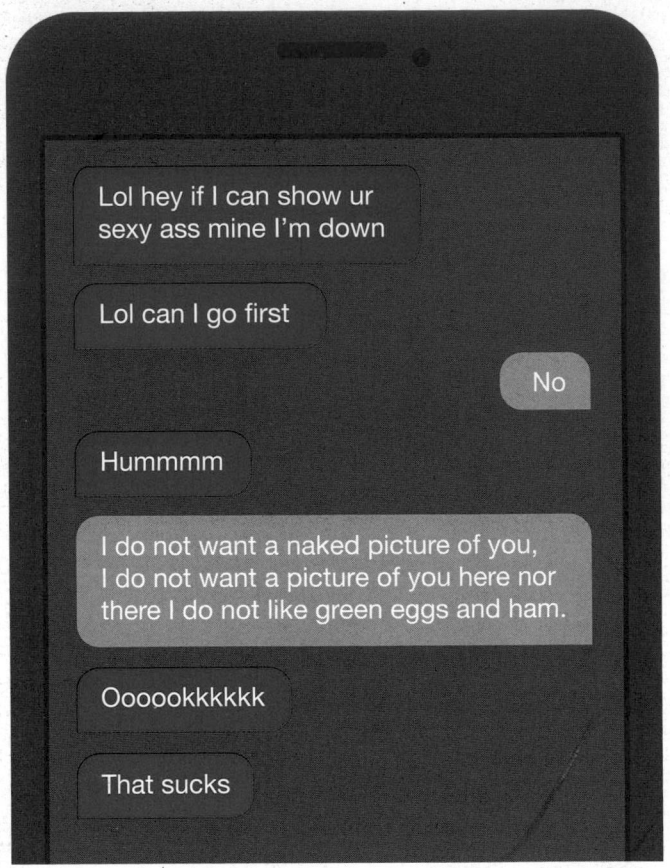

I don't think many guys will openly admit to sending unwanted dick pics. Pretty much anytime I bring up the subject of dick pics with a group of men, they all immediately go, "I would never!" and "I just don't understand why anyone would do that!" But *someone* is sending the dick pics! It's obviously happening frequently because my inbox is bursting at the seams with dick submissions! This further illustrates my point that men generally don't care about understanding women. They are also either clueless about what we think of dick pics or they know that we think they're gross and send them anyway. The survey also asked men: **Which, if any, of the following words do you think *women* would use to describe dick pics? Please select all that apply:**

WHICH WORDS DO YOU THINK WOMEN WOULD USE TO DESCRIBE DICK PICS?

In order, men of all ages answered:

In comparison, all women answered:

→ ALL MEN →		→ ALL WOMEN →	
Gross	38%	Stupid	48%
Stupid	36%	Gross	41%
Sad	23%	Sad	25%
Funny	21%	Distressing	17%
Sexy	21%	Prefer not to say	14%
Don't know	21%	Funny	13%
Distressing	20%	Threatening	12%
Threatening	17%	Boring	10%
Pleasing	14%	Sexy	9%
Prefer not to say	10%	Pleasing	7%
Boring	10%	Don't know	7%
None of these	3%	None of these	5%

	All Men	Men 18–34	Men 35–55	Men 18–55	Men 55+
Stupid	36%	29%	39%	34%	40%
Gross	38%	32%	43%	38%	40%
Sad	23%	25%	21%	23%	23%
Funny	21%	19%	25%	22%	18%
Distressing	20%	13%	22%	18%	23%
Sexy	21%	30%	23%	27%	12%
Threatening	17%	15%	18%	17%	18%
Don't know	21%	16%	18%	17%	29%
Prefer not to say	10%	117%	10%	14%	5%
Pleasing	14%	18%	16%	17%	8%
Boring	10%	13%	8%	11%	10%
None of these	3%	3%	5%	4%	2%

All Women	Women 18–34	Women 35–55	Women 18–55	Women 55+	Everyone
48%	48%	49%	49%	46%	47%
41%	49%	49%	45%	36%	40%
25%	24%	24%	24%	26%	24%
13%	21%	16%	19%	6%	18%
17%	15%	15%	15%	19%	18%
9%	17%	9%	13%	2%	16%
12%	10%	12%	11%	14%	14%
5%	7%	4%	6%	4%	13%
14%	8%	10%	9%	22%	12%
7%	14%	6%	10%	2%	11%
10%	12%	8%	10%	10%	10%
5%	3%	5%	4%	6%	4%

I'm noticing some patterns. First, 21 percent of men "don't know" what women think about dick pics, which is also the same percentage that thought women find them "sexy" and "funny." Millennial men, in particular, severely overestimate how much we like dick pics: 30 percent said they thought women think dick pics are sexy. Only 17 percent of millennial women, and 9 percent of women of all ages, think dick pics are actually sexy.

Everyone is pretty much in agreement that dick pics are "gross," "stupid," and "sad." The discrepancy between men's guesses and women's answers is kind of sad, however. It seems to show that, even though some men know that women think dick pics are "distressing" and "threatening," 28 percent of men have still sent them. However, dudes over fifty-five seem more likely to know what's up. Maybe younger lads could take a lesson from them in the RESPECT department?

Even when we tell them how women feel about dick pics, they have to mansplain our feelings to us.

A note to any dudes reading this: IT'S BEEN STATISTICALLY PROVEN THAT WE DON'T WANT YOUR DICK UNLESS WE ASK FOR IT. I assure you, a woman does need to like you and your face in order to like your cock. That's just science. Cocks are very personal things that we like to carefully choose for ourselves, like haircuts. You can't just force someone to get a haircut that you pick out for them—they're going to hate it. It's the same thing with cocks. We need to warm up to one, think about it, get to know it for a while . . . I think this guy is actually just a sexual predator though.

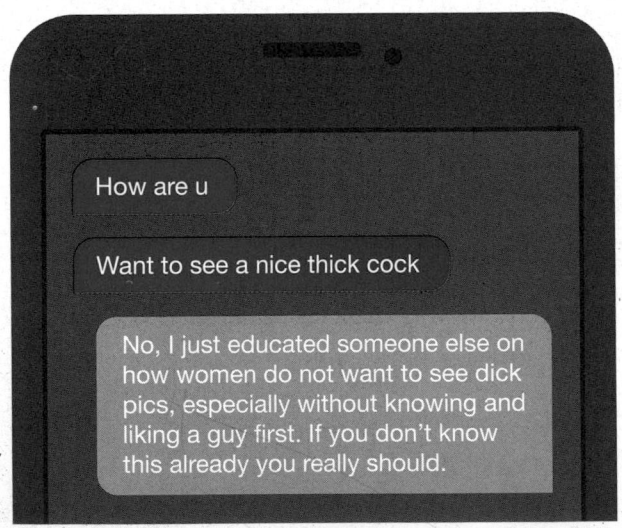

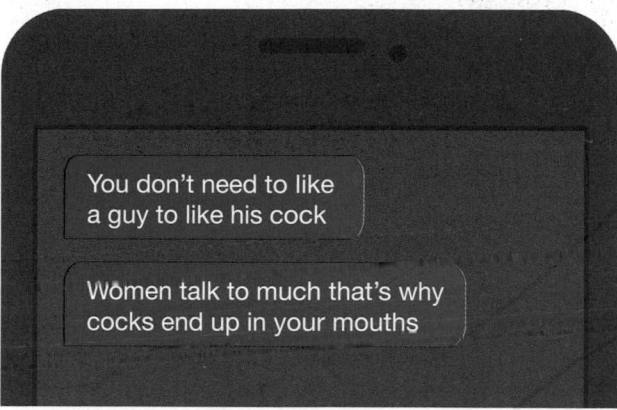

You don't need to like a guy to like his cock

Women talk to much that's why cocks end up in your mouths

I also really wanted to know how many women *do* actually want dick pics. The survey asked them, "Have you ever *asked* a man to send you a dick pic of themselves?"

"HAVE YOU EVER ASKED A MAN TO SEND YOU A DICK PIC OF THEMSELVES?"

11% said	"Yes."
73% said	"No."
1% said	"Don't know."
15% said	"Prefer not to say."

No surprises here. The dick pics don't really do it for most of us. I think the "prefer not to say" is being skewed by the women in the fifty-five-plus range, who were probably not too thrilled to be answering questions about dick pics in the first place. They've probably had enough man bullshit in their lives thus far and they are over it.

Of the women who said they have received a dick pic, we asked, "Has a man ever sent you a dick pic of themselves *because* you requested one?"

OF THE WOMEN WHO RECEIVED A DICK PIC, "HAS A MAN EVER SENT YOU A DICK PIC OF THEMSELVES BECAUSE YOU REQUESTED ONE?"

	All women	18–24	25–55	55+
Yes, they have	41%	69%	51%	6%
No, they have not	1%	2%	3%	—
Don't know	0%	1%	—	—
Prefer not to say	57%	28%	46%	94%

For this one, the spread was very different between the age ranges. Millennial women are actually pretty into dick pics, with 69 percent saying they asked for and received them. About half of thirty-five- to fifty-five-year-olds asked and received, but only 6 percent of women aged fifty-five-plus said the same. Older generations are, not surprisingly, more private about asking for it, but wouldn't it be kind of awesome if our grandmas were secretly the ones asking for all the dick pics?

What did we learn here? Something we already know: Dudes are pretty much clueless dolts. They sort-of know we don't like dick pics, but they also think that maybe we'll think they're sexy. NEWSFLASH: We don't, unless we ask for them. So, how the heck do you respond to the person who sent the disgusting, slimy, one-eyed-snake that's staring at you from your inbox/text messages/DMs?

REQUEST $$$

Request money via Venmo, PayPal, or whatever cash app you use. It's even integrated into Facebook Messenger and other apps. It's a win-win situation. You'll either make some money or they'll leave you alone!

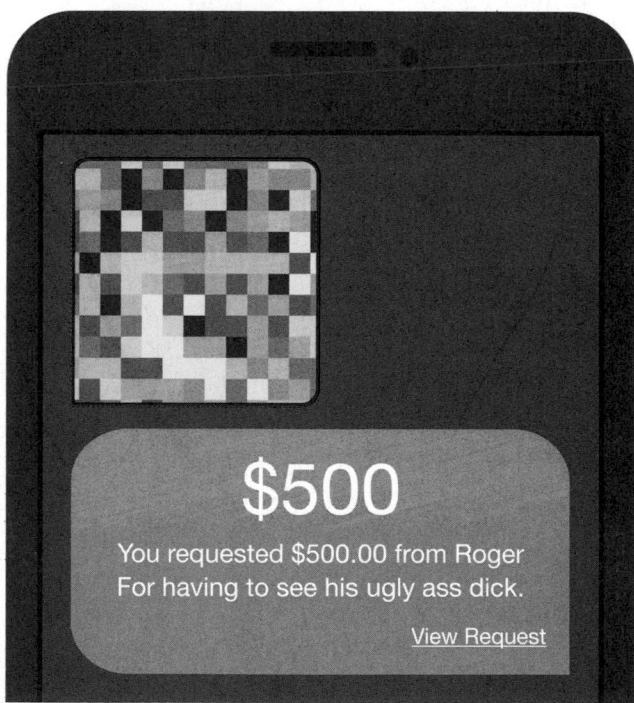

FIGHT FIRE WITH FIRE

Bombard him with other dick pics. Better dick pics. Dick pics that win awards. Samantha Mawdsley, a woman living in London, and now my friend, took it upon herself to blast an unsolicited dick pic she received on Facebook with more dick pics. Sometimes you have to fight fire with fire.

Samantha wasn't even single or on a dating website, but one day she received a comment on her Facebook profile under a review for a restaurant she had written months before.

facebook

Amazing food & the staff is so friendly! Definitely recommend.

✖ Hi Samantha, check my facebook dm please I would like to know your opinion.

"To begin with, my immediate reaction was a mixture of revulsion and humiliation. I am not ashamed to admit that I have been the victim of this kind of sexual harassment offline too," she wrote in a blog post. When she was fifteen years old, she had witnessed a man masturbating while looking at her at a public library. She said she had the same feeling, but this time instead of keeping quiet about it, she decided to make a scene.

"My first response came from a place of anger and wanting him to just go away," she said. "But I didn't want him to feel like he'd elicited any kind of emotional response from me. Yes, I fell back on the lazy and ridiculous notion that 'bigger is better,' but I have the feeling that was the level James was playing at and the lowest common denominator is always the easiest. So I Googled 'large dick pic' and found a somewhat lengthier penis to show James." That's where she thought it would end.

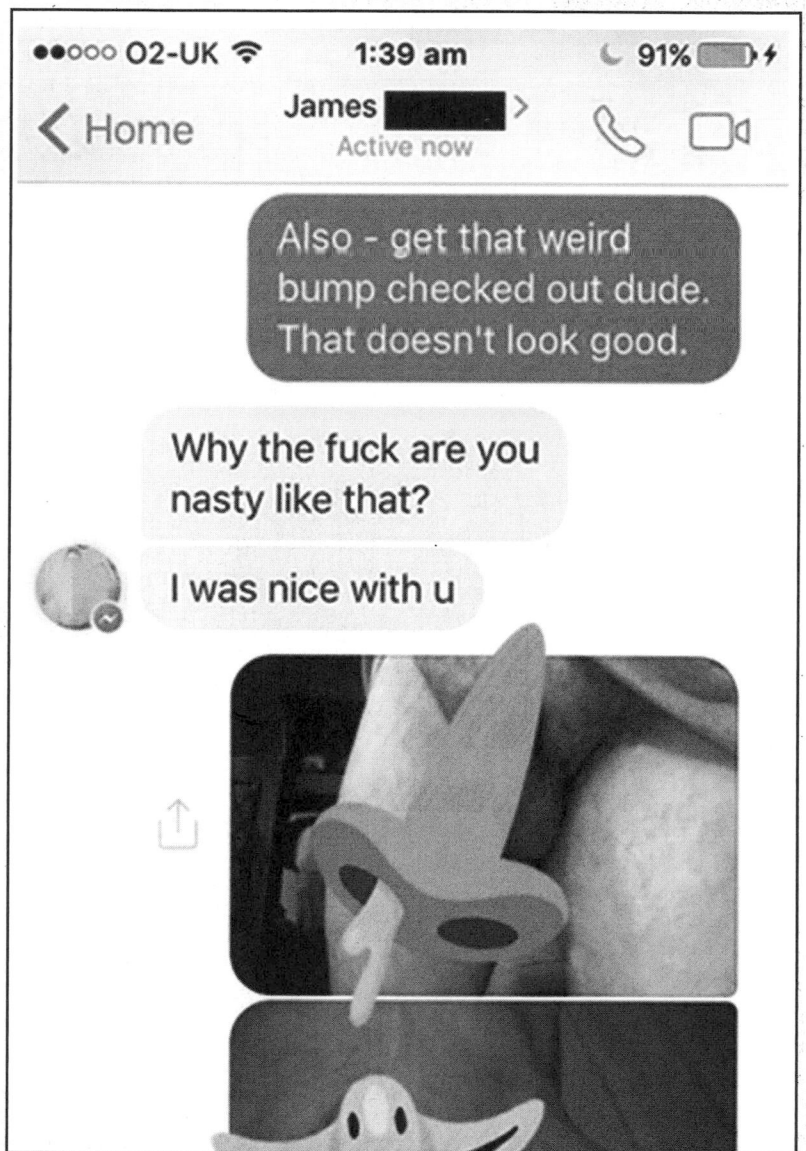

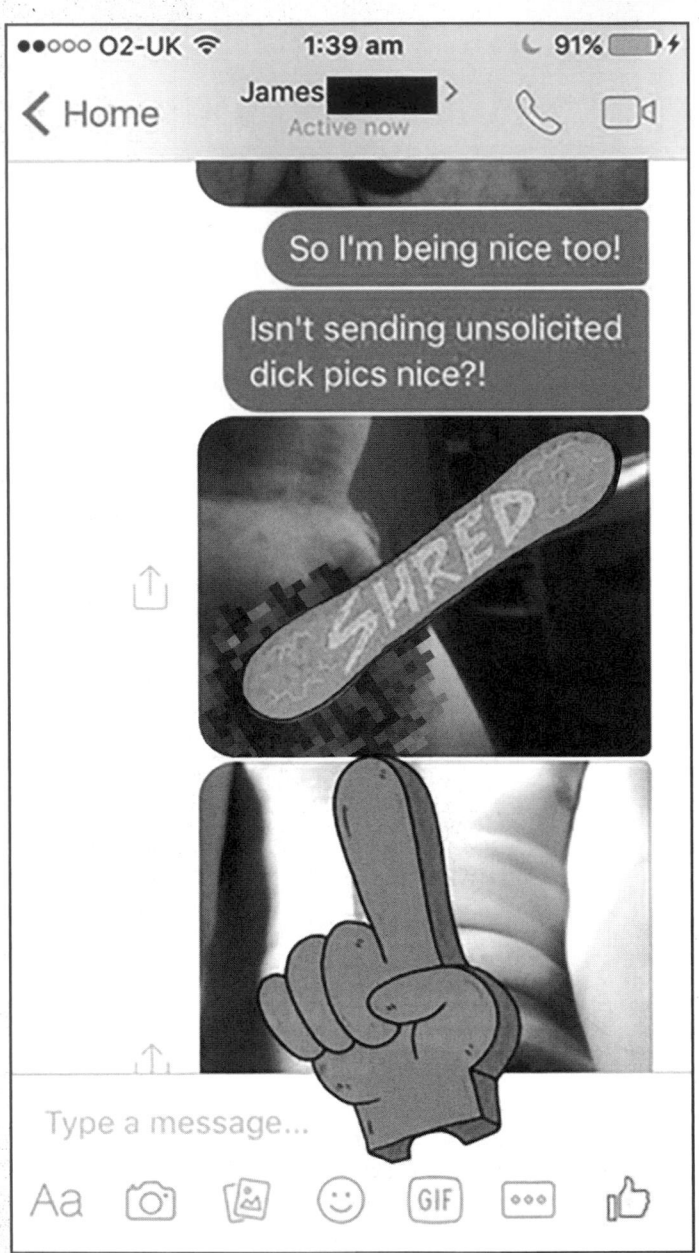

And she didn't stop until he called her "fucking crazy" and said, "I just want to puke! Please stop!" After all was said and done, Samantha had sent around fifty pictures and James had not apologized, so she decided to upload the entire conversation in a photo album on Facebook. Soon, the album had been shared tens of thousands of times, and her story went viral. She never heard from him again.

SEND IT TO YOUR FRIENDS AND GIVE FEEDBACK

Hey, he sent you something you didn't ask for, send him some opinions he didn't ask for.

I appreciate that they didn't promote toxic masculinity in their shaming, but instead commented on the context and why unsolicited dick pics are wrong.

HOW TO AVOID A DICK PIC

Sometimes, you can avoid a dick pic before it happens. You just have to be proactive. This Facebook dick pic sender was scared away not when the recipient said she was a lesbian, but when she threatened to send it to his family.

> Hey beautiful what's up
>
> Nothing. You?
>
> Wanna see something hjig beautiful
>
> Not really.
>
> Why not gorgeous
>
> Because I don't care.
>
> Why dont you care
>
> Why are you asking so many questions?
>
> I don't know just curious ig
>
> Mmkay.
>
> Have you ever seen a l in dick????
>
> I'm actually a lesbian and I don't really care about dick.
>
> ¯_(ツ)_/¯

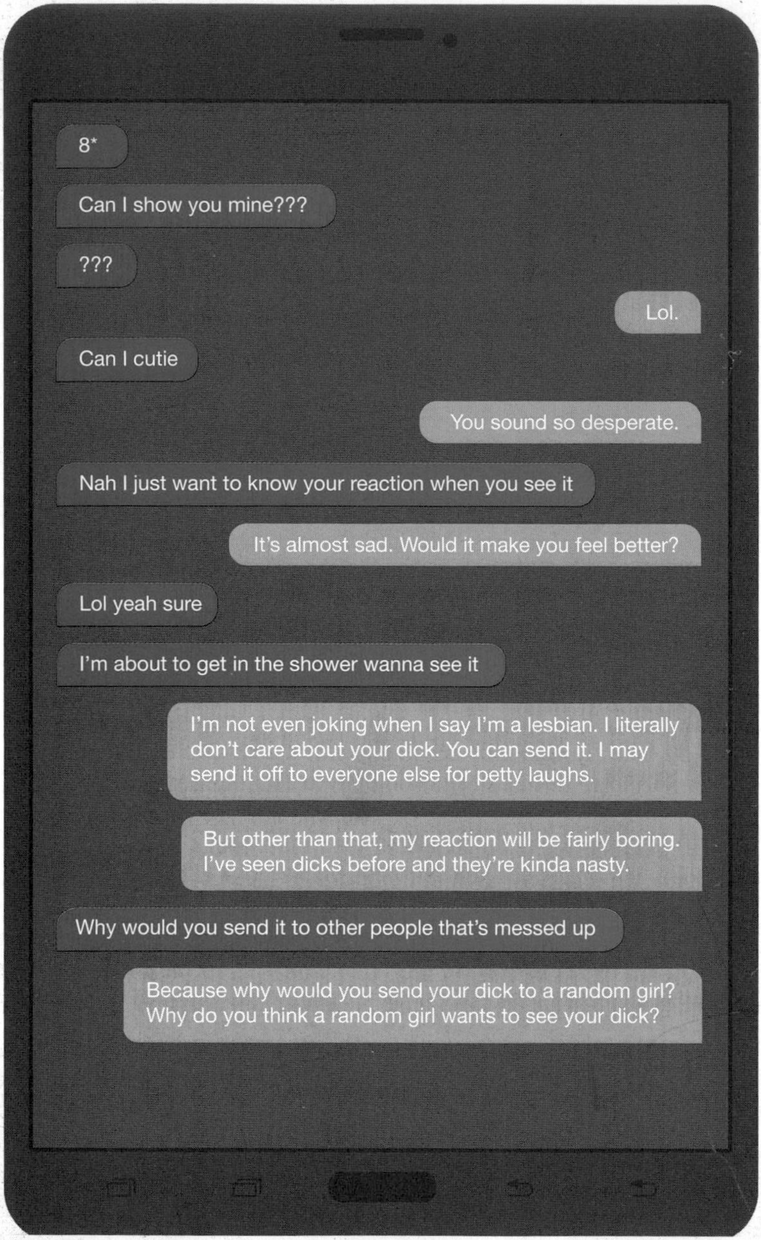

8*

Can I show you mine???

???

Lol.

Can I cutie

You sound so desperate.

Nah I just want to know your reaction when you see it

It's almost sad. Would it make you feel better?

Lol yeah sure

I'm about to get in the shower wanna see it

I'm not even joking when I say I'm a lesbian. I literally don't care about your dick. You can send it. I may send it off to everyone else for petty laughs.

But other than that, my reaction will be fairly boring. I've seen dicks before and they're kinda nasty.

Why would you send it to other people that's messed up

Because why would you send your dick to a random girl? Why do you think a random girl wants to see your dick?

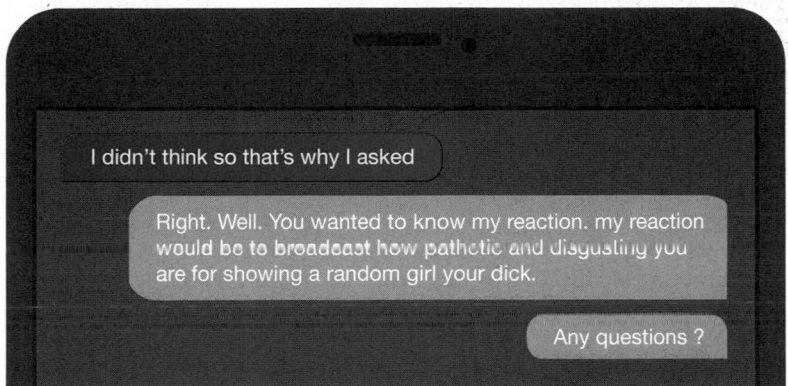

I didn't think so that's why I asked

Right. Well. You wanted to know my reaction. my reaction would be to broadcast how pathetic and disgusting you are for showing a random girl your dick.

Any questions ?

WHAT NOT TO DO: Size-shame. I am not a fan of size-shaming because it's not an effective tactic in the war on dick pics. If a guy sends you a dick pic and you say, "It's too small" or make fun of how it looks, you're only attacking something he can't really control. Yes, he shouldn't have sent it in the first place, but by saying it's small, he's not learning that it's wrong to send dick pics in the first place. While your intent was to make him feel bad, he should bemade to feel bad about harassing you, instead of for how it looks. Size-shaming is too indirect. You're only telling him it would have been OK to send that pic if his dick were bigger or more appealing. But that's not the case—we don't want unsolicited dick pics no matter what they look like. Also, if his dick is actually big or average, he can call you on it, as in this response:

"Received this text after telling him I wasn't impressed with his unsolicited dick pic . . . Oh and we'd only been talking for an hour."

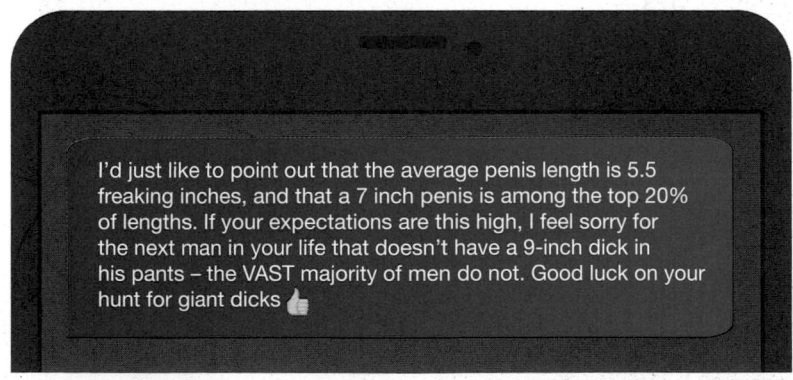

I'd just like to point out that the average penis length is 5.5 freaking inches, and that a 7 inch penis is among the top 20% of lengths. If your expectations are this high, I feel sorry for the next man in your life that doesn't have a 9-inch dick in his pants – the VAST majority of men do not. Good luck on your hunt for giant dicks 👍

A better approach might look like this:

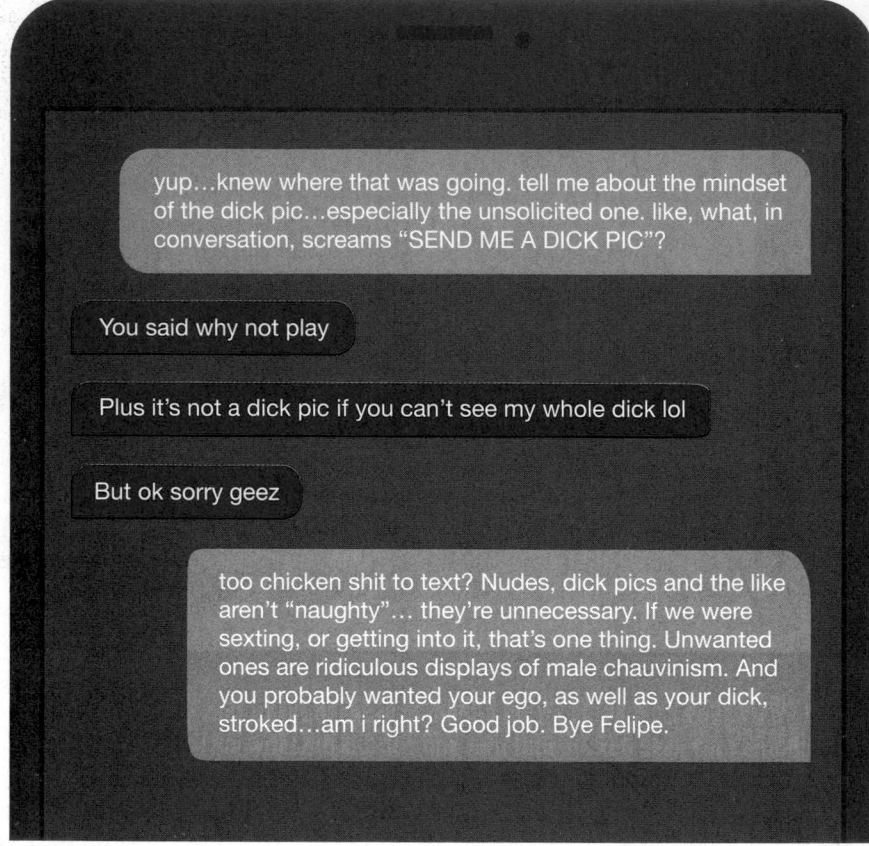

Ever notice how MUCH worse you feel when your mom says, "I'm not mad; I'm just disappointed."? Taking the time to explain to him that you're disappointed, and that you're a real person with feelings really drives the point home. Sometimes guys forget that they are talking to another person on the other side of the internet. But you should only educate them if you feel like it. It's not our duty to teach men how to behave, so only do it if the mood strikes you.

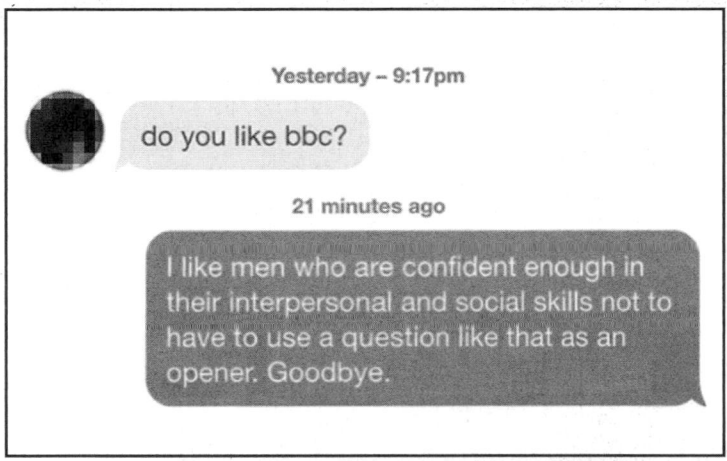

Yesterday – 9:17pm

do you like bbc?

21 minutes ago

I like men who are confident enough in their interpersonal and social skills not to have to use a question like that as an opener. Goodbye.

*BBC: big black cock

If you're feeling vengeful, name and shame him on your own social media platforms. Post his picture to Facebook and Instagram and Snapchat or whatever platform you have. Or, post the screenshots on his own page. One of my favorite submissions was when a guy named John sent a woman an unsolicited dick pic via Facebook messenger.

"No way, are you really sending me dick pics," the woman replied. "Is this even your dick? I really doubt this is your dick."

"Yesss, it's mine," John said. "Just take it now."

"OK, that's cool just making sure," she said.

She went to his Facebook wall and found his most recent post, a picture of some birthday cupcakes one of his friends had posted that said, "Happy Birthday, John!" She replied to the birthday message post, "Can you tell your friend John to stop adding random women and sending them his dick pics? It's actually a form of sexual assault." And she even included the dick pic in question (edited to cover the dick so as to meet Facebook's Community Guidelines.

"Why you mention me in comment," John asked.

"You should totally be able to send random women sexual photos with no consequences, right," she replied.

"In others' post?"

"Well you know, fair's fair, right? You sent me the dick pic, now I get to do whatever I want with it."

SEND HIM TO THE POLICE

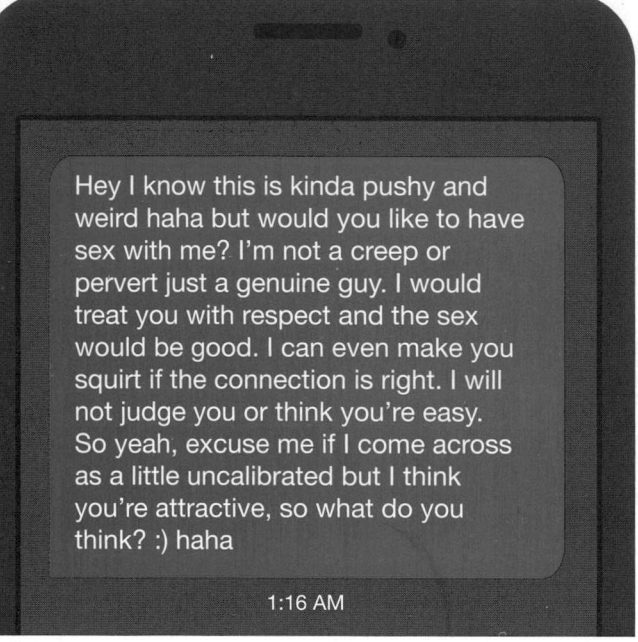

Hey I know this is kinda pushy and weird haha but would you like to have sex with me? I'm not a creep or pervert just a genuine guy. I would treat you with respect and the sex would be good. I can even make you squirt if the connection is right. I will not judge you or think you're easy. So yeah, excuse me if I come across as a little uncalibrated but I think you're attractive, so what do you think? :) haha

1:16 AM

I see this copypasta (internet crap that gets copy-and-pasted over and over again) message in the Bye Felipe inbox so many times, and each time, it fills me with a rage I did not anticipate. It's called The Apocalypse Opener, and it was invented by a pickup artist circa 2014 for use on Tinder. The PUA advice was to match with as many women as possible and send them all this asinine message begging for sex. It's a numbers game. They know it won't work with the majority of women, but they probably read that it worked for someone once, so they keep trying.

When a guy sends you the apocalypse opener, please troll the fuck out of him. (*A word of warning: before you decide to prank a PUA, know that he might get angry. So, be sure to protect yourself and lock down your profile so he won't be able to find you.) One way to do this is to take the bait. Act like you're interested. Reply with something like, "Wow, that's bold. I wouldn't normally say yes, but you sound pretty confident, so I might be interested ;) " He'll want to meet up. Don't give him your phone number, only chat on the app. When he asks for your address, give him the address of the local police department. Tell him you'll be there at 9. Wait until he gets there and then unmatch him. Laugh to yourself and know he'll never use The Apocalypse Opener ever again.

FIND HIS WEAKNESS AND EXPLOIT IT

My friend Sabrina Cognata is a brilliant writer, storyteller, and firecracker of a woman. If I were a man, I'd be terrified of her. One of her entire raisons d'etre is to take the sexist objectification she has experienced because of men and fling it back to them. "Men hate it when you treat them like women," she has told me. Sabrina started a project in 2015 called Dickoupage.[24]

DICKOUPAGE: *n.* The art or technique of decorating something with cutouts of dick pics over which varnish or lacquer is applied.

She started by collecting all the unsolicited dick pics she had received and decoupaging them to her coffee table as part of an art piece to display. The other part of Dickoupage was to post each dick online and write about it. "Dickoupage really started 'cause I was angry and wanted to make men feel the sort of looming shame women have to feel every damn second of their lives," Sabrina said. "The problem being—these unwanted dick pics helped me establish a community of likeminded people with a common goal of equality—and that made it really hard to stay upset." Dickoupage has now morphed into a sort of ideology.

SEND IT TO HIS MOM/GIRLFRIEND/WIFE/GRANDMA

It's usually as easy as clicking on his profile, if he's on Instagram or Facebook, finding out who his girlfriend or mother is, and sending them a nice message about what he's done. My friends, models Emily Sears and Laura Lux, have used this tactic with great success. Because they receive an amazingly high number of unsolicited dick pics, at least one or two daily, they decided to do something about it.

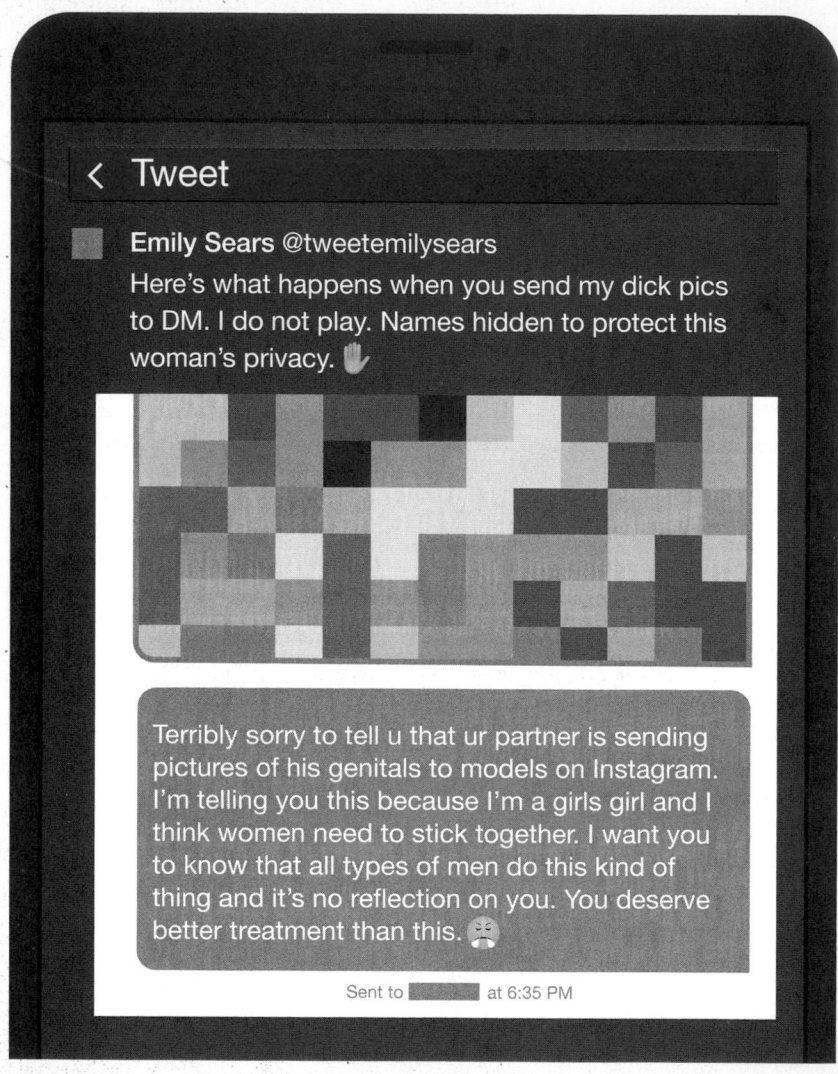

"I think the first time I decided to contact a girlfriend was probably close to two years ago when I opened my Instagram inbox to yet another dick pic with an explicit caption about wanting to fuck me from some random guy I'd never spoken to," Laura told *Buzzfeed News*. "I wrote back, telling him that his behavior was terrible, and he replied with a string of sexual slurs and abuse, and kept calling me a slut."

Looking at his Instagram profile, Laura discovered pictures of him with his girlfriend who described him as "the best boyfriend ever!"

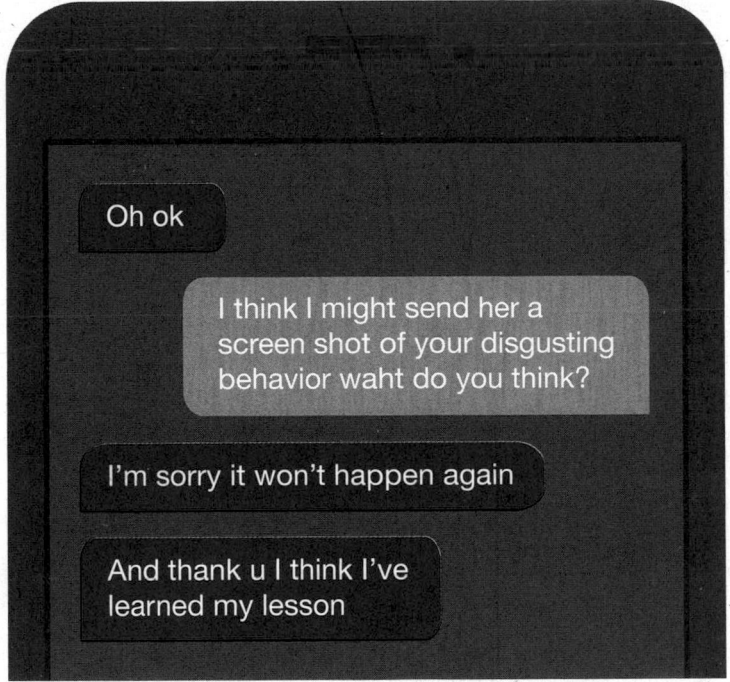

Oh ok

I think I might send her a screen shot of your disgusting behavior waht do you think?

I'm sorry it won't happen again

And thank u I think I've learned my lesson

"We send the photos as a reminder for them to have respect for women," Emily said. "I think it provides an accountability that people seem to lose online. Being behind a screen gives people a false sense of anonymity.

"I have noticed since posting my responses as a warning that the number has been significantly lower. I think my followers are slowly getting the message."

SEND IT TO HIS BOSS

Let his employer know:

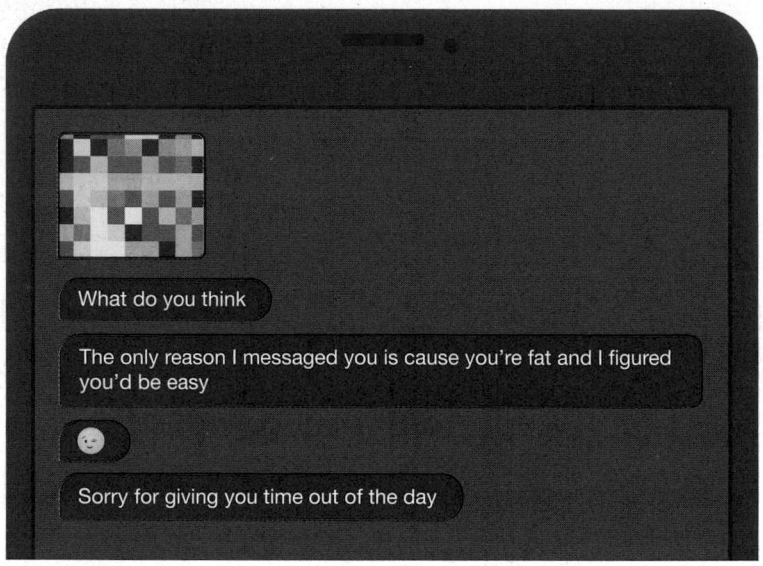

The submitter said, "He proceeded to block me. So I found him on Facebook, found out where he works, called his job and sent an email to HR with screenshots of his dick. #byefelipe"

A NOTE ABOUT PUBLIC SHAMING . . .

Public shaming is serious and can be unhelpful if it is used for the wrong reasons. But if used carefully and aimed well, it can be a powerful tool. It should only be used in extreme cases and where you are absolutely sure that the person committed an egregious action.

Now that you have the weapons to respond to the worst of the worst men, you'll be prepared to go wading through the muck that is online dating.

CHAPTER 5

Being a Boss: How to Take Control of Your Dating Life

I have not always been the boss bitch of my dating life. When I first tried online dating, I was waaaaaaaaay too forgiving. I kept my options open. I gave millions of chances and benefits of the doubt.

"Maybe he'll turn out to be a good person," I thought. "Maybe one day he'll text me back before 2 a.m. Maybe he'll care about my day or ask how I'm doing. Whatever, we'll see what happens! Don't let him think that you care—you might scare him away with your feeeeelings! Do NOT mention 'relationship' or he will run for the hills."

I was all about the carefree, easygoing, giving-people-second-and-third-chances style of dating. It took me an embarrassingly long time to realize that if you're sick of dating and somewhat serious about meeting a person who is not trash, this strategy is all wrong.

It's taken me hundreds of dates, but I've learned a lot of lessons through trial and error. Some of them straightforward, and others not so straightforward. When I think about my early dating life, the mistakes are obvious in retrospect. It's bizarre thinking about your past relationships because your mind is filled with fog when you're in them, but once you leave an unhealthy relationship and give it time, you look back on it, thinking, "What was I doing???"

I met "Marshall" on Tinder in February 2014. We immediately clicked. You know when you meet someone, and you don't really have to explain yourself. They just know what you're talking about, and you know what they're talking about? You have the same sense of humor. You can talk to them on the phone for hours and it's not weird. And when you meet a hot one you have chemistry with, watch out, because you will be DICKMATIZED. (Hypnotized by the dick.)

Marshall was a cool, edgy art photographer. In fact, when we first met, I thought he was way too cool to be interested in me. Insanely hot, he had the most pillowy lips you could imagine. Tall, covered in lowbrow-as-highbrow tattoos. He dressed like every photographer artist you've ever seen: horn-rimmed glasses; an over-sized, artfully ripped soft white shirt; black skinny jeans with holes in the knees; Nike Roshe sneakers. *Of course*, he was an art school dropout. *Of course*, he was "Instagram famous" (65,000 followers, which, at the time was huuuuuge). He was sweet, but with a bad-boy exterior. Extraordinary at texting, he knew just what to say and how to make you feel like he wasn't like other guys. He used emojis liberally, especially the smiley with heart eyes.

When I met Marshall, the word "fuckboy" wasn't yet a word being used to describe player-type guys. It's extra hard to see something when it hasn't been named yet, but that's what he was. He had the bad-boy reputation online, but in real life, he was surprisingly down-to-earth. After Marshall and I hung out the first time, it was just easy. He would text me while I was at work, "Thinking about you 😜" and "Let's hang soon." Every time he did, my heart did a flip.

His art was controversial. He was like a millennial Terry Richardson, focused on parties and drugs and messed-up kids. It was a lot of "trashy" nudes as art. I knew he wasn't creepy like Terry Richardson, even though he used a similar flash style. He was a normal guy, it just *looked* like he was a partying playboy from his online persona.

"People think I'm such a creep, but I'm not like that," he would say.

He really just liked to drink wine, cuddle on the couch, watch movies. It was so fun hanging out with him because we'd laugh at ridiculous jokes. He loved my cats. I couldn't believe he liked me.

Looking back on it, I'll admit, I was kind of an idiot. From the get-go, he talked about being fresh out of a relationship. And yes, he gave the dreaded get-out-of-jail-free card at the beginning: "I'm not looking for anything serious right now."

"We're friends, right?" he would say.

"Yeah," I'd reply.

One week, my roommate was out of town, and Marshall came over. He was leaving the country soon to speak about his art for the first time. He had to give a thirty-minute speech, and he had no idea what he was going to say because according to him, there wasn't actually any message behind his photos. He'd never talked about them in public before. I asked what they were about.

"I don't know—I just shoot what looks cool," he admitted.

"I'll help you write your speech," I said.

So that week, we talked all about it and I basically BSed my way through talking points about his art: I knew anyone who saw these photos could potentially call them out for being problematic to women. But I knew he was just capturing interesting images. He wasn't a misogynist. So I coached him about sex-positive feminism and the male gaze and how our generation is making art in a different way. I helped him put together his slideshow. I gave him all the answers.

He stayed the entire week at my house. I love cooking for other people, so I made him dinner every night. We had fun. Still, there were a few things that bothered me. When I would talk to him, he'd always have his phone in his hand. Marshall was flaky. Sometimes we'd make plans, but he wouldn't set a time so it ended up not happening. Or I'd ask what he was up to and he wouldn't respond for a day. I learned that I couldn't trust plans with him. I didn't realize it at the time, but it always made hearing from him exciting. I never knew when he was going to respond or when he wasn't, so when he did, it made my heart jump even more. I was falling for him. And, yes, I knew I needed to keep my distance and not "catch feelings," but I couldn't help it. He drew me in. I talked about him all the time with my friends.

My roommate hated him because I told her all the annoying things he did.

"But he's different," I'd say. "He's not like that."

When Marshall left for his speech, it all started to fall apart. We'd been hanging out for almost three months. We never talked about what was happening between us, but I felt as if we were going in *a direction*. (That direction being to relation-shipville.) I dropped him off at the airport. I said I'd take care of his car while he was away. I liked doing it. I liked taking care of him.

A few days into his trip, I used my iPad to check my email and saw that he hadn't signed out of his account. So, duh, of course I peeked. I knew that I shouldn't, but for some reason, I didn't think it was all that bad. I would never normally snoop in a boyfriend's email, but he wasn't my boyfriend; and I was thirsty to know what was going on. I thought maybe there would be a clue.

His phone service didn't work where he was, so he had to email everyone. I saw that he was getting drinks with a woman. Annnnd, yep. They definitely slept together. I broke down, crying. We had never talked about being exclusive, but I thought it was sort of implied. I knew that I should have been dating other people since we hadn't had *the talk*, but I didn't want to sleep with anyone else.

In retaliation, I went on a date with another guy. Marshall called me while I was on the date and left a voice-mail message. He was wondering if I could pick him up from the airport. I felt terrible. We were never exclusive. There was never a label. I couldn't even be mad that he slept with someone else. I had no right to be upset. I also wasn't even supposed to know about it.

Of course, I picked him up from the airport when he returned. I didn't want him to know that I had snooped, so I pretended like everything was normal and fine. He was exhausted from his flight, so I let him lie down in my bed. We cuddled. But I had to know.

"What's going on with us . . . ?" I started.

"What do you mean?" he replied. "Really? We're having this conversation right now?"

"Yeah, I care about you."

"I care about you too, but I told you, I just got out of a relationship and I'm not ready."

I told him I didn't think we should keep seeing each other because I didn't want him to hurt my heart.

Despite my best efforts, we kept seeing each other for a few months, but eventually that summer we slowly just stopped talking. I thought that if we remained on good terms, maybe when he was ready we could try to make it work, but I eventually realized that it wasn't ever going to work. I was wrecked for months.

The thing that sucked the most about this nonbreakup was that I felt that I didn't have a right to be sad about it because he had given me his disclaimer in the beginning. It seems so obvious now, looking back, that he was emotionally manipulating me, although not intentionally. I don't think he was actively trying to hurt me. He was just clueless and selfish. I was incredibly naive. After Marshall, I swore that I'd never make the same mistakes again.

Eight months after Marshall and I met, I started Bye Felipe. I'm not going to lie: I was inspired by his Instagram account when I created it. The concept was a collection of images grouped together with a common theme behind it. I viewed it as an art project of sorts in the beginning. I was also angry and bitter from having to deal with men's bullshit, and that anger definitely showed through in the first posts. Marshall and I remained on speaking terms, though.

Two years later, I got a text from Marshall: "I met Alison Stevenson. You guys need to be friends."

I knew of Alison because she's a hilarious stand-up comedian/writer who talks about dating as a feminist, body positivity, and just being a badass in general. We had a bunch of mutual friends, and people were always telling me, "Do you know Alison Stevenson? I feel like you'd be friends with her." We were Facebook friends, but had never met in person. I always assumed we'd meet at a party eventually.

Marshall texted both of us in a group thread. "You guys need to meet!"

"OK!! We will!" I said.

So, we made a friend date to have lunch. Marshall was right. Alison and I immediately clicked. Alison had met Marshall on Tinder, and they'd been on some dates. I tried to broach my backstory with him. That we'd dated and he was not really a trustworthy guy, even though he makes you think he is. I wanted to warn her not to develop feelings for him. Alison and I decided to work on some projects together. I invited her to be on my podcast, and we planned a feminist comedy event.

After we met, I didn't see her again for a few weeks, but we got drinks one night. She told me that she'd been seeing Marshall, and it was like an exact transcript of what had happened when I was seeing him. I told her about suspect things he did, like taking full advantage of me cooking him dinners. Sending strings of nonsensical emojis to be purposely ambiguous. He once admitted to me that he would respond to texts and emails in emojis if he didn't want to give someone an actual answer. That way his reply couldn't be used against him. He was a master at dodging questions. If you ever asked him about something straight up, he would change the subject, or if you were texting, just pretend not to see it.

He had given both of us the same exact lines. "I can't give you what you want right now—I don't have the time. I need to figure my life out."

We'd both been bamboozled. He'd latched onto us, reaping all the benefits of having a relationship, but then got upset when we suggested becoming more than "friends."

"Gaslighting AF," Alison said when I told her my story.

How could we both have fallen for it? We're both outspoken feminists. We've both been around the dating block. We're known for not taking bullshit or letting men manipulate us. We both loved him. Looking back, I feel like an idiot. I had all the evidence that he was taking advantage of me, but I had convinced myself otherwise. I swore to never let my feelings get involved with anyone who showed the obvious warning signs again. After the night of comparing stories, Alison and I agreed that we wanted to warn other women, because we knew he'd continue doing it to more women in the LA area.

Alison has a bit about Marshall in her stand-up routine: "I beat the boss of fuckboys." And he truly is the boss of fuckboys. As in, when you're playing a video game and you make it through all the levels only to come to the last battle to fight the "boss" in order to win. The boss is generally the strongest and most difficult enemy to fight, and you have to have a special strategy to defeat him. Alison and I both feel that we overcame the biggest of bosses and are game champions.

Dating in your twenties is treacherous. You know the warning signs about what not to do, but you ignore them. You know, deep down, that what you're getting into is an emotional minefield. You convince yourself that you're OK, that you know what you're doing. But one wrong step, and boom. Heartbreak. You can learn about how to avoid it, but in reality, you just have to make the mistakes and learn from them in your own way. You don't truly know what it's like until you're in it. If you've made it through your adolescence and early adulthood without ever experiencing heartbreak, congrats. But I truly believe that getting into a messy relationship makes you stronger after you make it out on the other side. As long as you learn something from every relationship, you'll be on your way to being the boss bitch. In the end, I'm glad that I dated Marshall, and I'm glad that he told me we weren't right for each other. I take it as a sign the universe needed to teach me something.

Be Your Own Dream Girl

One of my best friends is Kate Dwyer: girlboss, entrepreneur, badass band chick, sage advice expert. She and artist Penelope Gazin created the website Witchsy.com, a digital store that sells uncensored art in response to Etsy's banning of witch-craft spells. Their story went viral in 2017 when a Fast Company article came out describing the innovative way they boosted their company's development. When they were first trying to get Witchsy off the ground, they created a man's alias, "Keith Mann," to answer emails because they weren't being taken seriously. (Their book is forthcoming.)

Kate and I became Facebook friends through a mutual friend. She messaged me one day, saying, "Hey Alexandra! I always see you liking the same stuff as me and we have a solid group of mutual friends. I normally don't really reach out to people I don't REALLY KNOW on FB, but I was thinking it might be cool if we got to REALLY KNOW each other! I live in Silverlake and I am always interested in a drink of coffee/smoothies/beers. Let's be buds!" And so, we made a friend date to get some dinner together. I am infinitely thankful we did because she is a powerhouse of knowledge and wisdom. We immediately clicked. We talked about life, our goals, and what we wanted to do. I told her about all the terrible men I'd been dating. And that's when she bestowed some of the best advice upon me: "Be your own dream girl."

As soon as I heard it, it was like a light bulb above my head illuminated.

"What do you mean?" I asked.

"I decided to be my own dream girl," Kate said. "Like, what did you think about when you were a little kid, and you imagined the coolest girl? That's why I do everything I do. That's why I started a band, because my dream girl plays in a band. That's why my hair is blonde. That's why I drive a convertible. I do all of these things not to impress guys, but because it's what *I* want."

I had never thought about my life like that. I thought that I was doing what I wanted, and being a strong feminist woman, but I also saw myself bending to what I thought guys wanted. What did my dream girl look like? She definitely rode a motorcycle and wore a badass leather jacket. She didn't give a fuck about what dudes thought of her. She also probably drove a vintage Mustang. She was her own boss, and owned her own house, filled with things she loved, like a dog and a cat, maybe some chickens. So, the next year, I saved up, went to a motorcycle safety class, and bought a bike and a totally badass leather jacket. I'm still working on the rest.

It's kinda cheesy, but Kate's advice makes sense. Live your best life—not what you think anyone else wants or thinks is cool, but what *you* think is cool. People are attracted to other people who are authentic. Even if I never have a boyfriend, at least I'm happy with myself and where my life is. If there's anything that I've learned, it's that friendships are significantly more important than any boyfriend.

HOW TO DATE LIKE A BOSS

I know I said this wasn't a book about how to catch a man, and it isn't, but anyone reading this knows that dating is the worst. I know SO MANY amazingly intelligent, shining, beautiful people who are single: "What's wrong with me?" they say.

First of all, NOTHING is wrong with you.

Most conventional dating advice will begin, "Just stop trying so hard. You'll meet someone when you aren't looking." I HATE hearing this. It's like, ummmm, if I wasn't looking for a boyfriend, I'd be sitting in my house binge-watching TV and never talking to men. If I wasn't putting in effort, I'd be hanging out with my friends doing things that didn't involve straight men, like going to brunch and like, organizing Planned Parenthood fund-raisers or something. Yes, friends are awesome, but I don't want to bone my friends. So, unless you are content with being celibate, (nothing wrong with that, but it's not my style), you have to put yourself out there.

How can you stop making it such a big deal? PRACTICE. The way I did it was to go on tons of dates with different guys. I basically just said yes to every guy who I thought was vaguely attractive, didn't have any glaring red flags, and who asked me on a date. Six years, lots of dating experience and casual sex later, and I am out of fucks to give. It's great! I encourage everyone to date so much that they get sick of it, because with experience comes knowledge. You'll figure out what you're looking for, what your life goals are, what qualities your ideal person has.

- Step outside of your "type." Meet up with the kinds of guys you've never talked to before. Branch out of your scene. Soon, you'll get the hang of it. You'll become an expert dater. It's actually really fun! It's supposed to be fun, not agonizing.
- Adopt a CEO mentality. Know that you're the shit. Establish your standards. If he doesn't cut it, fire him. Guys who don't live up to what you want will get the boot.

- Be your own dream girl. Always be your authentic self, because otherwise what's the point? What if most guys don't like you? That's OK! You're only trying to find one who does. Let shit roll off your back, and don't let the trolls and Felipes make you feel bad about yourself.
- Go on terrible dates. At least they make amazing party stories! If you do all of this, being single will be a lot more enjoyable, and you'll be that much closer to finding a gem who loves and appreciates you.

ON GIRL GROUPS

I don't know what I'd be doing if I didn't have Girls Night In, the secret Facebook group where Bye Felipe started.

Born out of another "secret" group, Girls Night Out (GNO), which has more than twenty thousand members, GRLCVLT originally started because a group of women just wanted to post nudes, and GNO was too big. After a thread where there was drama about someone posting a suggestive/vaguely NSFW picture (now nostalgically referred to as "buttholegate"), a core group started their own offshoot, Girls Night In. They needed something more intimate, where all the members were on the same page. The principles of GNI were sex-positive feminism (consensual sex is cool, no slut shaming, and sex workers are people too) and intersectionality (gender, race, class, sexual orientation, and disability all overlap to impact oppression). If you can't get down with listening to and lifting up those more oppressed than you, you can't stay.

The Facebook group name changes frequently, according to inside jokes, but I mostly refer to it as Girls Night In, GNI, or my secret girls group. The types of conversations women were having in there were the fun things that happened at sleepovers when you're in fourth grade—crushes and boys—but also emotional things like grief, low moments, embarrassing stories, fears; we ask questions that we wouldn't feel comfortable asking just anyone. There was an immense feeling of community. It was here that I saw firsthand what happened when women supported each other. Many of us have still never met in person, but that doesn't stop us from lending each other money when someone needs it or sending them care packages when they're having a tough time. A few of the amazing things that have come out of GNI include:

- A real-life slumber party complete·with bouncy castle, burlesque show, movies, a dance party, a hundred blow-up mattresses, booze, a weed-smoking tent, face masks, huge fifty-four-inch pizzas, cupcakes, and more, all acquired through social media sponsorships and a small ticket fee.
- A massive fund-raiser and letter-writing campaign, called "Fuck Rape Culture," to unseat Judge Aaron Persky, who issued the light six-month prison sentence to the Stanford rapist Brock Turner in 2016
- A Democratic Debate watch party/fund-raiser at the Ace Hotel with comedians like Hannibal Burress.
- Countless gift baskets and flowers for those who needed them while going through breakups or bereavement.
- Donations to charities and volunteering projects.

We operate outside of patriarchal structures in the group, and it's pretty much a paradise. We have our own economy. Whether you're looking for a haircut, a mechanic to fix your car, help with PR or marketing—basically anything you can think of—you check if there's someone in the group who can do it first.

We enabled each other to be more confident and know that each member is important. If someone was feeling bad about something a dumb man said on the internet, everyone was there to comfort and reassure them.

Of course, GNI was not without drama. There have been a few divisive issues that have led to members being removed from the group: leaking sensitive information to parties outside, saying anything hurtful to another member, and saying things that didn't accord with intersectionality. Ultimately, it disbanded, for the most part, but many of the members are still close friends and have forged other smaller groups.

Tons of women's groups have been popping up across the internet. A newer, but no less badass group I was added to is called Banmanuary. It was started in January 2017, fueled by the anger after the election. Banmanuary is a women/femmes-only space where we do not validate men and we do not do free labor for men.

The group states: "Banmanuary is an initiative that can be celebrated many ways, one of which is this Facebook group, meant to facilitate open and honest discussion of gender roles and to provide support to one another. The group is invitation only but meant to be inclusive—we want members from all generations and walks of life. Please invite other women and LGBTQ friends liberally. If you would like to be anonymous on this forum, make another FB account and invite yourself. If you would like to follow the rules of Banmanuary without participating in this forum, that's cool too."

THE RULES OF BANMANUARY* ARE:

1. In Banmanuary, we will not like a man's social media posts. We will not repost, favorite, or share, and we definitely will not feature a photo of a man on our social media accounts.

2. In Banmanuary, we will not say "I am sorry" to a man.

3. In Banmanuary, we will laugh sparingly at the jokes of men. We will never fake laugh.

4. In Banmanuary, we will not talk negatively with each other about our bodies.

5. In Banmanuary, we will not nod along while a man is explaining something to us we already know.

6. In Banmanuary, we will not send many texts to a man. Just give it a rest.

7. In Banmanuary, we will not allow a man to be the focal point of our conversations with women. We will not ask shit like, "So is she dating anybody?"

8. In Banmanuary, we will object or leave the room when a man is saying something offensive or even just when we are bored by a man.

9. In Banmanuary, we will not invite men to very many events. We will focus on spending quality time alone or with female/LGBTQ friends.

10. In Banmanuary, we will not do unrequited emotional labor for a man.

11. In Banmanuary, we will seek more media made by women and LGBTQ people and we will be critical of gender roles in film, TV, journalism, business, science, art, medicine, criminal justice, etc.

12. In Banmanuary, we will not do more than a man does around the house and workplace. We will question why we are assigned certain roles.

13. In Banmanuary, we will not sleep with any assholes.

*Exceptions to rules on rare occasion as needed. Consultation with others encouraged.

Being in a relationship with a man does not mean you cannot participate in Banmanuary. It is an opportunity for you to examine your relationship and explore its gendered influences. Share your experiences with the man. Celebrate Banmanuary in a way that moves forward and don't let a man get away with any bullshit.

If you are in a relationship with a bad man, Banmanuary is the time for you to BAN him!

Although Banmanuary was created by a white cis woman who primarily identifies as straight, we want this to be an inclusive, safe space for everyone. Please post topics that are important to you and you will be supported. We can learn from your experiences.

Girl groups are revolutionary because they allow us to crowdsource advice and support without the fear of being judged or ridiculed by men. There are specific groups for every woman. They are safe spaces for women of color, LGBTQ, and disabled. Professional groups for women comedians and women in art, groups for moms, basically anything you can think of. These groups have solidarity that allow women to speak freely in a way they wouldn't normally on regular social media. It's a way to take power back and have a brief respite from dealing with exhausting men.

That's why I've created a Facebook group for Bye Felipe. It's a place where we can complain about dating, get advice, post about terrible men, and support each other. You can join at byefelipe.com/group.

Start your own group! Add your close friends, and tell them to add other friends who they think would get along. Be sure to include rules like these:

- Whatever happens in the group, stays in the group. Anyone caught leaking information will be removed.
- No slut shaming.
- Intersectional feminism is enforced.

My Dating Motto

"DICK IS ABUNDANT AND LOW VALUE"

I first read this magical slogan when I came across Alana Massey's article, "Dickonomics of Tinder,"[25] where she credits two tweets by Madeline Holden, the creator of the blog *Critique My Dick Pic*[26] (where men submit dick pics to receive objective, honest feedback).

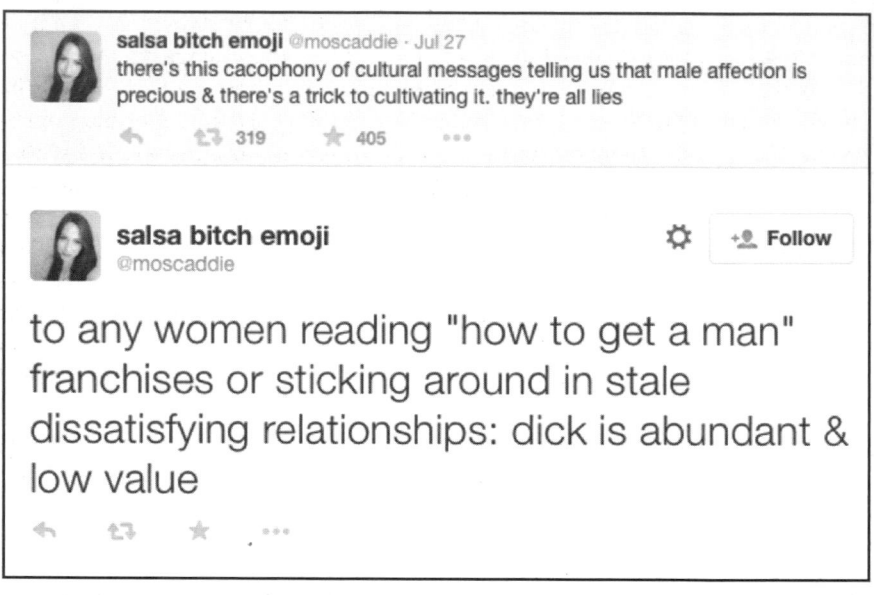

There are men out there who don't commit egregious acts of selfishness. I have to continually remind myself of this fact. When I roll my eyes yet again at that guy who only texts me back at 2 a.m., I think, "Dick is abundant and low value." Kick him to the curb and find someone else!

It made me think about all the women who put so much effort into cultivating relationships and working on themselves. They're constantly reading about it in magazines, going to therapy, asking their friends about what they should do in certain dating situations. They read books about how to get a man. They stick around in terrible relationships because they are under the impression that there's nothing better out there. Well, guess what? YOU'RE FINE. Dick is abundant and low value.

Men are the ones who need to buck up·and put in some effort. But I see it all the time, and I used to do this as well: I was always bending over backwards for trash men, expecting them to come around. We are entirely too accommodating of men who don't put in the effort to understand us or our realities. Not enough men look inward and think, "How could I change myself? How can I become better?" Some men don't do this because they've been babied their entire lives. Or when a woman breaks up with them, they're too stupid to figure out why and that maybe they need to work on some of their personal issues. It's not fair that we as women are constantly told to smile. Be polite. Make him happy at all costs no matter how you feel, even if he doesn't do the same. We need to stop clamoring for breadcrumbs and the scraps that these garbage men sprinkle near us to keep us interested. We need to stop the minute we realize they're "breadcrumbing" us and either address it or move on to the next guy. I know there are wonderful guys out there who are emotionally intelligent and who are great partners, but we need to stop coddling the ones who aren't.

If you want to meet a gem, you've got to be brutal. Throw away the trash at the first red flag. It may be difficult, but it's the fastest and most efficient way to find the right one and save your sanity. Once you've been screwed over by someone you had previously given a second chance, it gets easier. The first time he fails to text you back, just consider it over. I've learned the hard way: Ghost me once, shame on you, ghost me twice, don't be surprised because he's going to do it again. "He's just bad at texting" or "He was busy," you'll say.

NO. If a guy likes you, he'll figure out a way to talk to you. If he wants to hang out with you, he'll make it happen. If you're interested in him, let him know, but don't give more effort than you get from him.

Some men like to act like their dicks are the most special things in the entire world. They send them to us expecting us to drop what we're doing and sleep with them. And when we don't, we get, "You're never going to find someone else. You're lucky that I'm interested in you." This is when I want to rage-scream at the top of my lungs, "ARE YOU KIDDING ME?" Women are drowning in dicks. We couldn't escape them if we wanted to. Ask any woman, and you'll find that she's been hit on at work, at the post office, at the coffee shop, in the grocery store, on Facebook, on Twitter. She's seen an actual live dick on public transportation before. She's seen creeper dudes masturbating on the corner. So when guys try to say that we're lucky we've been harassed, I just wish that I could create a way for them to magically experience life as a woman for one day.

These boneheads obviously don't understand the basic rules of economics. The scarcity principle means that only scarce commodities have economic value. This makes a strong incentive to make everything into a scarce commodity. These men are trying to convince us that dicks are a valued commodity, and we sometimes fall for it. We think, "If I don't take this one, I don't know when the next one will come along." And it's true that decent emotionally intelligent men *are* a commodity. **Only 35 percent of men are emotionally intelligent.**[27] So, yes, if we're talking about men who genuinely respect us, they are absolutely a commodity. Men who understand us. Men who put in effort: effort into improving themselves and being well-rounded, intelligent, and kind people. Effort into listening to women and seeing perspectives from their point of view. Effort into learning what makes relationships work and how to be in one.

DUDE'S CRITERIA FOR WOMEN: *hot, fit, smart, fun, good sex, big boobs/butt, interesting, listens, cooks, cleans*

WHAT DUDE HAS TO OFFER: *boring personality, maybe looks OK in certain lighting, basically nothing*

"Emotionally intelligent" means that, even in an argument, these men can find "something reasonable in a partner's complaint to agree with," which leads to happier relationships. But the other 65 percent of men are *incapable* of being a good partner. Let that sink in. And those are the dudes who try to convince women that their dicks are special. This means that the majority of men will increase negativity when they argue and refuse to be influenced by women. (Hmm, sounds familiar . . . like The Red Pill/PUA men whose worst fear is being "overpowered by the feminine"?) But we must remember that GUYS WHO ACT LIKE DICKS ARE ABUNDANT AND LOW VALUE.

> *Carry yourself with the confidence of a mediocre white man.*
>
> —Feminist Proverb*

*based on a quote by Sarah Hegi

WHAT CAN WE LEARN FROM FUCKBOYS?

At one point in my ill-informed dating past, I stuck around and actually dated a fuckboy on purpose. He was the epitome of fuckboy, and I knew it going in: Hot ✓, never texted back in a timely manner ✓, never asked me out on dates ✓, never cared about me as a person ✓, was only interested in sex ✓, was a director (of cool indie music videos) ✓.

I met Jeremy on Tinder. We traded nudes regularly. He was annoying as hell. He'd always argue with me just for the sake of playing devil's advocate. He was insufferable. I hated his personality, but that's what made him perfect for a casual sex situation. (It's easier to not catch feels.)

Something I noticed about Jeremy was that he asked for everything he wanted, and he wasn't ever afraid of being told no. He'd just move along to the next thing. I once observed him go up to a musician in a successful indie band and blatantly ask him if he could direct his next music video. Even if the chances were slim that the answer was going to be yes, he asked anyway. That's when I realized I need to take a cue from Jeremy the fuckboy. What would happen if I, instead of being polite, just asked for what I wanted? What if all women just asked for what they wanted? *Carry yourself with the confidence of a mediocre white man.* It would be revolutionary. Jeremy didn't care if you thought he was a dick. He was just trying to do what he wanted to do, and if he got turned down, he didn't give one fuck. He just moved on and asked others until someone said yes.

Have you ever noticed that there's just a certain decisiveness that fuckboys have when they request something? They have no shame. Women are often conditioned to be "nice" and go along with whatever other people want to do to be polite. We are taught to ask for permission, say we're sorry, be empathetic, use manners, think of others' needs first. And these are not bad things. But how many times have you slept with someone and not been satisfied in the least? If the answer is even once, this is a tragedy. More often than not, when the man is done with sex, it's over. Why? Do you know what fuckboys care about? Themselves. Shouldn't we care about ourselves even half as much as fuckboys care about their own sexual needs? The answer is YES. Have less shame asking for things. What if women were taught that they deserved to receive equal compensation, respect, and sexual pleasure?

As a reformed polite girl, I've taken inspiration from the guys who had a no-fucks-given attitude to ask me to "send tit pics." The confidence is, frankly, astonishing. That's why you should ask for something *you* want in life. Channel your inner fuckboy to ask for something you think you deserve. Have you been taking on more responsibilities at work and know you should be getting paid more? Take some inspiration from the last dude who demanded to hook up, and march into your boss's office, asking yourself, "What would that asshole fuckboy do?" and don't apologize for asking for that raise. *Side note*: Obviously, don't model it after that fuckboy's spelling or grammar skills ("ay, u up? i need more $$$"). But the important thing is to ask. Maybe you'll get the thing you're asking for or maybe you won't, but don't feel bad if you get a no. Do fuckboys stop asking for tit pics when someone says no? They just ask five more women. Be assertive, ask for what you want, get yours, don't be afraid of being called a bitch, have fun.

BEING STOOD UP

While engaged in online dating, you might run into some bad experiences, but you can still use them as learning opportunities. Once I matched with a guy on Tinder—an artsy type who wore pants with paint splattered on them. We decided to go on our first date to get a drink and then see an art-house movie. I showed up to the theater and bought two tickets, since I was concerned it might sell out. I waited outside because we were supposed to meet there and then get a drink. After twenty minutes, I went to the restaurant next door and got a drink.

I texted him, "Hey, I'm outside." No response. "Are you still coming?" About ten minutes before the movie was supposed to start, he finally texts, "I'm so sorry, but I fell asleep."

"Umm, I already bought the tickets," I said.

"I really apologize, I just laid down for a nap and I totally forgot. I don't think I'll make it there in time."

"OK, I'll figure it out," I said.

I had never gone to the movies by myself, but I went up to the window and explained that I had been stood up for my date. Could I please return one of the tickets? Even though they don't normally do refunds, the cashier felt sorry for me and made an exception.

And so, I went to the movies by myself. But guess what? It was actually the best! Previously, I had always thought, in my early twenties, "Why would anyone go to the movies alone? What's the point?" But I realized that, after doing it, it's amazing. I could sit anywhere I wanted, eat all the popcorn, not pay attention to anyone else, and the biggest surprise to me at the time, probably because I was still kind of socially awkward, was that no one cared.

Being stood up on this date opened up a whole new world for me. I started going to concerts by myself. I went to movies all my friends had already seen. I went at the last minute. I started doing other social things I would never normally do by myself. So, thanks, guy who stood me up on that date when I was twenty-four. You actually did me a favor.

QUESTION: I met this guy on Instagram—he slid into my DMs—and he's ridiculously beautiful and talented. We had been sending each other flirty messages, and we hung out when he was in town. It was great, we meshed really well, and he was fun to be around. We were supposed to hang out again, but then he flaked and went on tour for a few months. Well, now he's back in town and he apologized for being flaky. Should I hear him out or tell him to get lost? I know he's not boyfriend material, but he's a megababe and I wouldn't mind having a night of fun.

ANSWER: As someone who has dated multiple musicians, and they are usually good-looking and charming, that's literally all they bring to the table. Not all, but most are incapable of having a serious relationship. That doesn't mean they're bad people, they just spark a lot of unnecessary drama that most people don't want to deal with. Only you know how you feel about him, so I would say if you are able to hang out with him and have some fun without getting attached, go for it! If you're the type of person who might get hurt when he never talks to you again (which there's a good chance of happening), I'd say let him go.

Sexting 101

Sexting gets a bad rap. You always hear about women whose nudes have leaked, or who are victims of revenge porn, and it ruins their lives. Yes, of course, this is terrible. However, there are always the victim blamers who reply, "Well, he couldn't have leaked those pictures of her if she hadn't taken them in the first place."

Well, guess what? A lot of people are doing it. Over 80 percent of adults have sexted, according to a 2015 study, and it's not going away anytime soon.[28] I'm going to preface this section by saying that, before you sext, think about your reasons for doing it. Are you doing it to impress a man, or are you doing it because you want to and you enjoy it? Do you know how the person will react? Do you completely trust the person? Think about how you will feel after you send it.

Maybe you're not interested. That's OK! Some guys don't take no for an answer. They sometimes attempt to pressure you and bargain. These guys are working on the assumption that you're going to get tired of saying no. If this is the case, you've got to up the ante and get him out of your life. Block him. If it's on a dating site, report him.

WHEN NOT TO SEXT:
- When you're under eighteen—anyone caught with an image of someone underage can be prosecuted for child porn, even if it's consensual!
- When someone is pressuring you to send explicit photos.
- If you're looking to gain approval from a man.

WHEN IT'S MORE RISKY TO SEXT:
- When you haven't met the person you're sexting with.
- When you haven't slept with the person you're sexting.

WHEN TO SEXT:
- When *you* want to.
- When it's completely consensual.
- When you've set rules with the person about whether they can delete/keep/share them with anyone.
- When you're prepared to own it if anything gets leaked.

That said, it's always risky to send images of yourself to someone because laws have not caught up with digital privacy. However, it is fun, and, like anything that is fun (drinking, bungee jumping, skiing), you have to know what you're getting into. There are ways to minimize the risk of someone sharing, leaking, or getting hacked.

SEXTING SAFETY TIPS

- Ask the person you're sexting what they do for security measures. Make sure you're both on the same page.
- Crop, block, or edit out any identifying features. Not only your face, but tattoos or birthmarks. Think about items in the background too. Could they be used to identify you?
- Make sure the geolocation function is disabled. Go into the settings on your phone and make sure EXIF data is stripped. If you don't know how, Google it. There are apps you can use to do this.
- Get a vault app if you're going to keep sexy pics on your phone: There are many apps that keep your photos safe behind a password. Make sure the other person is doing this too.
- Make sure you're cool with whatever platform you're sending the pictures on (Facebook Messenger, Google Hangouts, iMessage, etc.). Does it keep images indefinitely until you delete them? Can you disable the Saving Chat History function? Think about using one with end-to-end encryption, like WhatsApp or Bleep.
- If you only want someone to have a glimpse, use an app that makes it hard to take a screenshot and only displays the picture for a set amount of time (something like the Privates app).
- Have a strong password on your phone.
- Know how to wipe your phone clean remotely in case you ever lose it.
- DO NOT back up sexy photos to your cloud service. Make sure this setting is off when you're taking the pictures; otherwise, they could end up on your other devices or in the cloud, where they could be hacked. Remember when all those celebrities had their nudes leaked because iCloud was hacked?

- If you delete a photo, make sure to completely delete it and empty the Recently Deleted file bin.
- Sometimes you're just feeling yourself, and you take a nude and want to send it to someone. Instead of sending it to a man who doesn't deserve it, send it to your best friend or your best friend group chat. (After asking permission.)
- Consider watermarking it with the name of the person you're sending it to, so that if it's ever leaked, you know who did it and you can prosecute them.

How to Take the Best Butt Selfie

Lie on your side with the bottom leg straight and the top leg bent. Hold camera at a 45-degree angle.

You Changed Your Mind and You Don't Want to Go on That Date After All

SMOOTH EXCUSES

Maybe, after doing some detective work, you find out he's a flat-earther. (I know, terrifying, but they're out there.) Maybe he says something else that's weird and makes you reconsider your interest. But you already agreed to meet him! Here are some ways you can back it up:

- The first line of defense is to just be honest. But it really depends on the reason you're canceling. If he seems to be a decent guy, but you just don't think it's a match, you can tell him the truth. "I didn't agree with that joke you made. I don't think we would be a good match. I'm sorry, but I'm going to have to cancel our date."

- If you don't feel comfortable telling him the real reason you want to cancel (maybe you found out he's got a criminal record), you're gonna have to come up with a different excuse, and one where he won't be able to reschedule. This is kind of lazy, but it should be effective: "Hey, sorry to have to do this, but I had a talk with my ex, and we're getting back together, so I'll have to cancel the date." I don't like relying on telling guys that I have a boyfriend in the context of being hit on in public because it reinforces the idea that men only respect women if they're "spoken for," but in this situation, I think it's a good answer. Another variation is this: "I'm sorry, but I'm going to have to cancel the date. I don't think I'm ready to date anyone yet." The only issue with this one is that if he sees you stay on the dating app, or another dating app, he could call you out. Awkward. So remember to block him after you do that. Or, "Sorry, I had a personal issue come up, and I have to cancel the date we planned." The caveat here is that he might contact you again or expect to reschedule.

- If none of these will work for you, try the slowfade. Say you're feeling sick, something specific like you threw your back out or you have a sore throat. But this only prolongs the letdown. He'll probably text you in a few days, asking if you're feeling better and then you'll have to ghost him or think of another reason to cancel.

- If he did something rude and you don't care and want to be petty, tell him you have to wash your hair.

EXCUSES FOR WHY YOU HAVE TO LEAVE THE DATE

It's always a good idea to have an excuse about why you have to leave in your back pocket before you even get to a date, in case it's awful. You're on a date, this guy is boring you out of your mind, doesn't look like his picture, and you're pretty sure he smells like fish. WYD? For goodness' sake, get the hell out of there and stop wasting your precious time!

- If you've made it through one drink, say you're tired and you have to get to work early in the morning.
- The classic: Text your friend and have her call you with an emergency. "I have to go comfort my friend. She's having an existential crisis."
- Go to the bathroom, put lipstick on your neck, and make it look like you're having an allergic reaction.
- "OMG! I totally forgot, I'm pet sitting and I have to feed my friend's cat right now."
- Your roommate is locked out of the house and you have to go back and let them in!
- Say you have plans later with a friend. "Oh, I have to go to a birthday party at 9."
- "I just realized I left a candle burning in my house! Gotta go make sure it's not on fire."

WHAT IF I LIKE HIM, BUT ONLY AS A FRIEND?

So you want to "friend-zone" a guy. Maybe you went on the date with him, and he's perfectly nice, you had good conversation, maybe you even went on a couple of dates. He's fun, but there's just something missing. You feel no chemistry or attraction, or maybe he has a deal-breaker, but you genuinely like hanging out with him. I haaaaaaaate doing this. Just thinking about sending the text makes me sweaty. It seems so cliché and fake, but sometimes it has to be done! I don't want to hurt his feelings, because he's a genuinely good person. But it's just not going to work out with him in the dating department. I only ever say this to someone if it's true and I do actually want to see him again as a friend. It's like a Band-Aid. You just have to rip it off. And the sooner, the better. I always think about how I would want to be treated, so just go with that. I'll preface this by saying that hanging out with him after you give the friend-zone line is probably going to be unlikely. Guys can sometimes still get their feelings hurt, even when you're polite. Or they might have just been looking for a hookup anyway so they're not going to want to hang out with you anymore.

- "I had a lot of fun the other day, but I don't see this becoming more than a friendship."
- "I really enjoyed hanging out with you the other day. I'd really like us to be friends."
- "I'm down to hang out again, but TBH, I think it would be better as friends. I liked getting to know you, just didn't feel that connection."
- "You are the bomb. I liked [something specific about the date]. Can we be friends? I got more of a platonic vibe."

Don't Let the Patriarchy Win

Dating straight men often comes with the distinct hazard of making you feel bad about yourself. Men have incredibly skillful yet subtle ways of stoking insecurity: They uphold bullshit beauty standards. They police other men who like or date women outside of "the norm." They make comments about our bodies that sound insignificant, but that can cut to our cores. They buy into rape culture.

When online dating straight men, there's a sneaking sense of shame that can accumulate when you aren't the conventionally attractive thin, white, blonde feminine girl. There's pressure to live up to being a man's status symbol that can be extremely harmful to your psyche.

The number one key to being a boss bitch in your dating life is knowing and believing that you are a boss bitch. It's absolutely critical that you DO NOT let the patriarchy succeed in making you feel like shit. That's why, if you're going to be online dating, you've got to arm yourself with this magical force field called *self-love*. Yeah, I know it sounds like some woo-woo bullshit, but it is the one thing I've found that actually works.

If you don't already have the base-level confidence not to give a shit about what other people think about you, online dating can be really unpleasant. (Duh!!) Sometimes, all it takes is one asshole dude to mention your biggest insecurity for a complete shame spiral to start.

However, here's what happens when you love yourself: You will be free. You'll stop seeking your validation from men, because it will come from within you. You won't depend on attention from other people, so you won't be needy. Self-love is a powerful decent-human bait and incredibly potent fuckboy repellant. When you love yourself, people notice and they treat you differently. You'll be more assertive and you won't bend over backwards for people who don't deserve it. You'll have standards and priorities, and you'll be doing what *you* want on your own terms.

How do you boost your self-love?

1. BE AWARE OF YOUR THOUGHTS.

It took me a long time to figure this out, but your thoughts are not always right, and you have the power to listen and act on them or not. They'll always be there, but the first step is acknowledging them. Are they negative? Positive? Are they rational? What are they driving you to do? Maybe they're telling you that you're a loser or you're lazy. You know what unhealthy inner narratives sound like. The first step is to notice them.

2. GET HOLD OF NEGATIVE THOUGHTS.

It's a looooong and winding journey on the road to body positivity. I'm thirty and still learning to accept and love my body. (Aren't we all?) But I've come a really long way. Like most women, I started off hating my body sometime in elementary school when an older girl called me fat. What followed was a brutal daily war with my stomach.

Yadda, yadda, yadda, we've all been there because we all live in the same fucked-up world. Anyway, one day in high school, I'm not sure where I got the idea, but I made a promise to myself that I wasn't going to say anything bad about my body ever again. And I didn't. When I'd be trying on clothes with my friends and they'd insult themselves in the mirror, I'd always reassure them that they looked great, but I'd be sure not to join in on the self-criticism. I made it a habit, and it has totally made a difference in my self-worth. It didn't happen all at once, but was more of a slow and steady climb. Once you master this rule, take it a step further and stop putting yourself down in your own thoughts too. That's some real Jedi concentration. Sure, I still have bad days where I look at myself and don't love what I see, but being conscious of what I say to myself is one of my healthiest habits.

3. CHANGE THE NEGATIVE THOUGHTS INTO POSITIVE ONES.

I'm still working on this every day. I constantly need to remind myself, "DO NOT COMPARE YOURSELF TO OTHER PEOPLE." I'm always repeating it to my friends too. Everyone's on their own path, and that doesn't mean yours is better or worse. ★♥✧ Love and light, y'all. ★♥✧ You already know all the cliché quotes. Spoiler alert: I'm sorry to say they're true. Refocus your attention on yourself and concentrate on making constructive improvements.

All it takes is practice. Once you get into the routine of being mindful, it gets easier and soon you will be reaping the benefits of knowing you're a boss bitch. Best of all: You won't take shit from men. Your life will be simpler and easier. You'll go with the flow. You will exude stability. You'll be happier.

Sometimes you'll think, "I like myself OK. I'm fine." But then you'll make a new breakthrough and be like, "OK, I love myself even more now and this is SO much better." Once you start making progress in your confidence journey, you'll look back at your younger self and say, "What was I thinking???? Why didn't I love myself this much back then??? I always had it going on!!! What a dum-dum." Stop wasting your time and LOVE YOURSELF NOW, YOU GLOWING, MAGNIFICENT, UNIQUE, MAGICAL BOSS BITCHES!

CHAPTER
6

WTF Do
We Do Now?

I started Bye Felipe at a point when I was over it with men. I'd recently been screwed over by the "boss" of fuckboys. I was going on multiple dates each week to get him out of my head and, in the process, meeting more fuckboys. I saw how men were hurting my friends too. We would regularly get together and complain about how "men are the worst," and why can't any of them just respect us? Is that too much to ask?

I was fed up with how the guys I was dating were treating me, and how the other guys online could callously ruin my day with a swipe of their fingers and a "fat whore" comment. I was supremely pissed off because women deal with this regularly, but most men don't understand or care about it. Creating Bye Felipe was a way to give men a taste of their own medicine, and to show other men what it was like to be a woman. It was a joke, and one that I thought only my friends who have dealt with straight men would understand. But it was also a way to let out the anger that I had been keeping inside. It felt good to mock abhorrent men. To reclaim a small piece of the pain they'd caused me and so many other women. It felt good to be able to give those women a voice and to start a conversation on a larger scale about what we were going through. It started a national conversation about online harassment and misogyny.

I don't like to admit it, but sometimes a troll just happens to touch a nerve when they hit our biggest insecurity. If the thing you struggle with the most is body positivity, and some random dude pops up in your inbox telling you you're an ugly whale who doesn't deserve to live, it's really hard not to believe him if you tell yourself the same thing all the time. But a helpful thing to know is that trolls say that to everyone, whether they're a size 2 or a size 22! They think that the worst thing a woman could ever be is "fat."

There aren't very many types of insults to choose from if you're a troll. The troll is usually the one who is hurting inside, so to make himself feel better, he tries to make women feel worse. He'll just take a stab in the dark and tell you that you have cellulite because men know that women are supposed to be insecure about that (regardless of whether or not you have it). If you tell any woman she's unattractive because of her weight, what are the chances that she already thinks that about herself? Uh pretty good . . . since women are more likely to have lower self-esteem than men, according to a 2015 global meta-analysis. We also know that over half of girls aged ten to seventeen globally don't have high body esteem, according to the 2017 Dove Global Girls Beauty and Confidence Report.[29]

That's because the whole damn system is rigged! Men have an incentive to keep women's self-esteem down because women with lower self-esteem are easier to control. Women with lower self-confidence will not put up a fight. The Dove study also found that seven out of ten girls with low body esteem said they were less likely to be assertive in their opinions or stick to their decisions. So it's really pretty simple:

Tell her she's ugly, and she'll be more likely to do what you want. This is why building self-confidence is completely vital for dating and for taking down the patriarchy!

> **"Caring for myself is not self-indulgence, it is self-preservation, and that is an act of political warfare."**
>
> —Audre Lorde

The best thing you can do is not to believe them and not to care! I realize this is very "I am rubber, you are glue . . ." but it's true. No one is perfect. But everyone can have self-confidence; it just requires acknowledging your strengths and weaknesses. It takes effort to challenge the irrational beliefs that keep you from being assertive. Write down the things you don't like about yourself, and then make a list of reasons why they aren't true. Save that list, and look at it often.

In my early twenties, I was low on the self-esteem scale and naive as hell. I wasn't assertive about what I wanted because, on some level, I felt unworthy. I was afraid of seeming too demanding, of scaring men off by not being a chill, "cool girl." I was way too agreeable. So much so that I let men do whatever they wanted instead of sticking up for my standards. But, slowly, I started to learn that I should be myself and communicate my standards the whole time. If some of the dudes I was dating couldn't handle that, then fuck 'em. There are always more dudes. The more confidence I built, the less I cared if a guy didn't text me back. "I'm fucking awesome, and if he's not completely stoked about hanging out, well, LOL, I'll just find another one." Yes, I just quoted myself. And once I stopped caring so much, I stopped being angry.

I eventually also gained a level of compassion. For noncommittal fuckboys, but also for some of the trolls. Lots of men I wanted to date, but who didn't want to date me, had deep-seated emotional baggage that they needed to deal with on their own. And the trolls, Felipes, and guys who were rude to women were all hurting in their own ways. Maybe someone hurt them, or they were dealing with another type of hardship, like an illness or an injury. I also thought a lot about how all men are also dealing with narrow gender roles.

> ## "Empathy is the most radical of human emotions."
> —Gloria Steinem

During the last week of 2017, Sarah Silverman dealt with a Twitter troll in one of the most brilliant ways I have ever seen. The troll, Jeremy Jamrozy of San Antonio, responded to one of her tweets with "Cunt."[30] Instead of ignoring him or putting him on blast, she looked at his profile and replied with compassion.

 Sarah Silverman ✔ @SarahKSilverman   28 Dec
Replying to @jeremy_jamrozy
I believe in you. I read ur timeline & I see what ur doing & your rage is thinly veiled pain. But u know that. I know this feeling. Ps My back Fucking sux too. see what happens when u choose love. I see it in you.

 Jeremy jamrozy
@jeremy_jamrozy

I can't choose love. A man that resembles Kevin spacey took that away when I was 8. I can't find peace if I could find that guy who ripped my body who stripped my innocence I'd kill him. He fucked me up and I'm poor so its hard to get help.

5:41 PM - Dec 28, 2017

💬 13   🔁 6   ♡ 53   ⓘ

Yikes. Does the fact that he's in pain give him the right to cause pain in others? No way. But at least he apologized.

Silverman responded with positive enthusiasm and told him he should seek help for his back pain. Like an angel, she then put a call out to her twelve million Twitter followers, asking for a San Antonio doctor to help him. Twitter came through, and a back specialist responded, saying they would help. Jamrozy went in for a consultation, where he learned that it was worse than expected—five herniated disks—and set up a donation fund to help with his treatment. Doing him one more, Silverman offered to pay for his medical bills.

 Jeremy jamrozy @jeremy_jamrozy   28 Dec
Replying to @SarahKSilverman
I will go. But I trust no one I've been burned so many times. I'd give the shirt off my back and everytime I get burned. I'm super antisocial. I have no friends. I'm sorry I gave u shit.

 Sarah Silverman
@SarahKSilverman

Im so psyched you'll go. KEEP ME POSTED. Don't give up on yourself. Be brave enough to risk getting burned. It's what happens when u fight for yourself. But it's worth it. I promise.

6:01 PM - Dec 28, 2017

💬 3   🔁 4   ♡ 80   ⓘ

While, yes, reading this type of heartwarming tale feels like hugs from a thousand puppies, it's not helpful to say that women should respond this way to every troll. The ability to offer kindness in situations like this is a massive privilege. Many people do not have the time, money, or mental space to respond the way Silverman did. Yes, it's wonderful if you have the means to show compassion to a bitter dude who called you a cunt for no reason, but it is still very much optional. Women should never be obligated to take on the emotional labor of fixing hostile men. How many times have you seen a rape victim pressured not to press charges because "He's such a good student" or "It's going to ruin his life"?

The obvious answer is that men shouldn't attack women in the first place. How hard is it not to attack other people? But a very low percentage of abusers ever change, according to statistics. The chances of a stranger on the internet rehabilitating a troll is infinitesimally small.

If we call them out by name, will they change? We are at a crossroads. Do we respond with kindness and understanding to hostile men? Or do we call them out and shame them? With the #MeToo movement, women have found a voice to talk about sexual assault and rape, and powerful men taking advantage of and coercing women in their industries. CEOs, highly regarded producers and directors in Hollywood, indie musicians, tech bros, men everywhere have been called out for their behavior. Women aren't taking shit anymore, and they've started to speak up loud and clear.

Toxic men are afraid. That's why there's such a backlash against feminism and women becoming visible—because these men feel threatened that we are gaining momentum. That's why we have a pussy-grabber–in–chief: Before the 2016 election, half of men felt American culture had become "too feminine," and that this had a negative effect on men, according to polls.[31] Men thought he could take us back to the time when men had more of a free hand to dominate women. They could feel their privilege and superiority eroding.

Men still have the power in our society. And why would they willingly give that up if it benefits them? Until we as a culture start to talk about, condemn, and work to change the harmful aspects of masculinity, dudes just aren't going to give it up on their own.

Toxic masculinity is a mental health crisis. It is hurting, not helping, men. Studies show that men who feel the need to display these qualities—stoicism, domination, sexual aggression, violence, and misogyny—have been linked to unhealthy relationships, depression, substance abuse, rage disorders, criminal behavior, and suicide.[32] "Conformity to the masculine norms of self-reliance, playboy [sexual promiscuity], and power over women were the norms most consistently associated with poorer mental health," according to Y. Joel Wong, the lead author of a 2016 Indiana University study on masculine behaviors.[33] This is why we need to call that shit out. Tell them firmly, "Stop it. I don't like that!" (Except when you're dealing with a sadist. Then, don't give them the satisfaction.)

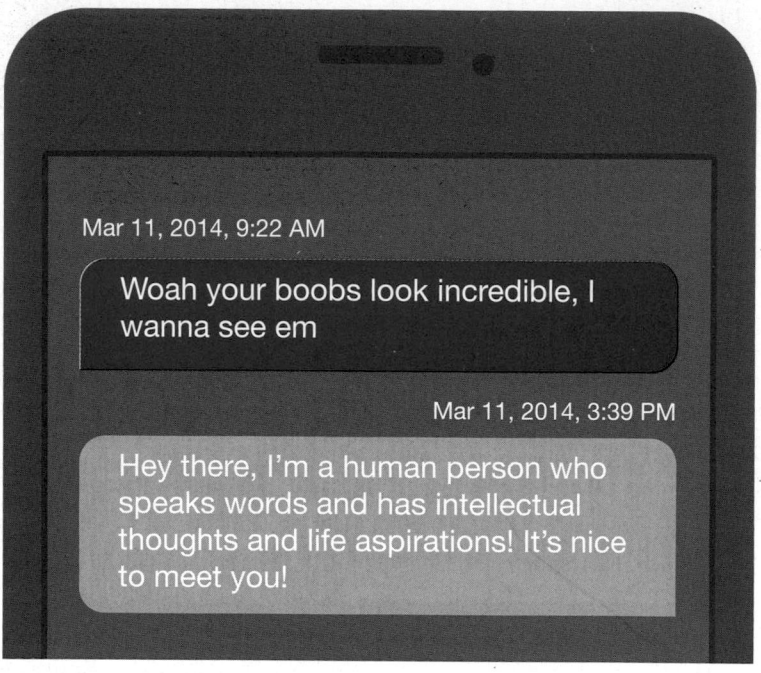

A Man Apologizes

I have received many well-wishes and nice comments from men apologizing for their gender. However, it's extremely rare to see an admittedly hostile man apologizing. A man—apologizing! While I never expected it to actually happen, I felt the need to acknowledge it here. The following is an email I received on November 3, 2014:

Subject: Thank you, from my heart

Hi,

I'm sending this message to thank you for your Instagram profile.

I admit I'm guilty of the wrongdoing -being abusive when ignored-. I've always [known] inside of me that it was wrong and shouldn't happen, but I've always allowed that asshole in me to take control and lead my actions.

Until I browsed through your posts . . . seeing it as an outsider -seeing someone else doing it , I know now how low I was. It feels awful to know that I was doing this to a woman just because she wouldn't reply or when I didn't like their replies.

I know there are women with issues, and maybe ignoring guys make them feel better about themselves or something, but I should have learned that this is THEIR issue, THEIR problem, and it doesn't give me any right to abuse or be mean to them.

I should have learned long ago to simply move on, unmatch and continue, just look forward to the next one.

I know now that abusing a woman -no matter how much she deserves it-, will only make less of a man of me.

Again, thank you for your profile. I'm sorry I'm sending this from an alias email, but my remorse is genuine, and I will work on whatever I have to work on to be a good man, a better man.

Thank you, and you will meet the person who will love and appreciate you just the way you are, and you both will sit together and laugh at other abusive assholes.

Peace,

I waver back and forth between appreciating this as a sincere apology and reading it like this dude is trolling me. I honestly can't tell. It's sooo close to being a real apology, but he juuuust barely misses the mark by thinking he's somehow valiant for not abusing women "no matter how much they deserve it." Um, hello, sir, you should never abuse a women . . . ever.

An Open Letter to Men

Dear men,

If you have read this book and are now thinking, "What can I do?" Here are some things you could do that would help A LOT:

- If you see your friends doing any of the things illustrated in this book, tell them to cut it out. I know it's uncomfortable, but if you really want to help, defending women is the best way.
- Likewise, if you are called out for something, step back and acknowledge it, instead of becoming defensive. Take responsibility and apologize. (Not by saying, "I'm sorry you were offended." That's not an apology.)
- If you want to send a dick pic, just ask first! And then honor whatever the other person says.
- All women/femmes/nonbinary/trans people are looking for is someone to treat them like human beings. It's pretty simple. If you're trying to hit on someone, compliment something that's not a physical attribute and try being sincere with no ulterior motives for once.
- If you're having relationship problems, please get help. Go to a therapist. Research how to forge healthy relationships. Read a book about it.
- If you see anyone coming forward about being sexually assaulted, raped, or otherwise harmed, DO NOT tell them what they should have done instead. This is victim blaming. Just listen and say something like, "Wow, that sucks. I'm sorry that happened to you. Is there anything I can do to help?"
- Stop enforcing toxic masculinity. Stop shaming other men who present themselves outside of harmful masculine stereotypes. That is, if they're not hurting anyone by being interested in knitting, don't tell other men that they're "pussies."
- If you could do us these small favors, that'd be greeeeeaaaat. OK, Thanks!

Non-Trash Men Exist Online

(I was told that the entire book can't be a cynical nihilistic diatribe against all men, so I'll leave you with an adorable Tinder success story for the ages.)

Casey Horan-Finemore has been a member of GRLCVLT since the beginning. She's a nurse, and she's known in the group for having an adorable elderly pug named Cheeto (he had that name before Trump), hating multilevel-marketing schemes, and being hilarious.

"I describe myself as a slightly lazy, underachieving, unathletic girl who wears secondhand clothing and takes enjoyment in cross stitching and crafts," she said. "I drive a Prius, do the bare minimum, and enjoy a good dose of trashy reality TV."

Like me, Casey was in a long-term relationship that began pre-Tinder days and ended "in the midst of the Tinder revolution." She too used it in complete rebound mode because she didn't know a lot of dudes outside her social circle in Los Angeles.

"I probably only went on maybe four dates, but it was pretty discouraging. In such a big city, and with so many fuckboys, I had a hard time," she said. "I met one guy off Tinder I really liked but he wanted to keep things casual for over a year, which was frustrating because all my friends would match with him unknowingly while we were actively seeing each other."

Soon, she was burned out on LA fuckboys and traffic, but she had always wanted to go work and travel in Australia. Her ex-boyfriend had never had any interest in that so, being single, she could finally live her dream. Of course, when she got there, she used Tinder "for meeting new people, for some dinners (which is awful I know but . . . oh well. I was backpacking and on a tight budget)."

Casey went on a handful of Tinder dates in the United States and Australia. "The Aussie dudes were far more attractive, but their dating techniques were so much worse than the American dudes, honestly. One dude took me to McDonald's and was super-homophobic. Another guy was unemployed, lived with his mom, and did sloppy mediocre graffiti on trains. I started realizing that maybe I was swiping right on the wrong type of guys."

So she switched up her strategy. "I can remember it as clear as day—I was on the train heading home from work, and there was a profile of an incredibly attractive, clean-cut guy on the beach with a greyhound. He seemed like the all-around good ole boy who probably had a degree, a stable family life, and liked sports. He couldn't be more opposite from me, but I thought, 'whatever,' swiped right, and it was a match.

"The one thing about Tinder that gets boring is how you match, but then the conversation just dies out or never happens—but he was different and witty and made dinner plans right away—which I found to be impressive. A man who knows what he wants, spells correctly, *and* has a dog: BONUS!

"We met up at this nice bar/restaurant. He nervously knocked his beer over ten minutes into the date and broke my smartphone (awkward). We kept seeing each other, and the thing that made him different and worth pursuing was the fact that he wasn't aggressive. Everything flowed naturally, he didn't try to get me to come home with him, and didn't just ghost on conversations. It wasn't the usual effort I had to put in with other guys. It just happened."

I'm sorry, what was that? Oh, he *wasn't* aggressive? Everything flowed naturally? He didn't try to get you to come home with him? He didn't ghost on conversations? I just don't know what that's like. Carry on.

"Eventually, after maybe like one or two months, we decided to be exclusive. We only dated for nine months before getting married, which is absolutely crazy, but I guess it just 'felt right.' I never had that feeling before in other relationships, and the thought of it creeped me out, but with him it was kind of like . . . OK. I was about to head back to America and we were sitting on the couch talking, and were both super-sad, so we basically just decided it was what we were going to do to be able to stay together.

"So yeah, super long story short, we have now been married for a year. There have been challenges, of course. Believe it or not, there are some cultural differences between Australians and Americans, and they have come up. We actually are complete opposites and I hate watching football with him because it's boring. He doesn't like the same music as me, and we have had to compile a completely weird mixture of our music in a playlist for road trips. Our sense of humor is slightly different. We come from completely different backgrounds and family styles, so that does become a challenge. He gets up at 5 to go to the gym, and I prefer sleeping until 11 a.m. and watching Netflix. Otherwise, I'd say we are pretty solid so far. I do think it's pretty crazy that if we didn't both swipe right on a silly app our lives would be completely different and we wouldn't even know each other. (Oh, and by the way, his dog in the photo was his ex-girlfriend's, so that didn't end up being a bonus.)

Bye, Felipe

This is a final reminder that *men are not in control of your happiness.* **You are in control of your happiness.** If a man doesn't make you feel happy, BAN HIM FROM YOUR LIFE. You're probably going to go through a lot of dudes who are annoying as hell and who aren't right for you. Most men *are* dickwads. They are stupid and selfish and socially unaware, but then most people in general are those things too. You aren't trying to date the entire world, you're trying to find one kind, emotionally intelligent person, and, because you exist, they also exist somewhere. But you're going to have to go through a lot of garbage to find them.

The antidote to dealing with dumb shit is to have your own shit going on. Be your own dream girl. Do whatever the fuck you want, and you will instantly feel better. When you feel better about yourself, you attract other people who feel good about themselves, and you create a circle of dopeness.

I see the worst types of men sending the worst messages every day, but ever since I started not giving a fuck and choosing the worldview that it's not my problem to change them, I'm doing what I want to at all times, and I've never felt more fantastic. Are there bullshit days? Duh, of course. But they don't matter as much in the big-picture context because, overall, I like myself. And that's all that truly matters. It is the key, and I want that for all women.

My goal always has been and always will be to create a community for women, and to lift up their voices; to take the harassment men fling at women, flip it around, and empower women in the process. I want to be here for you. Text me or call me and leave a message at (323-435-6919).

RESOURCES

OMG, if you are seriously being harassed and being made to feel unsafe, don't just crack jokes and send them dick pics, you have resources! There are a bunch of SUPER helpful nonprofits you can contact:

• **Crash Override (crashoverridenetwork.com):** Founded by Gamergate survivor Zoe Quinn and her boyfriend Alex Lifschitz, Crash Override helps anyone dealing with online abuse. It provides crucial tools, guides, and advice from people who have experienced it. They also connect you to legal and cybersecurity experts.

• **Hollaback! (ihollaback.org):** Their mission is to end harassment in public spaces. Download the Hollaback! app, and you can take a photo of your street harasser and upload your story with geolocation. They also have tons of helpful resources for dealing with harassment, a robust college campus program, and trainings around the world.

• **HeartMob (iheartmob.org):** A project of Hollaback! hyper-focused on online harassment. The website gives immediate assistance by connecting you with knowledgeable allies who can help you report and document your story, as well as provide emotional support. You can also sign up to be a helper to people experiencing harassment.

• **Cyber Civil Rights Initiative (cybercivilrights.org):** Founded by Holly Jacobs, a revenge porn survivor, CCRI provides victim services including emotional support, advice, and a free helpline (844-878-CCRI). They also work to educate the public, help tech companies come up with solutions to nonconsensual porn, and they provide legislative support and legal research for lawmakers.

• **Online SOS (onlinesosnetwork.org):** Provides tools and resources for people experiencing online harassment including an outbox tool for easily documenting your case, understanding your rights, guiding you through the process of formal reporting, and getting you expert help.

• **Without My Consent (withoutmyconsent.org):** Combats online invasions of privacy. The Something Can Be Done! Guide gives you tools for dealing with a nonconsensual porn situation: gathering evidence, how to get the images taken down, help with restraining orders, how to get a lawyer, and more.

ENDNOTES

1   http://consumersresearch.org/consumer-survey-the-best-way-to-swipe-a mate/

2   http://straightwhiteboystexting.org/important

3   https://www.technologyreview.com/s/609091/first-evidence-that-online-dating-is-changing-the-nature-of-society/

4   https://www.theguardian.com/lifeandstyle/2015/oct/10/neil-strauss-the-game-book-truth

5   http://www.attachedthebook.com/

6   https://www.reddit.com/r/AskReddit/comments/5mr6yf/men_of_reddit_what_thing_would_you_do_if_it_wasnt/

7   http://www.npr.org/sections/goatsandsoda/2017/06/15/532977361/why-do-men-harass-women-new-study-sheds-light-on-motivations

8   https://www.scribd.com/document/340345088/Trolls-just-want-to-have-fun-pdf

9   https://www.theglobeandmail.com/opinion/why-trolls-love-to-pick-on-women/article34336855/

10   https://thedebrief.co.uk/relationships/dating/dark-triad-attracted/

11   https://www.youtube.com/watch?v=Nn1ZbISu34Y

12   http://www.sandiegouniontribune.com/news/courts/sd-me-berlin-sentencing-20170201-story.html

13   https://www.reddit.com/r/TheRedPill/comments/5fihmu/how_to_get_laid_like_a_warlord_37_rules_of/?st=j92nwtp5&sh=40df9796

14   https://www.newstatesman.com/science-tech/internet/2017/02/reddit-the-red-pill-interview-how-misogyny-spreads-online

15   https://jezebel.com/ladies-quit-paying-attention-to-this-vile-troll-web sit-1469942571

16   http://www.rooshv.com/feminism-killed-the-nice-guy

17   http://www.rooshv.com/feminism-killed-the-nice-guy

18   https://www.quantcast.com/returnofkings.com?qcLocale=en_US

19   http://www.futurity.org/depression-opioids-rejection-865812/

20   https://www.reddit.com/r/MGTOW/comments/47azz6/welcome_to_mgtow_ready_
      to_change_your_life_this/?st=j92iohvl&sh=bba4090c

21   https://www.theatlantic.com/entertainment/archive/2015/10/neil-strauss-the-
      game/409789/

22   http://www.pewinternet.org/2017/07/11/online-harassment-2017/

23   https://lendedu.com/blog/tinder-match-millennials/

24   http://dickoupage.tumblr.com/about-dickoupage

25   https://medium.com/matter/the-dickonomics-of-tinder-b14956c0c2c7

26   http://critiquemydickpic.tumblr.com/

27   https://www.huffingtonpost.com/entry/emotionally-intelligent-husbands-
      are-key-to-a-lasting_us_5839f9cfe4b050dfe6187c74

28   http://www.latimes.com/science/sciencenow/la-sci-sn-sexting-sexual-satisfaction-
      20150807-story.html

29   https://www.prnewswire.com/news-releases/girls-on-beauty-new-dove-research-
      finds-low-beauty-confidence-driving-8-in-10-girls-to-opt-out-of-future-opportuni-
      ties-649549253.html

30   https://www.sacurrent.com/ArtSlut/archives/2018/01/05/san-antonio-man-trolls-
      sarah-
      silverman-on-twitter-but-she-responds-with-compassion;

31   https://www.prri.org/research/prri-atlantic-oct-11-poll-politics-election-clinton-
      leads-trump/

32   http://inthesetimes.com/article/20303/the-antidote-to-toxic-masculinity

33   http://education.indiana.edu/news/2016-12-15-wong.html

ACKNOWLEDGMENTS

Thank you to my mom, who taught me how to be a feminist and always just assumed I'd write a book one day. Thanks to my dad for his unwavering support and love.

THANK YOU to everyone who helped me write this book. I especially want to thank my agent, Anna Sproul-Latimer for believing in me and helping me at every step of the way, and to Jaclyn Friedman for introducing us.

Mountains of gratitude to the team at Running Press and my editor, Jennifer Kasius, for always being so supportive, patient, and helpful.

I can't thank Robin Eisenberg enough for her amazing illustrations and for sticking with me through this long process. Thank you, Kate Dwyer, for introducing me to Robin and for all the advice.

Many thanks and lots of love to:
- ♥ Iara Roa-Ferreira for being my ride-or-die, giving me all of the encouragement, and helping me with formatting.
- ♥ Umair Aleem for supplying me with endless hugs and for always being a trash person.
- ♥ Alison Stevenson for being an awesome friend throughout the process and being the best sounding board and podcast cohost for V Single.
- ♥ All GRLCVLT members.
- ♥ Everyone who submitted their terrible dudes to be ridiculed. This book couldn't have been written without you.
- ♥ My grandparents for being the coolest and supporting me always.
- ♥ My BFFs 4EVER for helping me become the person I am today, Kara Nesvig and Emily Moen.
- ♥ Eileen Beard for being a chill roommate when my writing mess was very extra and for being a dope podcast cohost (The Bye Felipe Podcast).
- ♥ Anel Salgado for taking my author photo, and to Joe Herzog for letting us use your studio.